Arab Politics in Palestine, 1917–1939

Volume 11

THE MODERN MIDDLE EAST SERIES
MIDDLE EAST INSTITUTE
COLUMBIA UNIVERSITY, NEW YORK

A complete listing of publications of
the Middle East Institute appears
at the end of this book.

Arab Politics in Palestine, 1917–1939

THE FRUSTRATION OF A NATIONALIST MOVEMENT

Ann Mosely Lesch

Cornell University Press

ITHACA AND LONDON

First published 1979 by Cornell University Press.
Published in the United Kingdom by Cornell University Press Ltd., 2–4 Brook Street, London W1Y 1AA.

International Standard Book Number 0-8014-1237-4
Library of Congress Catalog Card Number 78-32059
Printed in the United States of America
Librarians: Library of Congress cataloging information appears on the last page of the book.

Contents

Preface

This examination of Arab politics in Palestine covers the time from the beginning of British rule in 1917 until the outbreak of World War II. Although the British remained in Palestine until 1948, the interwar years were a distinct period in terms of the organization and actions of the Arab community as well as of the policies of the British government and the Zionist movement. The pattern of interaction among these three forces shifted drastically in the 1940s.

The history of the Zionist movement and of British policy in the Middle East has been analyzed in detail, but few studies have treated the political structure and behavior of the Palestine Arabs during the crucial years of the British mandate. Analyses have tended to stress the rivalries among individual leaders, the personality of the mufti al-Hajj Amin al-Husayni, and the factionalism within the elite, rather than assess the broad national movement of which they were a part and the profound historical currents in which the movement was caught. Such a context is essential for a comprehension of the limitations under which the movement and its leaders labored: the larger forces at work faced the Palestine Arabs with the virtual impossibility of achieving their goal of independence or even of limiting the growth of the Jewish community.

The voluminous documents in the Public Record Office in London provided essential information for my research. The documents include not only correspondence between British officials in Palestine and London and minutes circulated within the Colonial and Foreign Offices, but also lengthy memorandums by Arab politicians, interviews with Arab leaders, and numerous excerpts from the Arabic press. These materials were supplemented by records of the Palestine government and Arabic documents collected in the Israel State Archives in Jerusalem; correspondence and reports by Zionist leaders deposited in the Central Zionist Archives in Jerusalem; documents and Arabic-language books at the American University of Beirut, the Palestine Research Center in Beirut, and the Institute for Palestine Studies in Beirut; and private papers of British officials collected by Elizabeth Monroe at St. Antony's College, Oxford. I interviewed several Palestinians who were active in the political movement or were well versed in the events of that period; their names are given in the Bibliography.

I am grateful to J. C. Hurewitz of Columbia University for his careful and considerate attention to the manuscript at its several stages. My initial research was made possible by a National Defense Foreign Language grant, and completion of the manuscript was facilitated by a fellowship from the Foreign Policy Research Institute. I also thank Antranig Bakarjian for arranging interviews for me on the West Bank, Yehoshua Porath for assisting me with the archival material in Jerusalem, Richard W. Cottam and Fred Khouri for their informed critiques, and Wayland W. Schmitt for suggesting editorial improvements. Judith McQuown skillfully crafted the index. Above all, I must thank Jack, who patiently sustained me through the long process of researching and writing this book.

ANN MOSELY LESCH

New York, New York

Abbreviations Used in Notes

For complete bibliographical information on these collections, see the Archives section of the Bibliography.

CAB   Cabinet Papers
CO   Colonial Office
CZA   Central Zionist Archives
FO   Foreign Office
ISA   Israel State Archives
ZO   Zionist Organization

PART I /

THE BACKGROUND OF

PALESTINE NATIONALISM

Key:
- - - - International
      boundary
1937 partition
— Jewish state
1937 partition
— British enclave

LEBANON

Metullah

SYRIA

Lake
Huleh

Safad

Acre

Haifa

Lake
Tiberias

Tiberias

Athlit

Nahalal

Nazareth

Plain of Esdraelon

Umm
al-Fahum

Afulah

Jenin

Beisan

Haderah

JORDAN

MEDITERRANEAN SEA

Tulkarm

Qalqilya

Nablus

Petah Tiqvah

Tel Aviv

Jaffa

Lydda

Ramallah

Rishon le Zion

Ramlah

Rehovoth

Jericho

Amman

Jerusalem

Majdal

Asqalan

Bethlehem

Gaza

Hebron

DEAD SEA

PALESTINE

Khan Yunis

Beersheba

EGYPT

Jordan River

1 / Introduction

The success of nationalist movements in Asia and Africa after World War II can be attributed less to their intrinsic strength than to changes in the status and attitudes of the West European powers toward colonial rule. The attitudes of the later period contrasted sharply with those of the inter-war years, when Europe mastered Asia and Africa, the members of the League of Nations were hostile to indigenous independence movements, and aspiring powers such as Germany and Italy claimed "a place in the sun" for themselves. Although the British and French governments conferred a degree of self-government on some of their colonies before World War II, when such a policy did not conflict with imperial strategic interests, ultimate power remained firmly in their own hands. Lip service was given to the Wilsonian concept of self-determination by League of Nations supervision of the mandatory system, used to govern several Arab territories. But the League was dominated by the colonial powers and never questioned the premises of the imperial system.

Thus there was no correlation between the intrinsic strength of the national movement in a colony and the willingness of the imperial power to transfer political sovereignty to that movement. Britain concluded treaties with Iraq and Egypt in the 1930s, for example, and conferred internal autonomy on Transjordan, but Parliament opposed establishing even an advisory legislative council in Palestine. The Arabs' nationalist movement was no less active in Palestine than in Egypt or Iraq, but Britain's pledges to the rival Zionist movement precluded any similar concessions. The claim to national self-determination raised by the Jewish community won international recognition, while the claim by the Arab residents did not. The Zionists constructed their shadow government and autonomous society within the mandated territory, laying the foundations for the establishment of a Jewish state after World War II.

The historical circumstances in which the Palestine Arabs were caught prevented the achievement of the aims of their national movement: during the interwar period, Britain was unwilling to abandon imperial control, and the competitive Jewish national movement consolidated its position until it could not be dislodged. After World War II, the Zionists rather than the Palestine Arabs had the internal and external strength needed to seize control over the contested land.

Colonial powers held that European settlers not only buttressed their rule but also spread enlightened Western economic practices, social norms, and intellectual values among the indigenous people. In practice, however, the settlers tended to be less benevolent than acquisitive, exerting pressure on the home government to grant them valuable land and mineral resources and to obtain a predominant role in government. The economic advance of the local population was often delayed, and their economic requirements were subordinated to those of the settlers. The reinforcement of racial barriers by communal forms of representation and racial job quotas further sharpened the sense of discrimination and separateness and accelerated nationalist mobilization among the indigenous people.

As areas of conflict widened between settlers and indigenous peoples, independence was further delayed, each group grew more embittered, and antagonism against the imperial power deepened.[1] The bitterness and mutual hostility produced violent clashes. Where the settlers were stronger, as in Palestine, they could defeat or expel the indigenous groups. Where the political claims of the local people were recognized by the ruling power and the international community, as in Kenya and Algeria in the late 1950s, they could prevail after a long, bitter struggle. In an era when the colonial powers were determined to maintain control and when international forces did not press against such rule, nationalist movements were unable to achieve their aims. Moreover, when a competitive ethnic group strove for national self-realization in the same territory the difficulties faced by the indigenous movement were exacerbated. When the competitive group had greater cohesion and militancy than the indigenous movement, the latter was placed in a sharply disadvantaged position. This situation was most apparent in Palestine, where the Jewish nationalists' political claims negated those of the Arabs and won acceptance from the British government and the international community.

The Roots of Nationalist Movements

A common language, religion, race, culture, and historical background contribute to a group's sense of identification as a nation, although no single element is essential. The contrast between the indigenous group and foreign officials or settlers also fostered the growth of national self-identification by enhancing feelings of subordination or discrimination.

This gap was underlined by the disparity in wages offered to European and local workers. In Palestine, the problem was

1. This was also true in India, where the Hindu-Muslim antagonism complicated the drive toward independence. Margery Perham, *Colonial Sequence, 1930 to 1949* (London: Methuen, 1967), pp. 187, 226, contrasts African colonies on the basis of whether they did or did not have settlers. See also Rupert Emerson, *From Empire to Nation: The Rise to Self-Assertion of Asian and African Peoples* (Boston: Beacon, 1966), p. 79, Karl W. Deutsch, *Nationalism and Social Communication* (Cambridge, Mass.: M.I.T. Press, 1966), pp. 183–186, describes the effect of social mobilization of the underlying population on national development.

exacerbated by the Zionist policy of *avodah ivrit* (Hebrew labor), which forbade the hiring of Arabs by Jewish colonies and industries. The General Federation of Hebrew Labor (Histadrut) sought to replace Arab workers by Jews in every sector of the economy. In addition, Arab merchants had to compete with immigrant merchants, who established their own cooperative marketing networks and had greater familiarity with European commercial practices. Arab government employees feared that they would be squeezed out by British and Jewish officials, and educated Arab youths found their avenues of personal advancement limited in that bureaucracy and their leadership potential blocked by colonial rule.

The alienation of land caused resentment and agitation in many colonies.[2] In Palestine, Zionist land companies purchased tracts from absentee landlords and indebted peasants, dispossessing villagers and replacing them with Jewish agricultural settlements. These colonies, bolstered against failure by the Jewish National Fund (JNF), were often established as politico-military outposts to stake territorial claims. They became the focus for violent attacks by Arab villagers, which caused the settlers to reinforce their military character and their isolation from the surrounding Arab villages.

A nationalist movement would not engage all social groups. Some members of the traditional elite opted to support the colonial power in order to retain their social prerogatives. Minority groups sometimes clung to foreign protection. The middle class might divide politically: administrators gained a vested interest in the colonial system, and businessmen and traders tended to have greater ties to the status quo than politicians drawn from the liberal professions.[3] Wealthy absentee landowners might benefit personally from land sales to settlers and therefore remained unresponsive to efforts to

2. See Carl G. Rosberg, Jr., and John Nottingham, *The Myth of Mau Mau: Nationalism in Kenya* (New York: Praeger, 1966), on Kikuyu anger at the loss of land in the "white highlands" of Kenya as a major factor in the Mau Mau revolt.

3. See Lucian W. Pye, *Politics, Personality and Nation-Building: Burma's Search for Identity* (New Haven: Yale University Press, 1962), pp. 97–99.

hold onto land as the basis for the future of the nation. Most of the peasantry remained too isolated, ignorant, and poor to play a real part in the movement, except when a rebellion swept across the country.

To mobilize the public, nationalist movements sometimes used the traditional social institutions and also developed new organizational structures borrowed from Europe. Nationalist ideas filtered down to the rural peasantry through the clan or tribe, which provided the organizational structure. Villagers in Palestine, for example, followed the political guidance of the local and regional families and of their clan (*hamulah*) leaders. Such ties were not immutable, however, and leading families competed for influence in the villages and towns. Alternative sources of information and influence were also opened up by the spread of radios and newspapers to rural areas. And the village guesthouse and town café served as centers for political discussion.

In urban areas, mosques and churches provided centers to disseminate political doctrines and organize public action. Similarly, artisan guilds and labor societies provided the basis for political as well as economic organization. Middle- and upper-class literary and sports clubs also assumed a political identity, serving as forums to debate programs and elaborate strategy. Organizations adapted from the West played an active part in politics: trade unions protested discriminatory hiring and wages; political parties merged with the family and club groups; boy scouts and private schools spread nationalism among the younger generation; and the press helped to diffuse political ideas.

Stages of Nationalist Movements

For analytical purposes, the evolution of nationalist movements may be separated into three broad phases, during which their structure became more complex, their aims more clearly articulated, and their tactics intensified. In the first phase, the educated elite formed political clubs, often disguised as literary societies, whose platforms emphasized constitutional reform: representative government, leading roles in the administrative and judiciary systems, and educational and economic opportunities. Rupert Emerson explains, "They seek to appeal . . . in rational and constitutional terms, demonstrating that they are responsible persons rightly to be entrusted with a share in colonial management."[4] This generation of "liberal" politicians[5] existed in Palestine in the last decades of Ottoman rule and carried over into the first decade of the mandatory period.

If the colonial ruler established a legislative council and granted the liberals some self-government and economic opportunities, the elite might be temporarily satisfied with these limited measures. When, however, the imperial power felt that it could safely ignore the petitions presented by the moderate and gentlemanly liberals, forces leading into the next phase would be generated, supported either by the liberals themselves when they realized the limitations of their methods or by the younger generation, repudiating its elders. In practice, this second phase tended to begin while the liberals still sought reforms and thus complicated their efforts.

"Radical" politicians[6] in the second phase mobilized larger numbers and adopted aggressive pressure techniques against the colonial power. The radicals organized political parties and national fronts that reached out to the less-educated classes for broader support. Their techniques included petitions and deputations to the ruling power, as in the previous phase, but these were now supported by boycotts, strikes, and civil disobedience campaigns. Although pressure tactics could occasionally disrupt local administration and dramatize grievances, the movement had difficulty sustaining mass in-

4. Emerson, p. 243; L. H. Gann and Peter Duignan, *Burden of Empire: An Appraisal of Western Colonialism in Africa South of the Sahara* (Stanford, Calif.: Hoover Institution Press, 1971), p. 324.

5. William B. Quandt, *Revolution and Political Leadership: Algeria, 1954–1968* (Cambridge, Mass.: M.I.T. Press, 1969), pp. 25ff.

6. Ibid., pp. 43ff.

volvement, given the obstacles facing the population and the relatively low level of public awareness and organization. Because the nationalist movement would incorporate many different groups, it had difficulty working toward any common economic or social goals, beyond the single goal of political independence. Factions within the national movement—formed along family, political party, or class lines—might compete with one another for influence and control and thereby provide the colonial power with opportunities to divide the movement and undermine its effectiveness. In Palestine, the Arab Executive, a committee of politicians who attempted to coordinate the struggle in the 1920s and early 1930s, was subject to severe internal strains as a result of rivalries among the leading Palestinian families. In the mid-twenties it was reduced to serving as the instrument of only one faction, although it succeeded in reincorporating rival groups at the end of the decade and thereby reinvigorated itself and reasserted its dominant position.

The nature of the final phase depended on the degree of success already attained. If pressure tactics succeeded in winning substantial political concessions from the colonial power and independence appeared imminent, the national movement swelled with people seeking political favors and careers after independence. The politicians began to articulate social and economic programs they would want the new state to implement. Party organizations became more elaborate as they were transformed from pressure groups into electoral and governing machines.

If the colonial power still blocked independence, reorganization would be postponed until the end of a militant, sometimes revolutionary, phase.[7] In this final phase, the movement turned to organized violence to achieve its goals. Urban riots and rural guerrilla warfare raised the price of control for the imperial power, but the strategic requirements

7. Ibid., pp. 66ff.

of that power remained the decisive determinant of the response made to such violence. In contrast to Iraq and Egypt, where negotiations were accelerated after disturbances, in Palestine militancy and violence yielded no tangible results until the full-scale revolt of the late 1930s.

Throughout this militant phase, the national movement would be confronted with fundamental dilemmas. Its ability to mobilize the public was enhanced by the seriousness of the perceived threat, but violence tended to strain the united national front, alienating those who opposed the use of force. Moreover, militancy was a source of strength in the confrontation with the rival national movement in the colony, but also caused that movement to increase its own strength and further polarized the two movements. The gulf between the Arab and Jewish communities in Palestine widened with every outbreak of violence. Each side hardened its demands and accelerated the mobilization of its followers.

Tactics and Dilemmas

In addition to organizing within the colony, nationalist movements attempted to attract support abroad from members of the same ethnic group, dissidents within the ruling country, countries that opposed the ruling power, and members of international organizations. The most important and concentrated efforts were directed toward the ruling power. For nationalists in British colonies, lobbying in Parliament and sending delegations to the Colonial Office served to articulate and reinforce their drive and aims. But such efforts could be double-edged, since settlers could also rally support abroad and often had more intimate and effective contacts in London. In fact, the indigenous population tended to be less able than the settlers to reach the ear of foreign diplomats and to pressure the ruling power for concessions, as long as the prevailing climate of international opinion supported the colonial system. In Palestine, the Zionist Organization was much more effective in gaining external support for the Jewish community than was the Arab leadership. The Arabs appealed to the League of Nations and to British public opinion, but they could not sustain these efforts or win meaningful support. Only among the Arab and Muslim countries did the Palestinians gain support that provided them with some useful external leverage on the British government.

Nationalist movements faced a serious tactical dilemma over the issue of accepting constitutional offers made by the ruling power. In some situations, the offer of a legislative council was the first step toward independence and was followed by the incorporation of local leaders into the government and the attainment of responsible internal rule. In other situations, however, it meant the postponement of independence or the compromising of the nationalists' principles. In a settler colony, in particular, acceptance of a restricted constitutional arrangement might compromise the nationalists' claims and legitimize the settlers' political role. If the nationalist movement refused a constitution, it could appear to be blocking a positive step and thus signal its own political immaturity and, from the viewpoint of the ruler, its obstructionism.

This dilemma was particularly acute in Palestine, where the continual growth of the Jewish population threatened the majority status of the Arab community. Arab politicians feared that, if they accepted a legislative council that could only advise the government and could not control immigration, they would find that such an institution would help the Jewish community legitimize its position and eventually become the majority. But the Arabs' refusal of a legislative council left them without any constitutional forum in which to articulate their grievances and caused the British government to brand them as backward and to exclude them completely from policy making.

The lack of a constitutional means to redress grievances, in a situation marked by economic difficulties, a keen sense of political injustice, and increasing political mobilization, could cause popular frustration to erupt into mass violence. Just as important a motivating force as frustration was the deep feeling that injustice had been done to the indigenous people, coupled with the absence of any nonviolent means to redress this injustice. An outbreak of violence might be triggered by a religious incident, might arise unexpectedly out of a demonstration, or might be fomented by guerrilla organizations and secret political cells. Violence flared up briefly in Palestine in the early 1920s and in 1929; demonstrations in 1933 degenerated into clashes with the British police; and a rural revolt swept the country in the late 1930s. Such violence could embarrass the dominant politicians: although it underlined the seriousness of the grievances, it appeared to damage their claims to political maturity. When settlers were present, they cited violence as further evidence of the need for European rule and for firm control over the "natives." Thus, violence could be politically counterproductive, although it increased popular mobilization and pressure on the authorities.

The tactics adopted and the manner in which the dilemmas were faced established the patterns of interaction between the nationalist movement and the European authorities and settlers. In the end, however, these actions could not determine the outcome of the struggle. Rather, the balance of force and influence between the indigenous movement and the settlers, the strategic requirements of the ruling power, and the international attitude toward colonialism were the overriding determinants.

2 / The Political Environment

The first phase of the Palestine Arab nationalist movement was played out in the context of a weakened and restive Ottoman Empire at the beginning of the twentieth century. Members of the Muslim Arab landowning and administrative elite and of the Christian Arab mercantile families articulated political grievances and concepts that sharpened discontent with the empire and provided the basic arguments against Zionism. The defeat of the Ottoman Empire in World War I marked the end of this phase and the beginning of the British mandate, which witnessed increasingly militant stages of the national movement.

The British government, seeking to maintain its power in the Middle East and committed to supporting the establishment of a Jewish national home in Palestine, found itself caught between the conflicting pressures of the Jewish and Arab communities. Its hold became less tenable in the 1930s, at the very time when the Italian and German threat underlined the strategic importance of Palestine to Britain. The Jewish immigrants were not merely seeking entry into Palestine. Part of a self-conscious nation even when they lived in their Diaspora, they sought to realize their messianic dream of recreating the ancient Jewish state. Moreover, they were fleeing from virulent persecution in Europe. Their special attachment and serious need helped them to persuade Europeans and Americans to support Zionism as the one legitimate national movement in Palestine, but could not diminish Arab opposition to Zionist aims.

23

The Ottoman Period

The Ottoman Empire was subjected to severe strains in the nineteenth century from both European powers and internal groups. The empire lost control over Greece, Egypt, North Africa, and the Balkans and was compelled to grant local autonomy to the Maronites on Mount Lebanon. Wars contributed to the empire's financial crises, which, in turn, enabled the European states to penetrate and control the Ottoman economy. To counter the centrifugal forces and stem European encroachments, the regime tried to modernize and centralize its administration, but these efforts further exacerbated strains between the central government and the provinces.

The centralizing trends accelerated after the Young Turk coup d'état in July 1908 and the suppression by the Committee of Union and Progress (CUP) of a counterrevolution in April 1909. Although the CUP initially promised political equality to all Ottoman subjects without distinction of religion or race, it soon outlawed political organizations based on ethnic or national groups and shifted its policy from equality to Turkification. This ideology glorified pre-Islamic Turkey and thus weakened the religious bond between Muslim Arabs and Turks that had been a basic element in Arab loyalty to the empire.[1] The CUP alienated a wide spectrum of Arabs when it decreed that Turkish should be the sole language used in administration, the judiciary, and schools in Arab provinces. Moreover, the CUP continued to lose control over the provinces, particularly suffering setbacks in the Balkans.

After the 1908 coup, the Arabs were allowed to organize politically and to express their views through newspapers,

1. By the 1880s and 1890s consciousness of the differences between Arabs and Turks was growing, but this was accelerated after 1908. C. Ernest Dawn, *From Ottomanism to Arabism* (Urbana: University of Illinois Press, 1973), pp. 129–140; Zeine N. Zeine, *The Emergence of Arab Nationalism* (Beirut: Khayats, 1966), p. 143; Kemal H. Karpat, "The Transformation of the Ottoman State, 1789–1908," *International Journal of Middle East Studies*, 3 (July 1972), 279, 281.

political parties, and the parliament. Local political groups, such as the Reform Societies of Beirut, Basra, and Jaffa, called for decentralization of the empire and Arab control over provincial administration. The Young Arab Society (al-Fatat), formed by Arab students in Paris in 1909,[2] and the Ottoman Administrative Decentralization Society in Cairo were less inhibited in their calls for autonomy because they operated outside the sphere of the Ottoman authorities.

The government ignored the societies' demands for decentralization articulated at a congress in Paris in June 1913, largely because the regime felt that the societies represented only a negligible element in Arab society. The failure of the moderate reform movement to win concessions from the CUP radicalized its members and induced a small group of Arab army officers to organize a secret society, al-Ahd (the Covenant), which established links with al-Fatat. Both groups were crushed by the Ottoman authorities during World War I, before they could have a significant impact. In fact, most Arab residents remained loyal to the empire until the British army actually occupied the Arab provinces in 1917 and 1918.[3] The elite, particularly in Palestine, continued to believe in internal reform, preferring Muslim rule to Christian and fearing European hegemony more than continued Ottoman control.

Palestine was divided between two provinces during the late Ottoman period. Provincial reorganization in the 1880s resulted in the formation of a *vilayet* (province) of Beirut, which included the fertile agricultural districts of Acre and Nablus (Balqa) in northern Palestine. The central and southern zones of Palestine were detached from the *vilayet* of Sham (Damascus) and constituted into the autonomous *sançak* (district) of Jerusalem, under the direct control of the imperial

2. Awni Abd al-Hadi and Rafiq al-Tamimi, both from Nablus, were active in Paris (Zeine, pp. 95–103).
3. Ibid., pp. 132–133; C. Ernest Dawn, "The Rise of Arabism in Syria," *Middle East Journal*, 16 (1962), 152, 159.

government in Istanbul.[4] This *sançak* contained three-quarters of Palestine's population and the two holiest cities in Islam outside the Hijaz, namely, Jerusalem and al-Khalil (Hebron).

The Muslim Arab elite in Palestine felt secure within the empire.[5] Members of the leading families in Jerusalem, Nablus, Acre, and Jaffa served in the imperial foreign service and central administration and controlled the municipalities, religious institutions, and schools in their towns. In Jerusalem, the Khalidi, Jarallah, and Alami families were most influential in the eighteenth century, but they were outranked by the Husaynis in the late nineteenth century, when Husaynis served as both mayor and mufti of Jerusalem. A fourth family, the Nashashibis, began to gain influence in the early 1900s, as its rural landholdings increased. In Nablus district, family rivalries centered on the Tuqans and Abd al-Hadis, whose armed skirmishes in the early nineteenth century were transformed into heated political battles by the century's end. In general, the urban Muslim families eclipsed the rural clans in the latter half of the century, as the provinces experienced enhanced administrative stability and economic growth. At the same time, Christian Arab merchants and professionals expanded their activities and began to acquire limited political rights. Within the Greek Orthodox church, Arab opposition

4. P. M. Holt, *Egypt and the Fertile Crescent, 1516–1922: A Political History* (Ithaca, N.Y.: Cornell University Press, 1966), p. 242; Zeine, pp. 28–30; Yehoshua Porath, "Al-Hajj Amin al-Husayni, Mufti of Jerusalem—His Rise to Power and the Consolidation of His Position," *Asian and African Studies,* 7 (1971), 126.

5. For detailed treatment of Palestine Arab society and politics during the late Ottoman period, see Ann Mosely Lesch, "The Origins of Palestine Arab Nationalism," in *Nationalism in a Non-National State: The Dissolution of the Ottoman Empire,* ed. William W. Haddad and William L. Ochsenwald (Columbus: Ohio State University Press, 1977). See also Moshe Ma'oz, *Ottoman Reform in Syria and Palestine, 1840–1861: The Impact of the Tanzimat on Politics and Society* (Oxford: Oxford University Press, 1968), pp. 4–11 on Ottoman rule before 1831, pp. 12–20 on the rule of Ibrahim Pasha, pp. 113–118 on Nablus area rivalries, pp. 118–122 on the Hebron-Bethlehem area, and pp. 130–134 on deteriorated conditions in midcentury. See also Elias N. Haddad, "Political Parties in Syria and Palestine (Qaisi and Yemeni)," *Journal of the Palestine Oriental Society,* 1 (1921); James Finn, *Stirring Times, or Records from Jerusalem Consular Chronicles of 1853 to 1856,* 2 vols. (London: Kegan Paul, 1878); and Laurence Oliphant, *Haifa or Life in Modern Palestine* (New York: Harper, 1887).

to the Greek hierarchy assumed a nationalist and anti-Turk coloration in the 1900s, fostering an Arab self-identification among important segments of the Christian community.[6]

But the Arabs did not unite around either anti-Turkish or anti-European stands. Rather, anti-Zionism formed the rallying point for the Arab community: Jewish immigration and the political ambitions of the nascent Zionist movement foreshadowed the political submergence and potential displacement of the local population and thus posed a greater danger than European occupation or Ottoman restrictions. Until 1908, the Arab leaders relied primarily on petitions to Istanbul and the influence of members of the Muslim elite in the capital as the means to curb Zionism. After the Young Turk coup d'état, the local Arabic press registered protests, and delegates to the imperial parliament articulated grievances that centered on the issues of Jewish immigration and land buying.

The character of the Jewish community in Palestine changed markedly in the late nineteenth century.[7] Before 1881 it was a mix of European and Sephardic Arabic-speaking Jews, many dependent on alms (*halukah*) collected by Jews living abroad. Later immigrants were secular and politically motivated, yearning to reconstitute the Jewish nation on its ancient soil. In 1880, the Jewish community in Palestine totaled perhaps 35,000 out of 584,000 residents. By 1900, Jews numbered some 50,000 out of the 640,000 total, and by 1914 their share rose to over 75,000 out of 650,000.

The immigrants of the first *aliyah* (ascent) of 1882–1903

---

6. Sir Anton Bertram and Harry Charles Luke, *Report of the Commission Appointed by the Government of Palestine to Inquire into the Affairs of the Orthodox Patriarchate of Jerusalem* (London: Oxford University Press, 1921), pp. 26–29, 250–271; Elie Kedourie, "Religion and Politics: The Diaries of Khalil Sakakini," *Middle Eastern Affairs*, 1, *St. Antony's Papers*, 4 (1958), 86, also 77–79, 92; James Parkes, *A History of Palestine from 135 A.D. to Modern Times* (New York: Oxford University Press, 1949), p. 241; Yehoshua Porath, *The Emergence of the Palestinian-Arab National Movement, 1918–1929* (London: Frank Cass, 1974), pp. 7–8.

7. On the pre-1881 Yishuv, see Finn, I, 101–132, II, 56–82, 320–335; Ma'oz, *Ottoman Reform*, pp. 205–209. On the new attitudes, see David Ben Gurion, *My Talks with Arab Leaders* (New York: Third Press, 1973), pp. 2–3.

established agricultural colonies that often hired Arabs as laborers and guards, thus tempering their hostility by providing employment. The second *aliyah* immigrants (1903–1914), however, upheld a socialist, egalitarian ideology that insisted upon *avodah ivrit* (Hebrew labor) in the agricultural settlements. They felt that Jewish farmers should undertake all agricultural labor and guard duty themselves, as part of their personal and national self-renewal. Although this policy was justified on grounds of Jewish nationalism, it antagonized their Arab neighbors and further isolated the Jewish colonies from the indigenous people.[8] Despite legal restrictions on land purchase, eight Jewish agricultural settlements were founded in the 1880s in the *sançak* of Jerusalem. Ignorant of local customs and unable to speak Arabic, the settlers refused to let neighboring villagers and bedouin tribes continue customary pasture rights on their lands. The settlers punished trespassers themselves, disregarding Ottoman civil law and its court system. Such misunderstandings over customary rights and over boundaries often resulted in violence.

Muslim and Christian notables in Jerusalem joined together as early as 1891 to send a telegraph to Istanbul urging that Jewish immigration and land purchasing be prohibited. The government responded by publishing edicts that prohibited the immigration of Russian Jews and the sale of state land (*miri*) to Jews. As a result, land purchase was radically curtailed from 1891 to 1900, when the regulations were revised. During that decade, Zionist land-purchasing companies had to turn their attention to northern Palestine, outside the *sançak* of Jerusalem.[9] The European powers opposed these restrictions on land sale and immigration and succeeded in preventing the enforcement of the edict against immigration after applying sharp pressure on Istanbul. But the Ottoman

8. Yaacov Ro'i, "The Zionist Attitude to the Arabs, 1908–1914," *Middle Eastern Studies,* 4 (April 1968), 201–202; Neville J. Mandel, "Turks, Arabs and Jewish Immigration into Palestine, 1882–1914," *Middle Eastern Affairs,* 4 (1968); Holt, p. 246.

9. Mandel, "Turks, Arabs," pp. 86, 90, 96; Oliphant, pp. 59–60, 62, 288.

regime continued to be alarmed by the Zionist movement's apparent aims. When the Zionist congress of 1905 resolved to direct all its efforts toward Palestine, the Ottoman government responded abruptly by suspending all land transfers to Jews in both the Beirut *vilayet* and the *sançak* of Jerusalem.

By then some Zionist leaders were aware of the dual Arab and Ottoman opposition. The manifestos issued in Paris in 1904 and 1905 by Najib Azuri, a Christian Arab who had served as an Ottoman official in Jerusalem, brought the concept of an Arab national awakening to the attention of Europe, where pro-Zionist newspapers noted that such an awakening could hinder the realization of their own aims.[10]

After the 1908 coup, the Palestine Arabs could argue their case directly in Istanbul. The three parliamentary delegates from the *sançak* of Jerusalem spoke out against Zionism in debates in May 1911.[11] They were supported by two former *qaimmaqams* (district governors) in northern Palestine, now serving as deputies from Syrian towns.[12] The deputy from Acre, Shaykh Asad al-Shuqayri, did not oppose the Zionist movement. As a conservative Muslim, he was primarily fearful of European Christian influence and believed that the Arabs and Turks could enlist the Zionists on their side to resist European encroachment.[13]

Newspapers founded in Palestine after 1908 analyzed and articulated objections to Zionism. *Al-Karmil* of Haifa and *Filastin* of Jaffa, both published by Christian Arabs,[14] were

10. Ro'i, pp. 198–199.
11. Mandel, "Turks, Arabs," pp. 92–95. The three delegates were Said al-Husayni, Hafiz al-Said (Jaffa), and Ruhi al-Khalidi. In 1912, Ruhi al-Khalidi was reelected, but the other two, who represented the Entente Liberale party, lost to the CUP candidates, Ahmad Arif al-Husayni and Uthman al-Nashashibi. The winning candidates in 1914 were Raghib al-Nashashibi, Faydi al-Alami, and Said al-Husayni.
12. These were Emir Amin Arslan, former Tiberias *qaimmaqam,* who had blocked a large land purchase from the Sursuq family of Beirut in 1901, and Shukri al-Asali, the former *qaimmaqam* of Nazareth, who had been unable to block a similar land sale to the Jewish National Fund in 1910.
13. Ro'i, pp. 224, 228.
14. Najib al-Nassar published *al-Karmil* and Isa al-Isa published *Filastin.* See Mandel, "Turks, Arabs," pp. 92–95.

particularly outspoken. Local societies were formed to combat Zionist land purchases, and the Muslim elite used its control of municipal and legal positions to block land sales.[15]

Despite the Ottoman regime's apparent opposition to Zionist aims, its desperation for funds to underwrite the First Balkan War in 1912 led it to negotiate with the Zionist Organization. The government offered to sell some crown land (*çiftlik*), and the Zionist Organization expressed interest in land along the Jordan River near Beisan. In fact, the Zionist Organization could not have afforded to purchase the land, and the lengthy negotiations were never consummated.[16]

Certain Arab politicians also believed that they could gain financial and diplomatic strength from a rapprochement with the Zionists. The Decentralization Society, which operated outside Palestine, suggested an Arab-Jewish detente in February 1913 and repeated this idea the next winter.[17] But the Zionist leaders were hesitant to join these Arab groups in opposing the Ottoman regime, with which they were negotiating for acquisition of land. In any case, contacts with the Zionists were strongly opposed by Arab leaders within Palestine.[18]

The Ottoman-Zionist discussions of 1912–1913 increased popular anxiety inside Palestine, especially when the government relaxed its restrictions on Jewish immigration and land purchase, and briefly closed down the most anti-Zionist Arabic newspapers.[19] Tension increased in northern Palestine when people heard that the Beisan *çiftlik* might be sold, and anti-Zionist societies sprouted in the port town of Jaffa. Popular animosity flared into the first serious incidents since 1908–1909.

15. Ibid., pp. 98, 102.

16. Herzl had already tried to purchase tracts in 1901 and 1902 from the Ottomans; see Marvin Lowenthal, ed., *The Diaries of Theodor Herzl* (New York: Grosset and Dunlap, Universal Library Edition, 1962).

17. Neville Mandel, "Attempts at an Arab-Zionist Entente, 1913–1914," *Middle Eastern Studies,* 1 (April 1965), 261.

18. Mandel describes an effort by Nasif Khalidi, a Palestinian living in Beirut, to convene a Jewish-Arab conference in June 1914, ibid., p. 263.

19. Mandel, "Turks, Arabs," pp. 101–102.

By then the younger generation was beginning to express its views on Zionism and Arab autonomy. Arab university students in Cairo, Istanbul, Paris, and even in the secondary schools of Nablus and Jerusalem had access to Zionist writings in translation or followed the Zionist press in Europe. Through these sources they came to fear Zionism's political ambitions and its economic and cultural separatism. The Zionist leaders were unable to stem these fears, since their writings in Europe were intended to arouse the hopes and support of European Jewry and to minimize the obtacles to be encountered in Palestine, especially the presence of an indigenous people. The head of the Zionist movement's Palestine Office, which opened in Jaffa in 1908, emphasized that tact was needed in relations with the Arabs.[20] But the leaders in Europe felt that good relations with the Palestine Arabs were less urgent than their need to win support from European powers and the Ottoman government. Even in Palestine, they remained preoccupied with their own national requirements, such as the implementation of *avodah ivrit* and the establishment of separate Hebrew-language schools.

The incompatibility of Zionist and Arab aspirations in Palestine was apparent by the outbreak of World War I. Although both peoples were still weak in organization, their aims were already fully articulated. Fear of Zionism accelerated the growth of an Arab political movement in the districts that comprised Palestine and hastened the establishment of a vigorous press that could explain Arab grievances to those outside the elite circles.

The period from 1908 to 1914 may be viewed as the phase of the nationalist movement led by liberal politicians. These men sought constitutional reform within the framework of the Ottoman Empire and thought that rational appeals would win redress of their grievances and stem the Zionists' advance into Palestine. The Muslim elite was relatively satisfied by its role in the local, provincial, and central governments. But Turkifi-

20. Ro'i, pp. 205, 210.

cation measures, the imperial parliament's ineffectiveness, the Balkan wars, and, finally, the government's occasional parleying with the Zionists undercut its acceptance. Schooled in this atmosphere, the men who were to lead the Palestine Arabs in the 1920s and 1930s recognized the limitations of the tactics of petition and later turned to mass action and noncooperation to counter the Zionists and the new British rulers.

Although the repressive policies pursued by the Ottoman authorities during World War I alienated many people, the ties with the empire were not severed until the British occupied the *sançak* of Jerusalem in late 1917 and the northern regions in September 1918. The British occupation marked the realization of the Arabs' greatest fear—the triumph of the Zionist movement, expressed through the Balfour Declaration of November 2, 1917.

The British Mandate

On the eve of World War I, the British Empire extended across Asia and Africa, centering on the Indian subcontinent and covering the route through the Suez Canal from Europe to India. After the Ottoman Empire joined the war on the side of Germany and the Austro-Hungarian Empire, its forces attacked the British army holding the Suez Canal in 1915. Palestine thereby acquired a strategic importance to Britain, which sought to cover the northern flank of Egypt and then to defeat the Ottoman forces, severing all the Arab provinces from Ottoman rule by the end of 1918.

During the war, the British government made several commitments concerning these territories, commitments that were later seen to be mutually contradictory. A secret pact with the French government and czarist Russia in 1916, known as the Sykes-Picot Agreement, divided the Ottoman Empire into spheres of control and of paramount interest that would be parceled among the three powers. Because of the special European interests in Palestine's Christian holy places, the agreement placed Palestine under an international administration.

In the winter of 1915–1916, however, the British high commissioner in Egypt, Sir Henry McMahon, initiated a correspondence with Sherif Husayn, the emir of Mecca since 1908. Husayn agreed to join the Allies if they would uphold the Arabs' claims to independence. The borders of the Arab zone were only loosely defined in the exchange of letters between McMahon and Husayn, and Palestine was not mentioned explicitly. Arab leaders assumed that it lay within the area to be granted independence, but British officials later argued that it was excluded.[21]

Still another agreement promised the Zionists a national home in Palestine. The Balfour Declaration of 1917 stated:

> His Majesty's Government view with favour the establishment in Palestine of a national home for the Jewish people, and will use their best endeavours to facilitate the achievement of this object, it being clearly understood that nothing shall be done which may prejudice the civil and religious rights of the existing non-Jewish communities in Palestine, or the rights and political status enjoyed by Jews in any other country.

In addition, Britain and the Allies issued statements that stressed the principle of national self-determination and supported the pledge of Arab independence.[22]

But Britain occupied Palestine de facto, and its real political authority derived from military occupation. Wary of French imperial ambitions among the Catholic peoples in the Levant, the British government wanted to ensure its own paramountcy in the area. Since the Russian Revolution had removed that power from an active role in the Middle East, only France needed to be taken into account in assessing the relative

21. Great Britain, Parliamentary Papers, Command 5957, *Correspondence between Sir Henry McMahon and the Sharif of Mecca, July, 1915–March, 1916* (London: HMSO, 1939). Also in George Antonius, *The Arab Awakening* (New York: Capricorn, 1965), pp. 413–427, and J. C. Hurewitz, *Diplomacy in the Near and Middle East,* 2 vols. (New York: Van Nostrand, 1956), II, 18–22.

22. These statements included President Woodrow Wilson's Fourteen Points, the Anglo-French Declaration to the Peoples of Syria and Mesopotamia (November 1918), and the Covenant of the League of Nations.

weight to be accorded to the Sykes-Picot Agreement, the McMahon-Husayn correspondence, and the Balfour Declaration. The British foreign secretary, Lord Balfour, admitted that the pledges were irreconcilable and decided to resolve the issue by pressing for a settlement based primarily on the Sykes-Picot Agreement. He also provided for Arab autonomy in part of the area outlined in the McMahon-Husayn letters, and he upheld the application of the Balfour Declaration to Palestine, arguing that the Allies were "committed to Zionism" and therefore could not even "go through the form of consulting the wishes of the present inhabitants" of Palestine concerning its future.[23] One member of the Foreign Office noted that this conclusion ignored the problem of reconciling the Arabs to the loss of Palestine: Lord Balfour promised to grant Palestine to the Zionists "irrespective of the wishes of the great bulk of the population, because it is historically right and politically expedient that [Britain] should do so. The idea that the carrying out of these programmes will entail bloodshed and military repression never seems to have occurred to him."[24]

As part of the imperial arrangement, France assumed control over Lebanon and Syria, forcibly ejecting the Arab regime from Damascus in July 1920. Britain consolidated its hold in Palestine and granted nominal autonomy to Iraq and Transjordan. Only the Arabian peninsula, never occupied by the Allied forces, became independent. Arab leaders continued to press for full independence and to argue that Palestine was included in the Arab zone. British rejection of that argument contributed significantly to the Arabs' loss of faith in its pledges and fed anti-British agitation.

The Balfour Declaration laid the basis for British policy in Palestine, but that policy contained serious inconsistencies.

23. Memorandum by Balfour, Aug. 1919, Foreign Office (FO) 371/4183/2117/132187, published in E. L. Woodward and Rohan Butler, eds., *Documents on British Foreign Policy, 1919–1939* (London: HMSO, 1952), 1st ser., IV, 343.
24. George J. Kidston, Middle East Department, Foreign Office, minute, Sept. 22, 1919, FO 371/4183/2117/132187, available in the Public Record Office, London.

The Zionists read it as a pledge by the British government, later reaffirmed by the League of Nations, to establish a Jewish state in Palestine. Their spokesmen argued that this pledge overrode any secondary obligations to maintain the political and demographic status of the non-Jewish indigenous population.[25] Chaim Weizmann, president of the Zionist Organization, maintained that Palestine should become a Jewish country in which the rights of the non-Jewish minority would be safeguarded. He told Lord Balfour that, just as a foreigner in England could settle, work, and participate in English social life, so would a non-Jewish citizen "enjoy all rights and privileges of citizenship" under the Jewish regime.[26]

Arab politicians generally agreed with this interpretation of the Balfour Declaration and therefore opposed the Zionists bitterly. They argued that the mandate for Palestine, which included that declaration, was inconsistent with Article 22, paragraph 4, of the Covenant of the League of Nations, according to which the former Turkish provinces were to become independent except for "the rendering of administrative advice and assistance by a Mandatory."[27] Palestine, however, was ruled as a crown colony of Great Britain, in the interests of the immigrant community. Supporters of the Palestine Arab case added the argument that the declaration should be viewed only as a statement of sympathy for the Zionist movement, not as a commitment to realize its aims, because the phrases the "government view with favour" and "will use their best endeavours" were permissive rather than obligatory.[28]

25. Bernard (Dov) Joseph, *British Rule in Palestine* (Washington, D.C.: Public Affairs Press, 1948), offers a forceful, legalistic argument to this effect.

26. Weizmann to Sir Eyre Crowe (FO), Dec. 9, 1918, enclosing a note on his discussion with Balfour, FO 371/3385/747/203091.

27. Leland M. Goodrich, *The United Nations* (New York: Crowell, 1959), pp. 344–345, and Hurewitz, *Diplomacy,* II, 61.

28. W. T. Mallison, Jr., "The Balfour Declaration," in Ibrahim Abu-Lughod, ed., *The Transformation of Palestine* (Evanston, Ill.: Northwestern University Press, 1971), pp. 83–95. See also the January 1918 Hogarth message to Husayn, drafted by Sir Marks Sykes, one version of the text in Sykes' telegram to Sir Reginald Wingate (Cairo), Jan. 4, 1918, FO 371/3054/86526/245810, another in Antonius, pp. 267–268, and Hurewitz, *Diplomacy,* II, 29.

The British government did not accept these arguments, but it never offered a consistent interpretation of the declaration. Cabinet members and officials in Palestine initially admitted that they expected eventual Jewish statehood there.[29] But after Arab opposition swelled in the early 1920s while Jewish immigration remained modest, these officials attempted to win Zionist acceptance of a limited conception of their position in Palestine. The Colonial Office, which administered the Palestine mandate after February 1921, tried to define British policy as building up "in Palestine a commonwealth, based upon a democratic foundation, in which all sections of the community will enjoy equal political rights."[30] Its officials argued that the Arabs and Jews must learn to share the country as a biracial state. Yet neither Zionist nor Arab leaders assented to this formula: each group wanted its community to be the majority, and each claimed title to Palestine.

Colonial Office personnel were well aware of the dilemmas facing them: pursuing a Zionist policy would earn Britain the enmity of the Arab population,[31] but denying the Zionists the possibility of becoming a majority in Palestine would incur their anger and cause serious political repercussions in England. In 1930, a White Paper that implicitly limited Jewish immigration and land purchases triggered outraged responses from Zionist leaders and resulted in their successful application of pressure—through the British press, Parliament, and secret meetings with the cabinet—to reverse these restrictions.

After each outbreak of Arab violence, the British government dispatched a commission of inquiry to Palestine to inves-

29. Sir Ronald Storrs, military governor, Jerusalem, private letter to Sykes, July 17, 1918, Sykes Papers, St. Antony's College, Private Paper Collection.
30. Quotation from the draft formula submitted by the Colonial Office (CO) to the Zionist Organization (ZO) and the first Arab delegation to London, Dec. 17, 1921, as the basis for futher discussions, CO 537/854.
31. See E. Mills, minute, Dec. 9, 1921, on a letter from Chief Secretary W. Deedes, Nov. 22, 1921, CO 537/852; J. Shuckburgh and H. Young, minutes, in February 1923 on High Commissioner H. Samuel, telegram, Feb. 11, 1923, CO 733/42.

tigate the causes of the violence and to propose ameliorative measures.[32] Although their terms of reference were limited, they invariably found the tension to be rooted in the Balfour Declaration and the fears raised by political Zionism. Marginal recommendations by the commissions—such as measures to improve police efficiency—were implemented, but the recommendations for political and economic reform had only short-term effects, if any. Despite the emphatic warning in 1921 by the head of the Middle East Department in the Colonial Office that the British "must be prepared to resist pressure from both sides,"[33] the government was buffeted from side to side, attempting to relieve the Arabs' fears by verbal maneuvers without precluding an eventual Jewish majority. Yet the British won few friends among the Zionists, who continually pressed for accelerated immigration, more land-buying opportunities, and more political influence.

By the mid-1930s, the government was considering plans to crystallize the growth of the Jewish national home in order to placate the Arabs. Such plans centered on the idea of cantonization, which would accord political autonomy to each community and thus enable the Jewish state to admit as many immigrants as it desired while the Arab state would be freed from the fear of Jewish domination.[34] This concept was embodied in the royal commission's report in 1937, which concluded that partition was the only way to handle the antagonistic Jewish and Arab national movements.[35] That this course would be difficult to implement and would necessitate

32. Richard N. Verdery, "Arab 'Disturbances' and the Commissions of Inquiry," in Abu-Lughod, ed., *Transformation,* pp. 273–303.
33. Shuckburgh, minute on a ZO letter, June 10, 1921, CO 733/16.
34. Archer Cust, "Cantonization: A Plan for Palestine," *Journal of the Royal Central Asian Society,* 23 (April 1936), 194–220; minutes, CO officials, Jan.–Feb. 1934, CO 733/257/37356; critical memorandum by the Palestine government, enclosed in High Commissioner Wauchope, dispatch, Oct. 28, 1936, CO 733/302/75288.
35. Great Britain, Parliamentary Papers, Command 5479, *Report of the Palestine Royal Commission . . .* (London: HMSO, 1937). Command papers 1700 (1922) and 3692 (1930) had argued that the pledges could ultimately be reconciled.

a major displacement of the Arab population was underlined by the report of the Woodhead Commission in 1938.[36] Therefore the government abruptly shifted back to a proposal for a unified state in the White Paper of 1939. But even the idea of a shared state in which neither community would dominate the other was denounced by Jewish and Arab leaders, whose political aims were by then irreconcilable.

During the mandate period, Palestine had been officially held in tutelage by Great Britain under the legal authority of the League of Nations. This status was largely a cover for the division of the spoils of war among the victorious powers, but it did place some formal limitations on Britain's authority. The government was required to report annually on its administration of Palestine to the Permanent Mandates Commission (PMC) in Geneva. That body, however, exercised almost no supervisory powers. At its first session, the PMC decided that the residents of mandated territories could neither present their case directly nor send petitions to it. Written appeals had to be sent to the territory's high commissioner, who would forward them to the responsible government, with his own comments attached. That government would then present the appeals to the League of Nations, along with its own rebuttal, thereby diluting the impact of any criticisms.[37] The PMC also lacked the authority to make on-the-spot investigations, as one Palestine Arab memorandum had urged in 1925. Britain and the other imperial powers passed a resolution in the Council of the League that required the PMC to make its "best judgment" about local problems based on the "information placed at its disposal" in Geneva.[38] Moreover, the PMC decided in 1928 that its role

36. Great Britain, Parliamentary Papers, Command 5854, *Report of the Palestine Partition Commission* (London: HMSO, 1938).

37. The Palestine Arabs had sent an appeal directly to the PMC which the League printed and circulated to all members. The British were alarmed and persuaded the PMC to reject all further appeals. See H. Young and T. E. Lawrence, minutes on Samuel, telegram, May 25, 1921, CO 733/3.

38. Permanent Mandates Commission (PMC), *Minutes, Seventh session*, 1925, p. 270.

did not even include recommending any particular form of government for the mandated territories.[39]

Almost all of the PMC's members were drawn from colonial powers—Great Britain, France, Italy, Portugal, Spain, Belgium, and the Netherlands. Two came from aspiring powers—Germany and Japan—and the only members who came from noncolonial states were Swiss and Norwegian. Therefore the interest of the majority lay in limiting rather than expanding the commission's powers, particularly when they risked exposing their own countries' colonial practices to an independent investigation.

The PMC examined the annual reports of the British government on its administration in Palestine, but its few criticisms were minor and, in any case, *ex post facto*. It regularly rejected the Palestine Arabs' claim to the right of self-government, and the European states sought to keep Palestine available as an outlet for their own Jewish citizens. The League and the PMC were subject to intensive propaganda campaigns by the Zionist Organization.[40]

The only active involvement of the League in Palestine—the Wailing Wall Commission of 1930—was initiated by the British government. In the aftermath of the 1929 riots, the British persuaded the PMC to establish a committee to resolve Jewish and Muslim claims at that holy site in Jerusalem. The recommendations of the commission, issued in December 1930, were implemented by Britain the following June.[41]

In practice, despite the provisions of the mandate that called for the introduction of self-governing institutions, Palestine was ruled along the lines of a crown colony. From December 1917 to June 1920 it was "occupied enemy territory," governed by military officers who were bound by the Hague Convention of 1908 to maintain the status quo. In

39. PMC, *Minutes, Fourteenth session,* 1928, Annex 9, pp. 213, 246–247.

40. Chaim Weizmann, *Trial and Error* (New York: Harper, 1949), pp. 326, 375–376.

41. Correspondence between the Palestine government and the CO concerning the commission, CO 733/179/77013.

April 1920, the Allied powers agreed to grant the Palestine mandate to Great Britain. Although the mandate did not come into force until September 1923, the British established a civil administration there in July 1920. Transjordan was treated as a separate political entity under Emir Abdallah after 1922, although the British high commissioner had responsibility for both territories. In contrast to Transjordan's semi-autonomy, Palestine was ruled directly by the high commissioner, who consulted an executive council composed of British government officials. British officials headed the departments and served as district commissioners, although their assistants were usually Arabs or Jews, as were the lower-level personnel. The top officials had virtually unlimited power over the local population: they were not accountable to an electorate but to the high commissioner and, in turn, the Colonial Office and British government.[42] At the local level, Jewish rural settlements were allowed considerable autonomy, but Arab villages and the towns with mixed populations were closely supervised.

The only serious attempt to establish a legislative council occurred in 1922–1923, before the mandate came into force. Elections were held for municipal councils in 1927 and 1934, but these councils had limited jurisdiction. Although Arabs and Jews participated together in the municipalities and voted in the same election, each community received a fixed number of council seats, and national issues often intruded, causing tension and acrimony.[43]

Communal separation was compounded by the British decision to maintain the Ottoman confessional system and to es-

42. Albert M. Hyamson, *Palestine under the Mandate, 1920–1948* (London: Methuen, 1950), p. 97; Mogannam E. Mogannam, "Palestine Legislation under the British," *Annals of the American Academy of Political and Social Science,* 164 (1932), 47–54; Abdul Latif Tibawi, *Arab Education in Mandatory Palestine: A Study of Three Decades of British Administration* (London: Luzac, 1956), pp. 213–214.

43. Hyamson, pp. 102–103; E. Mills, memorandum on the report by a commission on local government, March 23, 1925, enclosed in Haifa district commissioner, letter to the chief secretary, March 27, 1925, Israel State Archives (ISA), Jerusalem, Chief Secretary's Office Papers, 2/135, POL/480/5.

tablish autonomous organs for the Muslims as well as for Jews and Christian groups. The guarantee in article 15 of the mandate that education would be conducted in the language of each community, taken in concert with the Religious Communities Ordinance of 1925 granting the communities the right to tax their members for educational purposes, enabled the Jewish community to establish its own autonomous school system. The ordinance also formalized the elaborate political structure of the Jewish community, dominated by the Zionist Organization. Moreover, the mandate granted special rights to the Jewish agency regarding settlement, use of natural resources, and advising the authorities. This action was partly the result of the prevalent belief that only European settlers could provide the capital and technical know-how, as well as the cultural values, necessary to develop the country. The Arabs complained that they were viewed as "a sick child," who must take bitter medicine and would eventually learn "to appreciate the draught for its beneficent effect."[44]

The idea of the return of the Israelites to the promised land had special appeal for Gentiles whose knowledge of Palestine was limited to the Bible, who felt that Christians should atone for their sins against the Jewish people by helping them to reestablish themselves in their homeland, and who accepted the conventional wisdom that Palestine was empty and derelict. These sentimental and economic arguments merged with the continuing strategic reasons for retaining Palestine. The territory's strategic value increased sharply in the mid-1930s and therefore made its loss to the British Empire even more difficult to countenance. By then an oil pipeline from Iraq terminated at the enlarged Haifa port, a valuable air base had been established at Lydda, and the 1936 Anglo-Egyptian Treaty placed greater military weight on neighboring Palestine. The increased militancy of Italy and Germany, especially after the Italian invasion of Ethiopia in 1935 and the Axis

44. Michael F. Abcarius, *Palestine through the Fog of Propaganda* (London: Hutchison, 1946), p. 195.

involvement in the Spanish civil war, challenged British naval hegemony in the Mediterranean and reinforced the need for friendly ports and bases. Palestine therefore appeared indispensable to maintain wider British interests. But the cost of occupying Palestine escalated during the Arab rebellion in the late 1930s, compelling Britain to withdraw troops from Europe. And the Foreign and India Offices feared that support for the Zionist movement would permanently alienate the Muslim and Arab worlds.[45]

Great Britain remained impaled on the horns of the dilemma, unable to abandon Palestine and yet unable to bridge the gap between the Zionist and Arab nationalist movements. Throughout the 1930s, British officials felt that the "likelihood of His Majesty's Government giving up its control of Palestine seems so remote as to be almost negligible."[46] They could not imagine an era in which they would not have the imperial power that enabled them to rule Palestine and that made Palestine a valuable possession.

The Zionist Movement

When the Balfour Declaration was embodied in the mandate, the Zionist Organization won the right to advise the British authorities about their policies in Palestine, and it sought to dominate those policies. Through affiliated institutions, the Zionist Organization controlled immigration and settlement, enforced rules against employing Arab laborers on Jewish land or in Jewish industry, and built up autonomous institutions that formed a quasi-government parallel to the British administration. By the mid-1930s the movement was able to maintain its momentum despite serious crises: Nazi persecution of Jews in Germany, the rebellion of the Palestine Arabs, and British efforts to circumscribe the Zion-

45. J. C. Hurewitz, *The Struggle for Palestine* (New York: Norton, 1950), pp. 86–88; also Anthony Eden (FO) to William Ormsby-Gore (CO), Jan. 20, 1937, CO 733/332/75156 pt. 1.

46. O. G. R. Williams, Middle East Department, CO, minute, Sept. 23, 1933, CO 733/248/17627.

ists' domain. Even after World War II, when European powers began to relinquish their colonies, the legitimacy of the Zionists' claim to Palestine remained basically unquestioned in Europe and the United States. In fact, international support and sympathy increased dramatically as a result of the Nazis' brutal annihilation of European Jewry.

Political Zionism grew out of a combination of ancient messianic attachment to the land of Israel and modern political reaction to anti-Semitism and economic discrimination in Europe. Its adherents viewed the establishment of an autonomous state to which all Jews could immigrate as essential for the future existence of the Jewish people and for the normalization of their position in the contemporary world of nation-states. Some Zionist leaders provided a religious rationale for their aspirations, declaring that God had promised Palestine to the Jews.

Many Zionists characterized themselves as a progressive European people bringing Western civilization to the East. Some also argued that the Jews could serve as "part of a wall of defense for Europe in Asia, an outpost of civilization against barbarism," as Theodor Herzl wrote in *The Jewish State.*[47] Chaim Weizmann disparaged the abilities of the local population. He wrote to Lord Balfour in 1918 that "the *fellah* [peasant] is at least four centuries behind the times, and the *effendi* [gentry] . . . is dishonest, uneducated, greedy, and as unpatriotic as he is inefficient." Although "superficially quick and clever," the *effendi* worships only "power and success," Weizmann claimed.[48]

A principal Zionist argument was that the Jewish national home was vital to solve the problems of Jewish dispersion and virulent anti-Semitism. Weizmann asserted in 1930: "The Balfour Declaration and the Mandate have definitely lifted [Palestine] out of the context of the Middle East and linked it

47. Quoted in Arthur Hertzberg, ed., *The Zionist Idea* (New York: Atheneum, 1969), p. 222.
48. Weizmann to Balfour, May 30, 1918, FO 371/3395/11053/125473.

up with the world-wide Jewish community and the world-wide Jewish problem. . . . The rights which the Jewish people has been adjudged in Palestine do not depend on the consent, and cannot be subjected to the will, of the majority of its present inhabitants."[49] Zionists tended to view the Jewish people as one nation, scattered around the world. They argued that the claims of the million Palestine Arabs had to be balanced against the national claims of sixteen million Jews, not just the Jewish minority in Palestine. They also insisted that the Arabs did not need an independent Palestine, because they already had many Arab states toward which they could direct their national loyalty, whereas the Jews had only one rightful country.

By 1918, Jewish colonists had settled in the new town of Tel Aviv and in several agricultural colonies, as well as in the traditional Jewish holy cities, Jerusalem, Hebron, Tiberias, and Safad. Their leaders had made plans for rapid colonization by acquiring large blocs of land and controlling mineral and energy resources. Colonists settled largely on the coastal plain between Tel Aviv and Haifa, around Jerusalem, and in the Emeq (Esdraelon), a valley that runs eastward from Haifa toward the Jordan River. The Palestine Electric Company, headed by the Russian Zionist Pinhas Rutenberg, acquired monopoly rights in 1921 to electrify all of Palestine except Jerusalem. This concession was "the main economic pivot of the whole Zionist programme," according to one British official.[50] In 1927, Moise Novomeysky acquired a concession to exploit the minerals in the Dead Sea,[51] and other compa-

49. Weizmann to Shuckburgh (CO), March 5, 1930, CO 733/187/77105.

50. Young, minute, Aug. 19, 1921, on high commissioner, telegram to CO, July 3, 1921, CO 733/4. The Rutenberg concession was challenged by Euripedes Mavrommatis, a Greek who had received a similar concession from the Ottoman government in 1914; for a sympathetic treatment of his claims before the Hague Court, see Joseph M. N. Jeffries, *Palestine: The Reality* (London: Longmans, Green, 1939), pp. 580–592.

51. The high commissioner and the crown agents had recommended that the concession be granted to another company, but Colonial Secretary Leopold Amery and Undersecretary William Ormsby-Gore, both active Gentile Zionists, overrode

nies won concessions to reclaim sand dunes and marshes along the Mediterranean coast and to drain the Huleh marshes on the northern reaches of the Jordan River.[52]

With the exception of the electricity and Dead Sea minerals concessions and the prewar first *aliyah* settlements, the Zionist movement officially prohibited Arab labor on Jewish-funded and operated agricultural colonies and industries. Land bought by the Jewish National Fund was held as the inalienable property of the Jewish people: anyone subletting his holding to an Arab or even hiring an Arab to work there automatically forfeited his lease. The General Federation of Jewish Labor (Histadrut), which was founded in 1920, enforced *avodah ivrit* by means of militant pickets as part of the "conquest of work" in Palestine.

Although British officials had serious misgivings about the impact of their policy on Arab-Jewish relations and on the Arabs' economic status,[53] the British government in 1931 explicitly sanctioned "the principle of preferential, and indeed exclusive, employment of Jewish labor by Jewish organizations."[54] In fact, the policy negated Zionist claims that Jewish immigration and economic projects would directly benefit the Arabs, and it deeply embittered Arabs against the Jewish residents. The secretary of the Arab Labor Federation of Jaffa asserted resentfully in 1937: "The Histadrut's fundamental aim is 'the conquest of labour'. . . . No matter how many Arab

---

the recommendation. High Commissioner, dispatch to CO, Feb. 19, 1926, CO 733/112; CO minutes, Feb. 24, 1927 on the crown agents' report of Jan. 17, 1927, CO 733/132/33056; Moise A. Novomeysky, *Given to Salt: The Struggle for the Dead Sea Concession* (London: Max Parrish, 1958), pp. 146, 151–152, 223.

52. In the case of the Huleh concession of 1934, an Arab from Beirut had held the concession since the Ottoman period but had been unable to raise the necessary funds to begin reclamation. The British would not assist him but, as soon as he sold out to the Zionists' Palestine Land Development Company, the British agreed to support 20 percent of the cost of the company's operations.

53. See O. G. R. Williams (CO), minute, Nov. 5, 1930, CO 733/182/77050; Colonial Secretary Sir Philip Cunliffe-Lister, memorandum to the cabinet, March 28, 1934, strongly criticized the policy, CO 733/257/37356, pt. 2.

54. Text of the letter in *Annals of the American Academy of Political and Social Science*, 164 (1932).

workers are unemployed, they have no right to take any job which a possible immigrant might occupy. No Arab has the right to work in Jewish undertakings. If Arabs can be displaced in other work, too . . . that is good. If a port can be established in Tel Aviv and Jaffa port ruined, that is better."[55]

As the Jewish community grew from 11 percent of the population in 1922, to 16 percent in 1931, and to 28 percent in 1936, an immigrant could live entirely within a Jewish area, dependent in no respect on the Arab majority and coming into only incidental contact with Arabs, although in such towns as Haifa and Jerusalem, Jewish and Arab families lived side by side. The pervasive social isolation and economic autarky were paralleled and reinforced by the political consolidation of the Jewish community.

Weizmann headed a Zionist commission that came to Palestine in March 1918 and organized emergency relief for Jewish agricultural colonists and townspeople, reestablished Jewish courts to handle communal civil law cases, and built up a central administration composed of thirteen departments that paralleled the British military administration.[56] The commission also assumed control over most of the Jewish private schools, required instruction in Hebrew,[57] and organized elections for a Jewish constituent assembly in the spring of 1920, in violation of the military administration's ban on political elections.

55. George Mansur, *The Arab Worker under the Palestine Mandate* (Jerusalem: Commercial Press, 1937), p. 28.

56. Chief Administrator Sir Louis Bols, dispatch to chief political officer, Cairo, April 21, 1920, FO 371/5119; Palin Court of Inquiry report, July 1, 1920, FO 371/5121.

57. Such schools as the Eveline de Rothschild Jewish Girls School, which taught in English, and the Alliance Israelite schools, which taught in French, were actively boycotted (chief administrator, dispatch to chief political officer, April 21, 1920, FO 371/5119). The Zionists vetoed a British idea to form a joint Jewish-Arab agricultural training school (high commissioner, dispatch to CO, Jan. 11, 1924, and CO minutes, CO 733/63; ZO, dispatch to CO, and CO minutes, March 24, 1925, CO 733/107). High commissioner, dispatch to CO, April 24, 1924, and CO minutes, CO 733/67; Israel Cohen, *The Zionist Movement* (New York: Zionist Organization of America, 1946), pp. 175–176; Hurewitz, *Struggle,* pp. 39–40.

The Jewish Self-Defense Corps (Haganah) was organized in 1920, patterned on prewar units in the colonies. Arab riots in Jerusalem that spring and in Jaffa in 1921 accelerated the growth of the Haganah. By the 1930s, the presence and utility of this force were recognized tacitly by the British government. In 1937 the Haganah had ten thousand men trained and armed and another forty thousand available for rapid mobilization.[58] During the Arab revolt of 1938–1939, the British recruited Jewish settlers as supernumerary police to protect the railways, oil pipeline, and border security fences. They also manned special attack squads against guerrilla bands and guarded Jewish settlements.[59] Any violent Arab reaction to Jewish immigration and settlement only served to tighten the cohesion of the Jewish community and to accelerate its military preparations and political determination.

The Zionist movement itself contained a cross-section of Jewry: orthodox religious groups, egalitarian socialists, cosmopolitan lawyers, and cost-conscious businessmen. Such people differed profoundly over social, economic, and religious issues, but they shared a fundamental belief in Zionism and the Jewish return to Palestine. The Labor Zionists, who controlled Histadrut, became the majority in the Zionist congresses after 1923, although the Zionist executive generally comprised a coalition of groups.

The anti-Zionist, ultraorthodox Agudath Israel remained outside the movement.[60] Similarly, many American Jews stayed outside the Zionist Organization at least until the Jewish Agency was formed in 1929, with half its members intended to be non-Zionists. To the right stood the Revisionist party, whose program asserted that the Zionists must demand a Jewish state in both Transjordan and Pales-

58. Cmd. 5479, p. 200; Hurewitz, *Struggle,* p. 42.
59. See Chapter 9 and speech by David Ben Gurion, Dec. 12, 1938, delivered before the Vaad ha-Leumi in Tel Aviv, transmitted to CO, Jan. 9, 1939, CO 733/406/75872/12B.
60. I. Cohen, pp. 175–176. For detailed treatment of the political factions see Hurewitz, *Struggle,* pp. 44–49.

tine.[61] Founded by Vladimir Jabotinsky in 1925, the party broke away from the Zionist Organization in 1935, when it formed the third largest bloc within that organization. The Revisionist party itself spawned an offshoot, the Irgun Zvai Leumi, which engaged in terrorism and charged the mainstream Zionists with insufficient militancy against the British and the Arabs.

Weizmann served as president of the Zionist Organization from 1920 to 1931 and again after 1935. By the mid-1930s, his General Zionist party had to share power with the Labor Zionists, led by David Ben Gurion. Weizmann stressed the importance of diplomacy in London and the need to win the active support of Diaspora Jewry. Ben Gurion—who settled in Palestine in 1906, served as general secretary of Histadrut from 1921 to 1935, and thereafter was chairman of the Jewish Agency's executive—considered the Yishuv (the Jewish community in Palestine) to be the crucial element in creating a Jewish state: its deep roots and strength could enable it to withstand the vicissitudes of external diplomacy or weakened support from the Diaspora. Despite the tension between the two approaches—and between the two men—their aims and methods were complementary. Together they engineered the success and consolidation of the movement.

The Zionist Organization (after 1930, the Jewish Agency) was recognized as the appropriate body to advise and cooperate with the Palestine administration in economic, social, and other matters affecting the Jewish national home and to assist in the general development of Palestine.[62] Although Zionist leaders argued that this made them partners with the government, the government itself continually denied that assertion.[63] After the Zionist Organization's headquarters moved to London, its spokesmen lobbied in the Colonial Office, cabi-

61. I. Cohen, pp. 180–181; Hurewitz, *Struggle,* pp. 48–49.

62. Great Britain, Colonial Office, Cmd. 1785, *Mandate for Palestine* (London: HMSO, July 1922), Article 4.

63. Chief Secretary Deedes, demiofficial letter to Shuckburgh (CO), Nov. 22, 1921, CO 537/852.

48

net, and Parliament.[64] The success of these efforts was confirmed in the parliamentary debates of 1936, during which virtually all the participants supported the Zionist position that any representative institutions were premature in Palestine.

In the late 1930s, however, the Zionist leaders bitterly criticized Britain's failure to crush the Arab revolt in Palestine and its unwillingness to permit unrestricted Jewish immigration. Even Weizmann, the consummate diplomat, began to describe the British and the Zionists as antagonists, force being on the British side but justice on the side of world Jewry.[65] In 1939, when Britain abandoned the partition plan and reverted to the idea of a unitary state, many Zionists feared that their dream of independence was lost. Weizmann decried the idea that the Jewish people should remain a minority, reduced "to ghetto status in the very land where it was promised national freedom."[66] Ben Gurion called for militant action to counter this British policy; the chief rabbi theatrically tore up the White Paper before his congregation; and the Irgun bombed Arab markets and raided Arab villages.[67] As the Jewish situation in Europe deteriorated, the Zionists strengthened their commitment to establish a Jewish state. Reliance on the British was indispensable to the Zionists in the 1920s and early 1930s, but became a liability in the late 1930s, when the government wavered in its support of the ultimate Zionist aims and began to recognize the existence of Arab political rights in Palestine.

Zionist Relations with the Arabs

Weizmann felt that personal arrangements with leading Arab figures outside Palestine were the best way to reduce

64. Leonard Stein (ZO) to Paul Goodman, on efforts to persuade certain MPs to stop supporting the Palestine Arab position, Feb. 24, 1922, Central Zionist Archives (CZA), Jerusalem, Z4/1391/IIa.

65. Minutes of Weizmann and Ben Gurion, talk with CO, Aug. 31, 1936, CO 733/297/75156 pt. 4.

66. Weizmann, letter to Shuckburgh, Dec. 31, 1937, when rumors of the abandoning of partition were already spreading, CO 733/333/75156/30.

67. High commissioner, dispatches to CO, June 20, July 21, Sept. 1, 1939, CO 733/398/75156 pt. 2.

49

Arab antagonism to the Jewish national home. He cited his meeting with Emir Faysal in Transjordan in June 1918 and his formal agreement with Faysal the next winter in Paris as evidence of the importance of such efforts.[68] In the 1930s, Weizmann thought that an arrangement with Emir Abdallah of Transjordan or with Egyptian politicians might prove fruitful.[69] But he met with the leading Palestine Arab politicians only in the very early years of British rule, and he consistently disparaged them as "unscrupulous Levantine politicians."[70] Weizmann felt that the British authorities could build up "moderate" Arab leaders who could be bribed to reach an accommodation with the Zionists.[71]

A few long-term settlers did attempt to contact the indigenous Arab spokesmen. Chaim M. Kalvarisky, an immigrant in 1895 and a leading member of the binationalist society Brit Shalom (Covenant of Peace), drew up "A Judaeo-Arab Covenant" in 1930 that called for cooperation between the two Semitic peoples, parity of political rights, and nondomination of either people over the other.[72] But Kalvarisky's credibility as a mediator was undermined by his simultaneous

68. C. Weizmann, pp. 234–235. The Zionists also had contacts with Syrian exiles, particularly in Geneva, in the early twenties; see Porath, *Emergence,* pp. 112–122.

69. C. Weizmann, p. 408.

70. Weizmann to Shuckburgh, Dec. 31, 1937, CO 733/333/75156/30. Weizmann addressed a gathering of Arab notables assembled by the British governor in Jerusalem in 1918 to clarify his aims. But Weizmann's references to future large-scale immigration prompted the mufti, Kamil al-Husayni, to leave the room in protest (Storrs, dispatch to FO, April 30, 1918, FO 371/3398/27647/92393; Aharon Cohen, *Israel and the Arab World* [New York: Funk and Wagnalls, 1970], pp. 137–138). In late 1921, Weizmann met the first Arab delegation to London, under the CO's auspices. A British official noted that, although Weizmann's speech was moderate, he adopted the attitude "of a conqueror handing to beaten foes the terms of peace." See Chapter 7; E. Mills (CO), note, Nov. 30, 1921, CO 537/855.

71. Zionist Commission, minutes on Weizmann's talk with high commissioner, Dec. 11, 1922, CZA, Z4/4113.

72. Susan Lee Hattis, *The Bi-National Idea in Palestine during Mandatory Times* (Haifa: Shikmona, 1970), pp. 54–55. For an extended analysis of Brit Shalom, see ibid., pp. 38–58.

efforts to bribe Arab politicians and newspaper editors in order to win their support, thus displaying a basic contempt similar to Weizmann's.[73]

The Zionist Organization also spent substantial sums to establish two Arab political parties, the National Muslim societies of 1921–1923[74] and the Agricultural parties of 1924–1926. Some well-known Arabs joined the National Muslim societies in the hope of personal advancement or cash or in reaction to the attachment of rival families to the anti-Zionist Arab Executive.[75] The Agricultural parties initially attracted certain village families who resented the preponderant political influence of the urban elite and hoped to receive agricultural loans or other favors from the Zionists.[76] Whatever moderating influence these societies might have had was undermined by public awareness that they were funded by the Zionist Organization. When the Zionists could not provide them with government posts, failed to underwrite any loans, and even curtailed their cash payments, the members found that they had lost not only their standing in the Arab com-

73. Frederick Kisch to Kalvarisky, Aug. 31, 1923, CZA, Z4/2421. See also the ZO, political budget, Fall 1923, which included two £75 monthly payments to *Lisan al-Arab* and a £20 payment to al-Akhbar, and another letter from Kisch to Kalvarisky, Nov. 14, 1924, CZA, S25/518.

74. Palestine government's monthly political reports for October 1921 (CO 733/7), November 1921 (CO 733/8), and February 1922 (CO 733/19) report on the activities of the societies. See also Samuel to CO, Nov. 18, 1921, CO 733/7; dispatches between Kisch and Kalvarisky, Oct.–Nov. 1921, CZA, S24/1250; Zionist reports, March 1922, CZA, S25/4380, and Dec. 1922, CZA, S25/518. The latter memorandum notes that the National Muslim society in Jerusalem received £285 per month until July 1922 and suggests that the ZO resume the payments at the rate of £100 per month. See also Porath, *Emergence*, pp. 215–221.

75. Haydar Bey Tuqan wanted to become mayor of Nablus; Hassan al-Shukri wanted to become mayor of Haifa and succeeded; Shaykh Asad al-Shuqayri opposed the mufti of Haifa, who was a member of the Arab Executive and the Supreme Muslim Council.

76. Porath, *Emergence*, pp. 227–230. Report on Agricultural parties' program in district governor, Samaria, to assistant political secretary, Jerusalem, Jan. 17, 1924, ISA, Chief Secretary's Papers, POL/19, 2/173; district governor, Samaria, to assistant political secretary, Jerusalem, Aug. 25, 1922, ISA, Chief Secretary's Papers, POL/13, 2/168; political report, June 1924, CO 733/71; Kisch, letter, Nov. 9, 1925, CZA, S25/655; Said al-Shawwa (Gaza) to Kisch, April 25, 1924, CZA, S25/518.

munity but also the tangible benefits of associating with these parties.[77]

An extraordinary attempt to buy support inside the Arab Executive occurred in 1923, when the London office of the Zionist Organization made a payment to Musa Kazim al-Husayni, the leader of the Arab delegation to London. Kalvarisky reported that Musa Kazim Pasha promised "to assume illness and refrain from convening meetings and congresses until after the Muslim festivals" in April 1923.[78] He did not attend certain meetings, citing his ill health, and he postponed holding the general Arab congress until June, but he also emphasized to Kalvarisky that he must continue to oppose the aims of Zionism. Kalvarisky and Weizmann were jubilant at this opportunity to win help in the camp of their enemies but its impact was brief and minimal.

The advisability and efficacy of these methods were debated among Zionist leaders in the early 1920s. Weizmann asserted that "extremists and moderates alike were susceptible to the influence of money and honours"[79] and felt that an active effort by the Zionist movement to secure government positions for Arabs would put an end to Arab political hostility.[80] Kalvarisky and Colonel Frederick Kisch, the political officer in Palestine, also supported this method. Kalvarisky noted that economic cooperation between Arabs and Jews was a fine idea as a means to attract Arab support, but it would never be carried out:

> Some people say . . . that only by common work in the field of commerce, industry and agriculture mutual understanding between Jews and Arabs will ultimately be attained. . . . This

77. Kalvarisky to London office, June 4, 1923, on the erosion of support, CZA, Z4/2421. Examples of unsuccessful petitions include Abdallah Husayn, president of the Beisan branch of the Agricultural party, letter to Kisch, Oct. 28, 1924, requesting loans, CZA, S25/518; Musa Hudayb of Hebron to Kisch, Sept. 10, 1925, asking for a job for his son, CZA, S25/517.
78. Kalvarisky to ZO (London), April 12, 26, 1923, CZA, Z4/1392/IIB.
79. Weizmann, talk with Samuel, Dec. 11, 1922, CZA, Z4/4113.
80. Shuckburgh, minute on Samuel telegram to CO, Nov. 3, 1923, CO 733/50.

is, however, merely a theory. In practice we have not done and we are doing nothing for any work in common. How many Arab officials have we installed in our banks? Not even one. How many Arabs have we brought into our schools? Not one. What commercial houses have we established in company with Arabs? Not even one. . . . These left elements who talk about close friendship with the Arab labourers demand, and justly so in this period of unemployment, that we should help them to supplant the Arab labourers in the colonies by Jewish labour. . . . These methods are perhaps desirable, but they require too much time to be followed.[81]

But Leonard Stein of the London office called for exactly such cooperation and denounced "spasmodic largesse." He argued that the Zionists must seek "a permanent *modus vivendi*" with the Arabs by means of Arab participation in Jewish undertakings and the admission of Arab students to the Technical Institute in Haifa and the Hebrew University in Jerusalem. He pointed out that any political party in which "Arab moderates are merely Arab gramophones playing Zionist records" would collapse as soon as the Zionist financial support ended.[82]

In contrast, the militant Jabotinsky held that Arab national feelings could not be overcome by either bribery or economic gains. He warned against such "contempt" of the Arabs: "The Arab is culturally backward, but his instinctive patriotism is just as pure and noble as our own; it cannot be bought, it can only be curbed by . . . *force majeur*."[83]

The policy of subsidizing newspapers and political parties was abandoned by 1927, during the Zionist movement's financial crisis, and it was never revived systematically. The few attempts to meet Palestine Arab political leaders in the 1930s to explore grounds for a mutual understanding never moved beyond a preliminary testing of views.[84]

81. Kalvarisky to Kisch, July 2, 1923, CZA, Z4/2421.
82. Stein to Kisch, June 12, 1923, CZA S25/665.
83. Jabotinsky to the Zionist Executive, Dec. 29, 1922, CZA Z4/4113.
84. In early 1932, for example, two Zionist leaders met with Awni Abd al-Hadi of the Arab Executive to win his acceptance of the concept of parity (the nondomi-

The presence of an organized Arab community in Palestine remained an awkward reality for the Zionist movement. Their sense of superiority as Europeans prevented the Jewish leaders from facing the issue in the 1920s, when an accommodation might have been possible. Bribery was a stopgap method that in the long run won more enemies than friends. Basically, the Zionist leaders hoped that effective Arab action against them would be delayed and Arab influence offset by their own influence in London until the Yishuv became strong enough to withstand and prevail over any Arab opposition.

---

nation of one community over the other irrespective of numbers). But Awni Bey saw this as a means for the Zionists to acquire equal representation even though they comprised only 20 percent of the population and replied that he saw a fundamental clash of interests that could not be canceled through verbal agreements (Hattis, p. 101). Other meetings took place during the 1936 general strike and in late July 1937 after partition was proposed. In the first instance, meetings were held with the independent politicians George Antonius and Musa al-Alami, but broke off on the grounds that they could not speak on the authority of the principal Arab leaders. Judah Magnes, the binationalist chancellor of the Hebrew University, who had arranged the discussions, felt that the Zionist participants broke off the talks because they could not reduce their own insistence on 62,000 immigrants yearly (ibid.; A. Cohen, pp. 272–273). In July 1937, members of the Arab Higher Committee asked Kalvarisky to communicate to the Jewish Agency a proposal to open negotiations to prevent partition. But the negotiations never materialized, and the deportation of the Arab leaders in October precluded any further contact (A. Cohen, p. 276).

3 / The Social and Economic Setting

Arab society in Palestine underwent significant change and upheaval under British rule, partly as an aspect of the broader changes sweeping the eastern Mediterranean and partly as a result of specific policies and conditions of the mandatory regime. Along with a rapid rise in population, the value and extent of land planted to cash crops grew, and trade and small industry expanded. Despite educational, economic, and social improvements that compared favorably with the neighboring Arab countries, the Palestine Arabs inevitably viewed their situation as distinctly inferior to that of the Jewish community in Palestine. The wide gap in literacy, living standards, and economic power between the two communities necessarily had a profound impact on political attitudes among the Arabs.[1]

The 1922 and 1931 censuses and the June 1936 official estimate of the population provide useful benchmarks to illustrate the changing population patterns.[2]

1. Palestine Government, *A Survey of Palestine* (Jerusalem: Government Printer, 1946), II, 727–729.
2. The figures for Christians include the small number of non-Arab Christians. See Janet L. Abu-Lughod, "The Demographic Transformation of Palestine," in Abu-Lughod, ed., *Transformation*, pp. 144–145; Lister G. Hopkins, "Population," in Sa'id B. Himadeh, ed., *Economic Organization of Palestine,* (Beirut: American Press, 1938), pp. 7, 9, 12, 16; Jacob Shimoni, *The Arabs in Israel* (New Haven: Human Relations Area Files, 1956), pp. 118–120, 281.

Year	Total Population	Muslim	Christian	Jewish
1922	Over ¾ million	590,000 (78%)	72,000 (9.6%)	83,000 (11%)
1931	Over 1 million	760,000 (73%)	91,400 (9%)	174,000 (17%)
1936	1,337,000	848,000 (64%)	106,500 (8%)	370,000 (27.7%)

Only 3 percent of the increase in Arab residents came from immigration, whereas 70 percent of the increase in the Jewish community in the 1920s and 90 percent for 1931–1936 came from immigration. This surge shifted drastically the relative proportions of Arabs and Jews in Palestine and deepened the Arabs' fears of losing numerical preponderance.

The economic role of the Jewish community was more important than mere numbers would indicate. Throughout the period, three-quarters of the Jewish residents were urban, whereas only a quarter of the Muslims lived in towns. In 1922 the Muslim urban population was twice that of the Jewish community, but by 1935 the urban Jewish sector had outstripped the total Muslim urban sector. The urban Jewish community was already larger than the heavily urbanized Christian community in 1922 and was three times its size in 1935.[3]

Sharp contrasts in literacy and health indices provide evidence of the disparity in living standards.[4] In 1931, 93.4 percent of the Jewish males (over age seven) and 71.5 percent of the Christian males, but only 25.1 percent of Muslim males, were literate. Overall, Arab literacy rates improved only from 19 percent in 1931 to perhaps 27 percent by the end of the 1930s. At most, 20 percent of Arab children attended school in 1922, even after a two-year spurt in building schools in villages had doubled the number of government schools.[5] The number of government schools remained static

3. J. Abu-Lughod in Abu-Lughod, ed., *Transformation*, p. 147; Hopkins in Himadeh, ed., *Economic Organization*, p. 12.
4. Hopkins in Himadeh, ed., *Economic Organization*, p. 36; Shimoni, p. 534; Hurewitz, *Struggle*, p. 36.
5. There were 171 such schools in 1920 and 314 in 1922; see Abcarius, p. 102; Tibawi, pp. 270–271.

through the 1920s and 1930s, despite the rapid increase in school-aged children.[6] In contrast, nearly all Jewish children attended school and, in fact, the budget for the Hebrew-language school system that was run by the Zionist groups exceeded the budget of the government schools that largely catered to the Arabs.[7]

Despite the contrasting mortality figures for Muslims and Jews,[8] the Arab population increased rapidly. This growth resulted from the end of Ottoman-era military conscription, which had removed many young men; enhanced internal security and thus greater stability in village life; and improved health conditions, particularly in the towns. Arab economic activity also expanded: the extent of olive and citrus groves multiplied sixfold from 1922 to 1940, and the area allotted to vegetable gardens nearly doubled. The number of Arab traders, professionals, and industrial workers also increased, although at less spectacular rates. In 1940, the government estimated that urban Arabs employed in workshops, industry, construction, railways, and public works totaled twenty-eight thousand. Only three thousand of these were employed by Jewish firms or by the international concessions such as the Palestine Electric Corporation or the Dead Sea salts concession. The international concessions were required to hire a fair share of Arab workers, but the Histadrut pressured Jewish firms to hire only Jews. Because Jewish firms hired seven times as many workers as did Arab firms,[9] this policy cut deeply into Arabs' employment prospects. Arab workers re-

6. By the 1930s, many accused the government of *siyasat al-tajhil,* meaning a deliberate policy of keeping the Arabs ignorant. See high commissioner, dispatch, Dec. 31, 1932, enclosing a letter from the president of the Arab Executive, Sept. 1932, CO 733/130/17240.

7. Tibawi, p. 177.

8. I. J. Kligler, director, Straus Health Center, Jerusalem, "Public Health in Palestine," *Annals of the American Academy of Political and Social Science,* 164 (1932), p. 170. According to Kligler's figures for mortality, 1924–1930, Muslims averaged 31.3 deaths per thousand, Christians 19.2, Jews 12.4. His infant mortality figures for 1930 were Muslims 169.6 per thousand, Christians 134.4, and Jews 69.0 (the latter representing a sharp decrease from 105.7 in 1924).

9. Shimoni, pp. 251, 195–196, 293.

ceived only half the pay that Jewish workers received, largely because Histadrut set the wage scales of Jewish workers, whereas the Arabs' rates fluctuated according to supply and demand.[10] This disparity received official sanction from the British administration,[11] and Arab protests against it remained ineffective. Arab labor leaders resented the argument that the Arabs' low living standard justified giving them low wages: "It makes [the Arab worker] more embittered still when he is told to accept a low wage *because* his standard of living is lower than that of the Jews; as if it were a crime to raise his standard of living! The poor must remain poor, and the low must remain low. What a queer logic in a civilized Government!"[12]

Arab politicians argued against handing large-scale concessions over to Zionist firms on the grounds that the government should develop the natural resources for the benefit of the entire country. In the case of the Palestine Electric Corporation's hydroelectric concession, the local political clubs and religious leaders in Jaffa managed to delay the municipality's acceptance of electrification from the concession for several months in 1923, but, in the end, the municipality had no choice because the corporation had a monopoly on electrification.[13] Similar protests were registered against the concessions for the Dead Sea minerals in 1927 and the draining of the Huleh marshes in 1934–1935,[14] as well as against land purchases.

10. Palestine Government, *Survey,* II, 735; Mansur, p. 10; Sa'id B. Himadeh, "Industry," in Himadeh, ed., *Economic Organization,* p. 284.

11. The government's Haifa harbor works paid Arabs half as much as Jews for unskilled quarrying, for example. High commissioner, dispatch to CO, April 8, 1937, described disparities in pay for road work, CO 733/311/75528. Also CO to Trades Union Council, March 18, 1930, on Haifa harbor wages, and high commissioner, dispatch to CO, June 7, 1930, and telegram to CO, Dec. 13, 1930, CO 733/189/77130.

12. Mansur, p. 42; see also high commissioner, dispatch to CO, April 8, 1937, cited in n. 11.

13. For example, protest by Arab Economic Committee attached to Palestine government, political report, May 1923, CO 733/46.

14. Arab Executive, letter to the colonial secretary, 1927, CO 733/170/67232. National Defense party, protest to the government, Jan. 1935, enclosed in high commissioner, dispatch to CO, March 4, 1935, CO 733/278/75156.

Arab Society

At the close of the Ottoman era, a small stratum of upper-class Muslim families monopolized the key government positions and dominated the rural areas. Commerce and education attracted a disproportionate number of the relatively urbanized and literate Christian Arabs. The bulk of the population were peasants, poor and illiterate. The nomadic or seminomadic bedouin lived on the fringes of this rural society.

During the following decades, the social composition began to shift as a Muslim middle class emerged, composed of teachers, merchants, and professionals, who became increasingly active in politics. They demanded the right to play a role alongside the traditional elite, which had lost its monopoly position when the British took over the central and district administrations. Although rural society remained more stable than urban society, many peasants were compelled by economic pressures and loss of land to move into the towns, inhabiting shantytowns or slum quarters. This lumpenproletariat comprised a socially unstable and rootless element in the towns outside the control of the landed elite.

The leading Muslim families[15] lost their influence in government with the onset of British rule, but they retained considerable economic influence and social prestige, particularly in the rural areas. In addition to their ownership of many villages, their power derived from the patron–client relationships that were the norm in the society. The elite families had helped protect the villagers against bandits and had arbitrated family feuds. Moreover, they had obtained favors for the villagers from the government, such as tax remission, the release of prisoners, and clerical jobs in the bureaucracy. These patron–client relationships enabled the heads of the elite families to be the accepted political leaders of Palestine Arab society, at least through the 1920s.

15. Hurewitz, *Struggle,* pp. 35–36; Shimoni, pp. 256–263, 296, 314–318; Geoffrey Furlonge, *Palestine Is My Country: The Story of Musa Alami* (London: John Murray, 1969), pp. 9–10; Tibawi, pp. 15–16.

The elite was far from cohesive socially or politically. Factionalism was endemic in the society because each family felt itself to be the equal of the others and therefore found cooperation under the leadership of an individual from any other elite family difficult. Competition among towns and even within families exacerbated these divisions. In the rural areas, virtually all villages were divided into two or more *hamulahs* (extended families or clans), each patronized by a prominent family. Thus the villagers suffered from serious internal rifts that were overcome only when they faced an outside threat, whether from another village that might be encroaching on their land or from a bedouin tribe trespassing on cultivated areas or demanding tribute. The *hamulah* structure was linked to the patron–client system: a landowning family would protect the *hamulah* and in return the *hamulah* owed it political allegiance. Competition among the leading families thus extended down to the village level and, reciprocally, village-level disputes worked their way up to the elite level, further accentuating rivalries.

The middle stratum of society was composed disproportionately of Christians, who worked as merchants, lawyers, teachers, journalists, civil servants, and artisans. The Christians were divided into several religious sects, of whom the Greek Orthodox comprised about 40 percent. Conflicts within this sect between the Greek clergy and Arab laity were often severe because the Greeks monopolized the clerical offices.[16]

There were also tensions between Christians and the Muslim majority. The Christian Arabs were wary of any pan-Islamic thrust to Palestinian political life and often anxious about the influential role played by the Supreme Muslim Council, formed in January 1922 to handle Muslim commu-

---

16. Chief Political Officer Sir Gilbert Clayton to FO, Dec. 6, 1918, enclosing a report from Storrs, Nov. 16, 1918, FO 371/3386/747/213403; Porath, *Emergence,* pp. 197–198. Hurewitz, *Struggle,* p. 29, provides a breakdown of figures on the Christian communities.

nity affairs. Muslim Arabs, in turn, sometimes suspected the Christians of being less critical of the British authorities, queried their disproportionate role in the bureaucracy, and feared any signs of Christian missionary tendencies. But Muslim and Christian Arab leaders worked consistently together as fellow Palestinians facing a common enemy to defuse tension and promote political cooperation.[17] In this regard, the Christians' anti-Zionism was a crucial factor in promoting cooperation. This anti-Zionism arose from the Christians' difficulty competing with the Jewish immigrants—in professions, government employment, and skilled trades—as well as from their political opposition and the element of anti-Semitism present in Christianity but largely absent from Islam.

By the late 1920s, a significant number of young Muslim Arabs, educated in government or private schools, were aspiring to government, professional, or commercial careers. They resented not only the special position accorded the Jewish community in Palestine, but also the political dominance of the Muslim elite and the competition of Christian Arabs. This stratum began to comprise an important independent political influence in the 1930s.

The changing social patterns in Palestine produced new organizations and altered the activities of more traditional ones. The Supreme Muslim Council actively promoted an Islamic cultural revival in Palestine and the growth of a coherent Muslim political structure there. It supported schools, expanded Muslim welfare and health clinics, and repaired local mosques and the central sanctuary of al-Haram al-Sharif in Jerusalem. Young Men's Muslim Associations, modeled on the Young Men's Christian Associations, provided cultural and social centers for youths. Family and sectarian clubs developed political roles, societies of well-to-do women extended their activities from charity to politics, and a few

17. Porath, *Emergence,* pp. 299–301, 303.

strongly nationalist private schools were established that fostered a distinctly nationalist identity. The chambers of commerce and the Palestine Arab Bar Association worked to protect Arabs' standing in trade and the liberal professions.[18] Labor unions also attempted to play active political roles, but the only cohesive group was the Jaffa Lightermen's Society. The other labor groups remained weak and divided. Expansion of the Arabic press and publications also furthered the nationalist movement.

The main social and cultural centers for townsmen were the many clubs ranging from family-based societies, such as the Dajani Sports Club in Jerusalem, to denominational groups, such as the Orthodox (Christian) Clubs, and explicitly political societies, such as the Arab Clubs. In addition to providing activities for their members, some clubs sponsored lectures for the general public, held classes to combat illiteracy, published articles in the newspapers on health, culture, and politics, and worked for the Fund of the Arab Nation. During the 1936 general strike, the clubs organized food distribution and protest activities. The subjects of their public lectures ranged from Arab civilization and literature to current economic problems, the dangers from the Zionist movement, and the nature of Western imperialism. Special meetings were held annually on Balfour Day (November 2) and the anniversaries of the beginning of the Arab revolt in 1916, the execution of the Hebron "martyrs" in 1930, and the beginning of the 1936 general strike. Club members came from educated, urban strata—merchants, lawyers, teachers, students, government employees, and young landed notables. As Adnan Mohammad Abu Ghazaleh points out, "The number of Palestine Arabs who were immersed in the cultural nationalist climate was small in comparison with the total

18. Shimoni, pp. 68–72, 417–422, 494–500; Adnan Mohammad Abu Ghazaleh, "Arab Cultural Nationalism in Palestine, 1919–1948" (Ph.D. dissertation, New York University, 1967), pp. 130–136; see also his article, "Arab Cultural Nationalism in Palestine during the British Mandate," *Journal of Palestine Studies,* 1 (Spring 1972), 37–63.

Arab population of the country and was mostly limited to the towns,"[19] but it was the politically active sector and had a growing influence over wider public views.

Women's societies led by the politicians' wives were particularly active in Jerusalem, Jaffa, and Haifa. The First Palestine Arab Women's Congress convened in Jerusalem after the 1929 riots. Local women's societies cooperated on educational, welfare, and political issues. The Jerusalem society[20] opened a welfare center in the Old City in 1931, distributed food to poor families, and sent nurses to help mothers learn proper sanitation methods and care for their children. The society even bought two plots of land in Hebron and dedicated them as a trust to benefit the families of the three men hanged in 1930 for their role in the 1929 outbreak. All the women's societies held annual flower days, bazaars, and lotteries to finance their activities. Both Muslim and Christian women joined these societies, and women worked together even though their husbands might be leaders of opposing political factions. The executive committee of the Women's Congress submitted frequent protests to the high commissioner against Jewish immigration, land buying, and alleged educational and economic discrimination. During the revolt of the late 1930s, the executive committee protested against the treatment of detainees and against military searches in the villages. Although the Women's Congress of 1929 had confined its public role to a procession in closed cars through Jerusalem, by 1933 women joined the Jerusalem and Jaffa demonstrations, and they led protest rallies during the revolt.

Arab labor unions developed slowly because of the weakness of Arab-owned industry, the illiteracy and poverty of the workers, and the strength of traditional social ties.[21] Tradesmen, such as grocers, wholesalers, auto dealers, and textile

19. Abu Ghazaleh, "Arab Cultural Nationalism" (1967), p. 136.
20. Mrs. Jamal al-Husayni, Mrs. Husayn Fakhri al-Khalidi, and Mrs. Matiel Mughannam led the Jerusalem society (Matiel Mogannam, *The Arab Woman and the Palestine Problem* [London: Herbert Joseph, 1937], pp. 56–58).
21. Mansur, pp. 7–9; Shimoni, pp. 447–448, 472–474, 481–483.

63

merchants, were organized in each town and were represented on the local chambers of commerce. The initial labor organizations had a similar guild orientation. The Jaffa Lightermen's Society and the Motor Car Owners and Drivers Association, for example, included employers as well as employees. Some sectarian labor groups, such as the Orthodox Labor Union, originated as religious charitable societies.

The first attempt at a Western-style labor organization came in 1925 with the formation in Haifa of the Palestine Arab Workers Society (Jamiyat al-Ummal al-Arabiyyah al-Filastiniyyah), but the society remained virtually inactive until 1929, by which time the Jaffa and Jerusalem branches had broken off from the society and reconstituted themselves as the Arab Laborers' Federation. The labor societies were heavily politicized, and efforts to expand them in the 1930s were used by the various Arab political parties to increase their own bases of support, rather than to redress specific labor grievances.[22] Conflicts among labor societies in Haifa, Jaffa, and Jerusalem weakened their cohesion, and the societies' structure remained "rudimentary," as one organizer admitted.[23] They lacked funds to provide health benefits to members or to support strikes and therefore lacked practical inducements to attract a stable membership. Moreover, the workers were extremely difficult to organize because of their illiteracy and poverty.

The press, political writings, and school curricula were important in molding public opinion and spreading political awareness. Although the reading public was small, the town café and village guesthouse provided social centers where someone would read articles from newspapers and the men

22. Fakhri al-Nashashibi was active with labor groups in Jerusalem; Hanna Asfur in Haifa; and the Jaffa labor leaders were the Christians Michel Mitri and George Mansur (district commissioner, Northern District, monthly report, Dec. 18, 1934, ISA, Chief Secretary's Papers, G/184/34; 208; Jewish Telegraph Agency bulletin, Dec. 19, 1934, attached to CO 733/250/37211).

23. Mansur, p. 7.

would discuss political affairs.[24] The several weekly and daily Arabic newspapers expressed a wide range of opinions, reflecting the views of different political groups.[25] Poetry was the only literary medium that reached a wide public, through the press and recitation.[26]

Few political essays or novels appeared until the end of the 1920s and the mid-1930s. Two books published in 1929 argued that the Palestine problem could serve as a unifying force among the Arabs and urged young Palestinians to acquaint the rest of the Arab world with the nature of the Zionist threat.[27] Four more studies on the Palestine problem appeared in 1936–1937.[28] Palestinian novels included two that stressed the fate of villagers whose land had been sold to Jews.[29]

Historical studies also tended to relate to current difficulties. One scholar edited twelfth-century manuscripts about the defense of the Holy Land against the Crusaders, an obvi-

24. Abu Ghazaleh, "Arab Cultural Nationalism" (1967), p. 21; Shimoni, p. 539; Great Britain, Colonial Office, Cmd. 3530, *Report of the* (Shaw) *Commission* (London: HMSO, 1930).

25. Newspapers included *al-Karmil* (Najib al-Nassar, editor; Haifa), *Filastin* (Isa al-Isa; Jaffa), *Mirat al-Sharq* (Mirror of the East; Bulus Shihadi), *al-Jamiah al-Arabiyyah* (The Arab Community; Husayni; 1927–1935), *al-Liwa* (The Flag; 1933–1938), *al-Difa* (The Defense; established in 1934), *al-Jamiah al-Islamiyyah* (The Islamic Community; pan-Islamic; Shaykh Sulayman al-Taji al-Faruqi). See Abu Ghazaleh, "Arab Cultural Nationalism," pp. 65–66; Shimoni, pp. 559–580; Hattis, p. 63; Hurewitz, *Struggle,* pp. 384–386.

26. Abu Ghazaleh, "Arab Cultural Nationalism" (1967), pp. 90–92; Shimoni, p. 553; Isa al-Sifri, *Risalati* (My Essays) (Jaffa, 1937); Ibrahim Nuh, collection of poems in Arabic (Damascus: n.d.).

27. Muhammad Izzat Darwazah, *Filastin wa al-Urubah* (Palestine and Arabism) (1929); Isa al-Sifri, *Filastin al-Arabiyyah bayn al-Intidab wa al-Sahyuniyyah* (Arab Palestine between the Mandate and Zionism) (Jaffa, 1929).

28. Yusuf Haykal, *al-Qadiyyah al-Filastiniyyah Takhlil wa Naqd* (The Palestine Case: Analysis and Criticism) (Jaffa, n.d.); Hasan Sidqi al-Dajani, *Tafsil Zulamat Filastin* (Explanation of the Palestine Injustice); Muhammad Yunis al-Husayni, *Tahlil Wad Balfour* (Analysis of the Balfour Declaration); Sadi Basaysu, *al-Sahyuniyyah* (Zionism). Abu Ghazaleh, "Arab Cultural Nationalism," pp. 44–47, 52–53; Shimoni, p. 556.

29. Muhammad Izzat Darwazah, *al-Malak wa al-Simsar* (The Angel and the Landbroker), 1934; Najati Sidqi, *al-Akhawat al-Nazimat* (The Grieving Sisters), 1928. See Abu Ghazaleh, "Arab Cultural Nationalism" (1972), pp. 45–47.

ous comparison with the contemporary situation. Another scholar-administrator wrote lengthy books on the bedouin of Beersheba and on the history of several Palestinian towns, which emphasized their historical continuity and the depth of Arab ties to them.[30] Yet another translated the works of such political philosophers as Montesquieu and Rousseau into Arabic in order to acquaint the public with European political thought.[31]

Writers and politicians were also active as teachers and administrators of government and private schools. Although the government schools taught in Arabic, their teachers were required to refrain from political activism; the private secular schools therefore played a larger role in fostering Arab and nationalist outlooks among their students.[32] Moreover, only two government secondary schools offered complete four-year programs in the 1930s. As a result the foreign-run and indigenous private secondary schools played a crucial role in preparing youths for university examinations and, in effect, training the next generation of political leaders.[33]

Through the educational system, writings in the press and books, and discussions in the clubs, the literate urban public came to share a culture that articulated their claim to Palestine. This sense of national identity overlaid and reinforced the economic and personal objections to Zionism, providing

30. These writers were Ahmad Samih al-Khalidi, principal of the Government Arab College, Jerusalem and Arif al-Arif, a district official (Abu Ghazaleh, "Arab Cultural Nationalism" [1972], pp. 57–62).

31. Adil Zuaytir, lecturer at the Institute of Law, Jerusalem; Abu Ghazaleh, "Arab Cultural Nationalism" (1967), pp. 32–33.

32. The six national secondary schools were particularly important, notably: Rawdat al-Maarif in Jerusalem, which was partly supported by the Supreme Muslim Council; al-Najjah College in Nablus, headed from 1921–1928 by Izzat Darwazah; al-Nahdah College in Jerusalem, headed by Khalil Sakakini after 1938; and Bir Zayt, a coeducational boarding school established by the Nasir family in a village north of Ramallah in 1932 (ibid., pp. 38–43).

33. There were no Arabic- or English-language universities in Palestine, although both the government and the Supreme Muslim Council outlined plans to establish such universities. Students had to go to Europe, the United States, or the Arab countries for a university education, which effectively limited access to the sons of the wealthy families and a handful of scholarship students.

a rationale for political opposition and an impetus for organizing that opposition.

Conflict over the Land

Land was always a crucial political issue for the Arab and Jewish communities in Palestine because of its vital impact on their societies. Although only 20 percent of the Jewish immigrants settled in rural areas, and the Jewish community acquired only 5 percent of the total land area by 1940, land was essential to the Zionist movement as the symbol of the Jewish people's roots in the soil of *Eretz Israel*. Land was equally symbolic to the Arab community: their gradual loss of control over this land pointedly reminded them of their diminishing control over *Filastin*.

As early as 1921, when the Zionist organizations consummated their first large postwar land transaction, a Colonial Office official predicted: "Before . . . the Zionist Organization have finished with their land-development policy in Palestine we shall have really ghastly difficulties over the land, and not improbably bloodshed."[34] That particular sale, a transfer of land in the Esdraelon (Emeq) from the Sursuq family of Beirut, uprooted over twenty Arab villages. Since the sale required that the land be handed over free of encumbrances, all the resident tenant farmers had to leave. When the Zionist organizations began to buy land, the customary rights, under which tenancy was transmitted from father to son, could not stand up in court.[35] Tenants received compensation only for improvements they had made to the holding, and no recompense was paid to day laborers, blacksmiths, peddlers, and others who had formed an integral part of the rural economy. The government issued periodic ordinances designed to protect the tenant from arbitrary expropriation, but these were

34. Gerald Clauson (CO), minute on high commissioner's telegram to CO, Nov. 22, 1921, CO 733/7.
35. Abraham Granovsky (Granott), *The Land System in Palestine* (rev. ed., London: Eyre and Spottiswoode, 1952), pp. 80, 283.

easily circumvented. Not until 1933 were squatters included in the category of claimants who should be compensated.

Land purchases did not affect the Arab community seriously until the early 1930s. Before 1920, the Jewish community held 650,000 dunums (one dunum equals a quarter of an acre); they purchased another 514,000 dunums by 1930.[36] For each of the next three years, purchases averaged 19,000 dunums, but accelerated to over 62,000 dunums in 1934 and to almost 73,000 dunums in 1935. Paralleling these accelerated purchases was a drastically increased displacement of tenants and smallholders.

Each large purchase had a significant political impact. The Esdraelon deal sent shock waves through the Arab political community;[37] the Arabs expected other large-scale purchases and the rapid displacement of entire villages. Such fears were only partially allayed by the British government's land ordinances of 1921–1922 and by its granting of ownership rights to the Arab tenant farmers in the Ghawr Beisan çiftlik.[38] The lease to a Jewish company in 1923 of an area of sand dunes and marshes on the Mediterranean coast below Haifa—the Kabbara Concession—occasioned vociferous protests on behalf of the bedouin who cultivated small patches of land and grazed their goats and sheep throughout the area.[39] A similar conflict over bedouin rights in Wadi Hawarith, another area purchased by Jewish land companies, simmered from 1930 to late 1933, when the last Arabs were evicted.[40]

By the end of 1935, the Jewish community owned nearly

---

36. Palestine Government, *Survey,* I, 244.

37. Political reports, Aug. and Sept. 1924, CO 733/73. On the economic importance of this area, see memorandum by the Arab Bureau, Cairo, 1917, based on information supplied by the Jewish agronomist Aaron Aaronsohn, enclosed in Reginald Wingate, dispatch, Feb. 7, 1917, FO 371/3049/41442/41442.

38. Political reports, Feb. 1921, CO 733/1; Oct. 1921, CO 733/7; Nov. 1921, CO 733/8.

39. High commissioner, dispatch to CO, Oct. 19, 1923, CO 733/50.

40. The Wadi Hawarith conflict was described in a lengthy report from the high commissioner to the CO, March 1, 1930, CO 733/190/77182. Also see high commissioner, dispatches, Nov. 12, 1930 (ibid.) and in 1933, CO 733/234/17282.

1.4 million dunums[41] and leased additional land from the government. The overwhelming bulk of this land had been sold by non-Palestinian absentee landlords. The Zionist organizations estimated that by 1936 the Palestine Land Development Company had purchased 89 percent of its holdings from large landowners and only 11 percent from peasants.[42] By the mid-1930s, the British officials were alarmed at the rate of dispossession. Attempts to enforce compensation payments to tenants or to maintain a minimum *lot viable* for them had been widely circumvented. Moreover, the London government rejected proposals to provide loans at low interest rates so that tenants and smallholders could improve their plots, aside from a brief—and highly successful—loan program from 1936 to 1938.[43] Farmers could, therefore, obtain loans only on the private market at usurious rates.[44] When

41. Granovsky, p. 276; Palestine Government, *Survey*, I, 244.

42. Such as the Sursuqs and Twaynis in Beirut; also a former Lebanese, Sulayman Nasif. See Deedes to Forbes Adams, Nov. 8, 1920, FO 371/5124; Nasif's applications for land sales in 1940 and 1944, ISA, Chief Secretary's Papers, I/28/27/40. The acting director of development listed in 1933 several prominent Palestine Arabs who had sold land or acted as agents in land sales to Jewish organizations: Umar and Abd al-Rauf al-Bitar of Jaffa, Shukri al-Taji al-Faruqi of Ramlah, Salim Abd al-Rahman al-Hajj Ibrahim of Tulkarm, Dmitri Tadrus of Jaffa, and Abd al-Rahman al-Taji (an anti-Husayni member of the Supreme Muslim Council), comments, March 24, 1933, on Arab Executive, letter to the government, March 10, 1933, CO 733/230/17249, pt. 3. John Ruedy, "The Dynamics of Land Alienation," in Abu Lughod, ed., *Transformation*, p. 134.

43. The government provided postwar rehabilitation loans in 1919–1923, emergency loans in 1927 (after an earthquake), and development loans in 1936–1938, but it did not have a permanent loan program and did not reopen the Ottoman agricultural bank. Chief secretary, dispatch to CO, July 3, 1924, proposing reopening the agricultural bank; rejection by CO and Treasury, CO 733/70. Samuel had already urged reestablishing the bank, telegram, Aug. 26, 1921, CO 733/5. Reports on the success of the 1936–1938 loan program are in CO 733/362/75092. For a summary of loans issued 1919–1938, see Palestine Government, *Survey*, I, 349.

44. An official investigation revealed that the peasantry's total indebtedness was £P2 million, which meant an average of £P27 per family at a 30 percent interest rate. But the annual net income per family averaged £P25–30, and so the farmer could not pay the debt out of his income, even when the government remitted all the tithes (land taxes) (Report of the Johnson-Crosbie Committee, 1930; see George Hakim and M. Y. El-Hussayni, "Monetary and Banking System," in Himadeh, ed., *Economic Organization*, p. 497, and Shimoni, p. 253). Tithes were remitted up to 45 percent in the southern and Jerusalem districts in May 1932, with a further 45 percent remission that August (high commissioner, telegrams to CO, May 28 and Aug. 10, 1932, CO 733/224/97270).

drought or blight ruined the crops, their land might be sold by court order to satisfy the mortgage or they might succumb to the "temptingly high prices"[45] offered by Jewish development companies. By 1931, the high commissioner reported "sullen distrust" among the peasants, which could change to "noncooperation and hostility unless an early opportunity is taken of demonstrating that the Government appreciate their difficulties and is prepared to give them practical help."[46] In 1935, another high commissioner asserted that the fear that the Jewish community is "eating up the land" is felt

> in every town and village in Palestine . . . About one fifth of Arab villagers are already landless. Village communities are well aware that they have sold, or their neighbours have sold, large sections of their land to Jews and that they have not permanently benefited by the transaction. Their money has gone, the shortage of land has increased. Their fear that the process will continue till the bulk of the land is gone is genuine.[47]

Although some Arab farmers used the payments to improve their holdings, particularly on the fertile citrus-growing coast, many spent the compensation to meet debts, maintain their families, or purchase a few luxuries, and then joined the poor who crowded into shantytowns on the fringes of the cities. Living in huts fashioned from petrol tin cans, the shantytown dwellers lacked basic sanitation as well as health and educational services and competed for low-paying, menial jobs.[48]

45. Quotation from high commissioner, dispatch to CO, March 22, 1928, referring to purchases in the Ghawr Beisan that had resulted from crop failure and subsequent indebtedness, CO 733/155/57313. See also political report, Dec. 1923, CO 733/63 and a report on the Jewish National Fund's purchase of Shatta village, which uprooted sixty families, high commissioner, telegram to CO, April 11, 1931, CO 733/199/87072 pt. 2.

46. Chief secretary, reports to CO, May 16, 23, 1931, CO 733/207/87275.

47. High commissioner, dispatch to CO, Dec. 7, 1935, CO 733/278/75156; see also his telegram, Feb. 11, 1935, ibid.

48. Mansur, p. 14; Palestine Government, *Survey,* II, 694–696.

Arab politicians made sporadic efforts to buy land, take court action to prevent sales, establish banks and funds for long-term loans, and convince farmers to retain their plots. Wealthy individuals and local nationalist societies tried to preempt some Jewish purchases, without significant success. But the Supreme Muslim Council did acquire some land in the early 1930s, which it converted into inalienable *waqf* (endowed property). In addition, the Fund of the Arab Nation bought about a thousand dunums in Gaza in 1933, shortly before it was disbanded.[49] Arab-owned banks operated on a small scale in the 1930s. In fact, total Arab bank deposits amounted to only £P376,000 in 1939.[50]

To underline the opposition to land sales, the head of the Supreme Muslim Council, al-Hajj Amin al-Husayni, convened a conference of five hundred *ulama* in January 1935, which endorsed a *fatwa* (advice by a mufti on religious law) against land sale and land brokerage.[51] The conference threatened to excommunicate all land sellers and brokers. The Arab community, however, was caught in a vicious circle. Its capital holdings were almost entirely in property, a fixed asset. In order to obtain the liquid capital necessary for maintaining their own land-buying company, they would have had to sell some land. But the only purchasers were Zionist organizations: to sell to them would have defeated the very purpose of the transaction.[52]

49. Shimoni, pp. 456–458; *Palestine Post*, Feb. 14, 1934. The members of the Fund's board were Ahmad Hilmi Pasha, Jamal al-Husayni, Yaqub al-Ghusayn, Salim Abd al-Rahman, Fuad Saba, Umar al-Bitar, Yusuf Ashur, and Said Khalil.

50. The Arab Bank was founded in 1930 by Abd al-Hamid Shuman. His father-in-law Ahmad Hilmi Pasha managed that bank and then founded the Arab Agricultural Bank in 1933, as well as heading the Fund of the Arab Nation (Palestine Government, *Survey*, II, 307–308, 727).

51. Report on conference and text of *fatwa* in high commissioner, dispatch, March 4, 1935, CO 733/278/75156.

52. Problems resulting from the lack of liquid capital were also apparent in urban areas. In Nablus, for example, homeowners found it impossible to rebuild after the serious earthquake in 1927 without obtaining emergency loans from the government. Their money had been invested in the buildings, which were then rented. With the buildings destroyed, both the capital and the source of income vanished (chief secretary, dispatch to CO, July 20, 1927, CO 733/142/44626).

Although Arab lawyers fought major land-sale cases in the courts, they obtained a favorable result in only one instance. Most claims were based on custom rather than written documents and were therefore difficult to substantiate in a courtroom. Even when judges granted the occupiers of the land the first option to purchase, the tenant farmers could not raise such substantial funds and therefore had to forfeit their claims.

Arab lawyers and politicians stressed that government legislation to protect tenants and a government-supported agricultural bank were vital necessities. The cautious National Defense party petitioned the high commissioner in January 1935, requesting that he prevent further land sales to Zionist companies because of the inalienability clause in the companies' leases. The petition called the issue one of "life and death to the Arabs, in that it results in the transfer of their country to other hands and the loss of their nationality. . . . [Once] Arab lands are alienated from Arabs to Jews, it is immaterial whether the productivity of these lands is increased or decreased, so long as the Arabs cannot derive any further benefit therefrom."[53]

In their anxiety to prevent land sales, Arabs supported such economically harmful practices as placing rural tracts under Islamic *waqf* and preventing the partitioning of *musha* (communal) holdings. *Waqf* land could not be alienated from the Muslim community, but, like other tenancy arrangements, it discouraged lessees from making improvements. Under the *musha* system, village lands were redistributed periodically among the villagers and no one developed a stake in one plot or had an incentive to substantially improve it because the fruits of his labor might go to another villager the next year. At the same time, however, the *musha* system prevented the

53. Raghib al-Nashashibi, National Defense party, letter to high commissioner, Jan. 28, 1935, enclosed in high commissioner's dispatch to CO, March 4, 1935, CO 733/278/75156. See also Awni Abd al-Hadi's forty-three-page critique, written on behalf of the Arab Executive, of the report of the development director, March 10, 1933, CO 733/230/17249 pt. 3.

purchase of large tracts by outsiders. Companies had to buy options on an individual's share in the village and accumulate many such options before taking control over the village lands. By 1937, only 171 of about 850 villages had been partitioned into individually owned plots. Three-quarters of these partitioned villages lay in the Jaffa-Ramlah-Gaza citrus belt, where the largest number of individual land sales occurred.[54]

Villagers similarly resisted government efforts to prevent them from cultivating *mawat* (waste) lands. Under the Ottoman regime, anyone could cultivate such land by paying a nominal sum to the government; thus farmers could expand their holdings at a minimal cost. But the British imposed a fine on anyone who occupied *mawat* land without permission. And it sent commissioners to demarcate such land in 1922. The villagers obstructed these moves by either withholding information or refusing to accompany the commissioners to the fields.[55]

Arab politicians resented the prevalent Zionist argument that only the Jewish community could make the land fruitful. They called attention to the contrast between the heavy subsidization of the Jewish settlements and the lack of material assistance to the Arab villages.[56] To demonstrate that Arabs were capable of growing prize-winning vegetables and fruits, politicans persuaded villagers to display their produce in government agricultural shows and organized Arab fairs in Jerusalem in the mid-1930s.[57] Prosperous farmers and merchants formed an Arab Economic Development Society in early 1922, which complained about the lack of educational opportunities and health care for villagers and asserted that the government must assist them financially. But the society lacked

54. Moses J. Doukhan, "Land Tenure," in Himadeh, ed., *Economic Organization,* pp. 105–106.
55. Political report, June 1922, CO 733/23; for an analysis of *mawat* see Abcarius, pp. 126–129.
56. Arab Executive, letter to Lord Northcliffe, early 1922, ISA, Arab Documents, file 3046.
57. *Palestine Bulletin,* June 16, 1926; *Palestine Post,* April 12, 1934.

the funds and organization to do more than publicize its views in the Arabic press and sponsor an Arab Economical Agricultural Conference and an Arbor Day in February 1923.[58] Additional agricultural conferences were convened in 1929 and 1930; they stressed the need to reestablish an agricultural bank (which had functioned under the Ottoman Empire)[59] and demanded a wide range of village improvements, including constructing schools and paving the roads between villages.[60] The executive committee of the Arab Women's Congress, formed in 1929, submitted frequent protests to the government against rural conditions and urged it to promote cooperative credit facilities and to pass measures to prevent the eviction of tenants.[61] Arab leaders also discussed long-term plans to develop rural areas by planting fruit trees, establishing village industries, increasing mechanization, sponsoring hydrologic surveys and well drilling, constructing irrigation canals and reservoirs, and supporting health programs. But such ambitious projects were never begun.[62]

Rural problems, resulting from indebtedness and impoverishment as much as from land purchases, provided an undercurrent of dissatisfaction against the government and anger at

58. Chairman, Abdallah Mukhlis; secretary (and principal organizer), Najib al-Nassar, editor of *al-Karmil*. Members included the Reverend Salah Saba, Muhammad Ali al-Tamimi, T. S. Butaji, Rushdi al-Shawwa, Wadi al-Bustani, Rashid al-Hajj Ibrahim, and, from Nablus, Hafiz and Sulayman Tuqan, Abd al-Latif Salah, Awni Abd al-Hadi, and Abd al-Rahim al-Nabulsi. See S. Symes (Haifa district governor) to civil secretary, Jan. 23, March 21, 1922, Dec. 9, 1923, ISA, Chief Secretary's Papers, 2/159, POL/2; protest by the society against the Kabbara concession, May 23, 1922, in high commissioner, dispatch, July 13, 1922, CO 733/23; report on the February 1923 conference in political report, Feb. 1923, CO 733/43; and Abd al-Wahhab al-Kayyali, ed., *Wathaiq al-Muqawwamah al-Filastiniyyah didd al-Ihtilal al-Britani wal-Sahyunniyyah, 1918–1939* (Beirut: Institute for Palestine Studies, 1968), p. 67.

59. Vice-president, Economic Congress, Haifa, to Arab Executive, Nov. 25, 1929, ISA, Arab Documents, file 3593.

60. Report, June 3, 1930, ISA, Arab Documents, file 3593; *Falastin,* English edition, June 28, 1930.

61. See, for example, demands presented to the PMC, Jan. 28, 1932, attached to high commissioner, dispatch, Feb. 13, 1932, CO 733/221/97174.

62. Arab Executive, memorandum, n.d. (1931?), ISA, Arab Documents, file 3682.

the Jewish immigrants.[63] The peasantry's traditional wariness of the tax-collecting government was sorely exacerbated. By the mid-1930s, rural Palestine was a tinderbox, ready to explode at the first strike of a match.

63. High commissioner, dispatch, March 5, 1932, CO 733/215/97050/9.

PART II /

THE GROWTH OF THE

NATIONALIST MOVEMENT

ARAB POLITICAL ORGANIZATION, 1919–1939

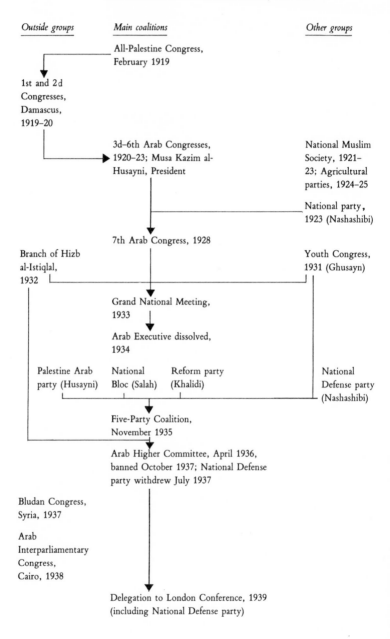

Outside groups   *Main coalitions*   *Other groups*

All-Palestine Congress,
February 1919

1st and 2d
Congresses,
Damascus,
1919–20

3d–6th Arab Congresses,
1920–23; Musa Kazim al-
Husayni, President

National Muslim
Society, 1921–
23; Agricultural
parties, 1924–25

National party,
1923 (Nashashibi)

7th Arab Congress, 1928

Branch of Hizb
al-Istiqlal,
1932

Youth Congress,
1931 (Ghusayn)

Grand National Meeting,
1933

Arab Executive dissolved,
1934

Palestine Arab
party (Husayni)

National
Bloc (Salah)

Reform party
(Khalidi)

National
Defense party
(Nashashibi)

Five-Party Coalition,
November 1935

Arab Higher Committee, April 1936,
banned October 1937; National Defense
party withdrew July 1937

Bludan Congress,
Syria, 1937

Arab
Interparliamentary
Congress,
Cairo, 1938

Delegation to London Conference, 1939
(including National Defense party)

4 / Mobilization from Above, 1917–1928

The nationalist demands of the Palestine Arabs were first articulated at their congress in December 1920 and further elaborated in the memorandum the first Arab delegation to London presented to the British government in August 1921. They called for the abolition of the principle of the Jewish national home, as expressed in the Balfour Declaration, and the annulment of British regulations favoring that principle; the establishment of a national government responsible to a parliament elected by the existing population, Muslim, Christian, and Jewish; an end to Jewish immigration until the national government could formulate its immigration policy; and the inclusion of Palestine in a federation with the neighboring Arab states.[1]

These demands were developed at length in a letter the delegation sent to the colonial secretary in October 1921. This letter stressed that the Balfour Declaration

> was made without our being consulted and we cannot accept it as deciding our destinies . . . .
>   The Declaration should be superseded by an Agreement which would safeguard the rights, interests and liberties of the people of Palestine, and at the same time make provision for reasonable Jewish aspirations, but precluding any exclusive po-

1. Muslim-Christian delegation statement, handed to the colonial secretary in London, Aug. 12, 1921, CO 733/14. On Palestine Arab ideology, see Porath, *Emergence*, pp. 39–62.

litical advantages to them which must necessarily interfere with Arab rights. . . . It is the claim of the Zionists that the People of Palestine, after practical experience, will recognize the advantage to the country of Zionist immigration. If that be so, the Jews may be confident that the future immigration policy of [the national government in] Palestine would not be unfavourable to them: but if the immigration policy of the Zionist Organization proves detrimental to the Palestinian people, this policy should be regulated, not in the interests of the Zionists, but of Palestinians.[2]

Despite the continuity in the Arabs' basic demands, their bitterness and despair intensified over the years, as Jewish immigration and land purchases increased and the possibility of independence under an Arab government receded. The demands articulated in the general strike of 1936 included suspending Jewish immigration, prohibiting land sales from Arabs to Jews, and forming a national government responsible to a representative council. The Arab leaders knew that they could not expel the Jewish community from Palestine, but they wanted the Zionist leaders to realize that the Arabs' needs must be accommodated if the two communities were to live together peaceably. The violence of the strike, however, exacerbated Jewish fears and accelerated their own national drive and separatism.

Obstacles to Unification

Several external institutional obstacles hindered the development of permanent, unified organs to express the Arabs' political views and complicated the political struggle. They made it impossible for the Arab community to establish a quasi-government of its own, paralleling the British institutions, as the Zionist were able to do. The Arabs were not one single religious community, for example, and therefore, unlike the Jewish community, they could not use this means to mold a unified sociopolitical structure. Separate religious and cultural institutions existed for the several Christian sects and

2. Muslim-Christian delegation to colonial secretary, Oct. 24, 1921, CO 733/16.

the Muslims. Although the powerful Supreme Muslim Council, which controlled the Islamic courts and *waqf,* played a key political role, it could never become coextensive with the national movement.

The British authorities refused to recognize the Arab political organs as the official spokesmen of the Arab community, despite evidence that the general public supported their basic demands. Although this refusal came ostensibly because the leaders were not actually elected by the public at large, government officials acknowledged in private that the real reason for "nonrecognition" was the Arabs' opposition to "the principles embodied in the Mandate," that is, the Balfour Declaration.[3] Thus the Arab politicians faced an impossible dilemma: if they gained British recognition by supporting the mandate, they would lose their popular backing and their stature as leaders of the Arab community.

During crises, such as occurred in 1929 and 1936, the British authorities turned to the Arab politicians as the de facto spokesmen of their people but, in less volatile periods, the authorities attempted to disregard them. This attitude was facilitated by the absence of a legislative council that would have provided a legitimate forum for airing grievances. Arab politicians had rejected such a council in 1922 because they still hoped to prevent the establishment of the mandate. When that effort collapsed and the mandate was consolidated, the politicians realized that a council could perform some useful functions, and they gradually came to want one. But the Zionist leadership placed its weight against formation of a legislative council because they realized that it would enable the Arabs to publicize their grievances effectively and might crystallize the political structure in Palestine before the Jewish community could become dominant.

Political life was forced to undergo major changes from the

3. Memorandum prepared by Government House, Jerusalem, on the Arab Executive's first report, March 30, 1921, CO 733/13. See also political report, Jan. 1921, FO 371/6374.

Ottoman era to the British period. The Arab politicians had engaged in limited forms of political action under the Ottoman regime. They had sought constitutional rights and had protested Jewish immigration, using the personal channels available to members of the elite and the new methods of petition and newspaper protests. These means were developed further under the British, but the close relationship between the ruler and the Arab elite was severed. The Arabs' attempts to organize and unite met with varying degrees of success during the mandate period. The shock of the Balfour Declaration propelled the Arab politicians into forming a united front in 1919–1920, which they maintained until 1923, attempting dramatic pressure politics—delegations to London, noncooperation, and demonstrations. But the mandate came into force in late 1923 despite these protests and on terms viewed with hostility by the Arabs. Their efforts appeared to have been fruitless, and the movement suffered a serious internal crisis, splitting into factions that were unable to reunite until 1928, when the possibility of negotiating with the government was renewed. The new umbrella organization formed by the politicians in 1928 included not only those active in the early 1920s but also younger men, critical of their elders' gentlemanly style and committed to fostering militant action.

The main political groups were integrally linked to the pyramidal family and clan networks. This enhanced their ability to spread views and mobilize all levels of society, but it complicated efforts to unify the movement. Each important family had a separate power base, and shifts in alliance were frequently the result of personal and family differences rather than political disagreements.

At the end of the 1920s, the nationalist movement shifted from organization and mobilization from above—by the elite—to mobilization from below. Youth, labor, scouts, and middle-class groups pressured the elite to act more militantly. These groups responded to the considerable disruption in Palestinian society by drawing support from the dispossessed farmers living in shantytowns around the main cities, the artisans and traders who feared Jewish competition, and the under- and unemployed educated youths. They challenged the established leadership, prodded it into increasingly militant tactics by the mid-1930s, and formed the backbone of the 1936 general strike and 1937–1939 revolt. This popular movement often criticized the various party factions for placing individual elite-level rivalries above national and social concerns and for not taking adequate steps to prevent Jewish immigration and land buying.

Popular pressure on the leadership climaxed with the general strike of 1936, which lasted for six months. The internal tensions generated by this violence, however, caused some politicians to try to reach an accommodation with the British and, through partition of the territory of Palestine, with the Zionists. A major split occurred in 1937–1938, when this faction broke away from the national front. Support for the concept of partition was rejected by the leading elements, so they resorted, for the first time, to assassinating their political opponents—and these assassinations further damaged national cohesion. The British finally quelled the revolt by the stick of severe repression and the carrot of major political concessions in 1939. By the time the Arab national movement reached the point of a full-scale rebellion, however, the Zionists' national movement was well entrenched, and the Arabs were unable to take advantage of the political concessions offered by the British.

Political Action under the Military Administration

Political clubs sprang up in most towns soon after the British occupied southern Palestine in late 1917. An official Zionist commission arrived in Palestine in March 1918, amid persistent rumors concerning the concessions made by the Balfour Declaration. Despite these indications, many Arab politicians believed that the country would become autonomous or join a federation linking Palestine, Syria, Lebanon, and Transjordan.

Palestinians were prominent in Emir Faysal's government and army in Syria, and the Palestine Club (Nadi Filastin) in Damascus pressed the Palestinian case on the Syrian government.[4] Other Palestinians, however, hesitated to support Faysal and the idea of a federation. Some urban Muslims distrusted a bedouin. Some Christians feared the pan-Islamic bent of a ruler whose father controlled the Islamic shrines in the Hijaz. Catholics tended to hope for French (Catholic) rule. Nevertheless, Faysal, as the de jure ruler in Syria and the Arabs' only spokesman before the peace conference in Paris, received tactical support from most Palestinian politicians, who hoped that he would help them realize their own goals.

Only three of the thirty or forty clubs formed in Palestine in 1918–1920 carried any political weight. The Muslim-Christian Society (al-Jamiyat al-Islamiyyah al-Masihiyyah) embodied the novel concept of political cooperation between people adhering to the two religions, based on their common fear of Zionism. The society claimed at least two hundred members in late 1919, drawn from the older generation of urban politicians. Many had been active under the Ottoman regime in local politics or in Instanbul. They tended to expect Britain to rule impartially and to uphold its wartime pledges to Sherif Husayn. They felt that they were the natural social and political leaders of Palestine and that they should be entrusted with responsible government positions.

The Arab Club (al-Nadi al-Arabi) and the Literary Society (al-Muntada al-Adabi) attracted younger members of the urban elite.[5] These groups opposed Zionism, criticized British

4. Its president was Shaykh Abd al-Qadir Muzghar (Muzaffar). Other participants were al-Hajj Amin al-Husayni, Izzat Darwazah, Salim Abd al-Rahman al-Hajj Ibrahim, Rushdi al-Shawwa, Muhammad Ali al-Tamimi, and Subhi al-Khadra (chief political officer, Cairo, dispatch, March 27, 1920, FO 371/5034; Zionist intelligence report, March 19, 1920, CZA, Z4/16078; Porath, *Emergence,* p. 77).

5. Porath, *Emergence,* pp. 74–77; Major J. C. Camp, report on the Arab clubs, Aug. 26, 1919, FO 371/4182/2117; Sykes, dispatch, Feb. 8, 1919, FO 371/4170/1051; intelligence report, Dec. 24, 1920, ISA, Chief Secretary's Papers, POL/2195/I, 2/155; Zionist intelligence report, March 20, 1919, CZA, Z4/16004; Zionist intelligence report, fall 1919, CZA, Z4/3886/I.

tutelage, and wanted Emir Faysal to rule "southern Syria," as they newly termed Palestine. The members of the Nadi were willing to support a British role in Palestine as long as Britain limited Zionist claims and supported Faysal's rule in Syria. But, as Syrian-French tensions grew, the Muntada criticized Britain—largely because the society's financing came from France—and therefore also criticized Faysal. In late 1919, the Nadi claimed over five hundred members and the Muntada some six hundred, although these figures seem inflated and may reflect overlapping membership. Within Jerusalem, Husaynis led the Nadi (al-Hajj Amin al-Husayni was president) and Nashashibis led the Muntada, but this family division was not perpetuated in the branches outside the capital city. The clubs maintained ties with such secret groups as al-Fidai (The Self-Sacrificer) and Jamiyyat al-Ikha wa al-Afaf (Association of Brotherhood and Purity), which organized in slum areas of Jaffa and Nablus and considered mounting terrorist operations against Jews. Jamiyyat al-Ikha wa al-Afaf was apparently used by the Muntada to maintain security at meetings, distribute pamphlets, and organize demonstrations.[6]

The Zionist commission sponsored a parade in Jerusalem on November 2, 1918, the first anniversary of the Balfour Declaration, displaying in public their political demands. A few days later, the Anglo-French declaration of November 7 held that the wishes of the people of Syria and Mesopotamia should determine their future form of government.[7] Anger over the Zionist parade and hopes raised by the Anglo-French declaration (even though it did not refer explicitly to Palestine) propelled the Arab organizations in Jerusalem to petition the British military authorities, proclaiming their support for the Damascus government:

We have noticed yesterday a large crowd of Jews carrying banners and overrunning the streets shouting words which

6. Porath, *Emergence,* p. 79.
7. See Chapter 2; the declaration is quoted in full in Antonius, pp. 435–436.

hurt the feelings and wound the soul. They pretend with open voice that Palestine, which is the Holy Land of our Fathers and the graveyard of our ancestors, which had been inhabited by the Arabs for long ages who loved it and died in defending it, is now a national home for them. . . . If it is meant that they should obtain national liberty in the country, why should this be confined to the Jews and not to others? . . .

We Arabs, Muslim and Christian, have always sympathised profoundly with the persecuted Jews and their misfortunes in other countries as much as we sympathised with the persecuted Armenians and other weaker nations. We hoped for their deliverance and prosperity. But there is a wide difference between this sympathy and the acceptance of such a nation in our country . . . ruling over us and disposing of our affairs. . . .

[We] expect that a Power like Great Britain well known for justice and progress will put a stop to the Zionists' cry. Furthermore, it will establish a just ruling for immigration to Palestine by Muslims, Christians and Jews equally, in order that the country may be saved from being lost and the inhabitants from being persecuted. In conclusion, we Muslims and Christians desire to live with our brothers the Jews of Palestine in peace and happiness and with equal rights. Our privileges are theirs, and their duties ours.[8]

Many politicians thought that joining with Syria would free them from Zionism and therefore resolved that Palestine should be included in Syria under sherifian rule and that the name of the sherif of Mecca should be pronounced as caliph in the Friday service at al-Aqsa mosque. The British governor opposed these moves and persuaded the mufti of Jerusalem, Kamil al-Husayni, to delay using the sherif's name until a decision on the caliphate was made in Mecca. He also warned the mayor of Jerusalem, Musa Kazim al-Husayni, and the director general of the *waqf,* Arif Hikmat al-Nashashibi—who

8. The protest was signed by the Muslim Benevolent Society, al-Nadi al-Arabi, the Greek Orthodox Benevolent Society, the Muslim Educational Society (the original name of al-Muntada al-Adabi), the Society of Brotherhood and Chivalry, the Greek Catholic Society, and over a hundred individuals. Gilbert F. Clayton, dispatch to FO, Nov. 8, 1918, transmitted report by Storrs which enclosed the protest, FO 371/3385/747/198575.

were leaders of the Jerusalem Muslim-Christian Society—that
their political activities were not consonant with their administrative posts. Both men agreed to withdraw from political
activities, but the governor doubted that he could persuade
the younger politicians to temper their activities.[9]

In early February 1919, a countrywide congress was convened in Jerusalem, largely at the initiative of the Jerusalem
and Jaffa Muslim-Christian societies.[10] Called the First Congress of the Muslim-Christian Societies, it sought to formulate a program to present at the Paris peace conference. The
military administration would not allow the societies to hold
elections of delegates to the congress, and so each society
nominated delegates, allotting two or three for each town.

The First Congress brought together, for the first time, the
politically active men from all around the country. Arif al-
Dajani, president of the Jerusalem Muslim-Christian Society,
presided. Dajani supported the idea of Palestinian autonomy
under British tutelage. In contrast, the secretary of the congress, Izzat Darwazah of Nablus, who was active in al-Nadi
al-Arabi and the Nadi Filastin in Damascus, supported Emir
Faysal and an Arab federation. Darwazah's approach pre-
vailed. The congress requested that Palestine remain an Arab
country, joined with Syria. Moreover, it rejected political
Zionism in a memorandum signed by twenty-five of the
thirty participants[11] and denounced French pretensions to
rule Palestine. The congress approved acceptance of assistance from Great Britain, on condition that such aid not restrict Palestine's fundamental independence.

9. Clayton, dispatch to FO, Dec. 6, 1918, enclosing Storrs, dispatches, Nov.
19, 24, FO 371/3386/747/213403.
10. Clayton, dispatch, March 2, 1919, transmitted a report on the congress, FO
371/4153/275. See also Chief administrator, report, Feb. 3, 1919, ISA, Chief Secretary's Papers, POL/2195/I, 2/155; Muhammad Izzat Darwazah, *al-Qadiyyah al-Filastiniyyah fi Mukhtalif Marahiliha* (The Palestine Case at Its Different Stages), 2 vols.
(Sidon, 1951), I, 35; Porath, *Emergence,* pp. 79–85, 274.
11. It was not signed by Yaqub Farraj, pro-British representative of the Jerusalem Greek Orthodox community, or by Abd al-Hamid Abu Ghawsh, Muslim agent
of the French and the Zionists (Porath, *Emergence,* p. 81).

The platform was not adopted unanimously. Minority re
ports were filed by the Catholic delegates, who objected to
the criticism of France, and by the pro-British bloc, led by
Dajani, who did not want to merge Palestine with Syria. In
analyzing the voting patterns, Yehoshua Porath has demonstrated that two coalitions emerged: the pan-Arabs and pro-
French voted together on the resolution to unite Palestine
with Syria, and the pan-Arabs and pro-British joined to reject
French claims.[12] Despite the tensions among these groups, a
schism was avoided and, after the congress, a compromise
agreement was reached on a proposal that Palestine have internal autonomy within the framework of Arab unity.

The British military administration prohibited the congress
from publishing and distributing its resolutions, and Britain
would not let the congress send a delegation to the Paris peace
conference, thereby forcing the Palestinians to rely on Emir
Faysal. Britain did, however, allow Palestinian politicians to
hold meetings and issue petitions in advance of and during the
visit of the King-Crane Commission, the American wing of
an international commission appointed by the Paris peace conference that toured Palestine and Syria in June and July 1919.[13]
The Arab community unanimously opposed Zionism in its
statements to the commission, but it continued to split on the
issues of unity with Syria or the acceptance of tutelage by
Britain, France, or the United States. The King-Crane Commission concluded that the majority would accept American
guidance, and this conclusion was also apparent in the resolutions passed by the First Arab Congress that assembled in
Damascus in July 1919.[14] While calling for the independence
of Syria (including Palestine) under a constitutional monarchy
headed by Emir Faysal, the congress accepted the idea of tutelage by the United States, as long as that would involve only

12. Ibid., pp. 82–83, 86.
13. See Porath, *Emergence*, pp. 89–92, and Harry N. Howard, *The King-Crane
Commission* (Beirut: Khayats, 1963).
14. See Antonius, pp. 440–442; Porath, *Emergence*, p. 85.

technical and economic aid and would last no more than twenty years. Britain was the second choice as mandatory, and France was rejected emphatically. The congress also rejected the Zionist movement's claim to a special position in Palestine.

The pan-Arab, pro-Syrian politicians assumed greater influence in late 1919, when they convened a special congress in Haifa that formed a committee to coordinate the activities of the various local societies.[15] Rashid al-Hajj Ibrahim of the Haifa Muslim Society presided, and Fakhri al-Nashashibi of the Jerusalem Muntada became secretary. The committee also maintained contact with the Nadi Filastin in Damascus, in preparation for the Second Arab Congress there. This congress proclaimed Syrian independence under Emir Faysal on March 8, 1920. The Nadi and Muntada sponsored demonstrations on that date to honor Faysal and celebrate the proclamation of independence.

The British administration feared that such public gatherings would become violent and suspended permission for further demonstrations. The young politicians then chose the annual Muslim festival of Nebi Musa (the prophet Moses) as an occasion for political protest. Musa Kazim al-Husayni, the mayor of Jerusalem, set aside his pledge to avoid politics and used the balcony of the municipality as the platform to deliver a speech praising Emir Faysal. Young politicians orated from the nearby balcony of al-Nadi al-Arabi, and the inflamed crowd raged through the Old City, attacking Jewish residents.[16] Although the violence shocked Musa Kazim Pasha, the British removed him from his position as mayor as a result of his speech. Some other activists—notably al-Hajj Amin al-Husayni and Arif al-Arif—fled to Damascus. Political allegiances shifted rapidly in the following months. The Husaynis became strong opponents of the British partly because they lost control of the mayoralty. The Nashashibis, in

15. Report on the Arabic press, Nov. 1919, and Zionist intelligence report, Jan. 1920, CZA, Z4/3886/I; Porath, *Emergence*, p. 93.
16. See Chapter 9 on the 1920 riots.

contrast, began to support the British as soon as Raghib al-Nashashibi succeeded Musa Kazim Pasha as mayor. This shift and the bitterness between the two families had long-term repercussions on Palestine Arab political life.

The Palestinians' political ties with Damascus were abruptly undercut in July 1920, when Syria fell to the French army and Emir Faysal fled into exile. The pro-French Muntada began to wane, and the pan-Arab Nadi began to find fault with Faysal, particularly for his dealings with Chaim Weizmann. Most important, the Palestinians were forced to reorganize their national movement on a purely Palestinian basis. This focus was reinforced after the British shifted from a military to a civil administration in Palestine in early July.

The Muslim-Christian societies, led by Musa Kazim Pasha and Arif al-Dajani, reemphasized their preference for an autonomous Palestine at meetings during the summer and fall of 1920.[17] The Palestinians who had worked in Damascus did not return to Palestine until the autumn, but their renewed influence was evident at the pan-Islamic meeting held in Haifa in October.[18] This meeting also opened the campaign to ensure that control over Muslim institutions remain in the hands of the Muslim community.[19] That demand was supported by the new British administration, which did not want to arouse Muslim religious fervor and had already granted substantial autonomy to the Jewish community.

The Arab Executive

The Muslim-Christian societies and newly returned Damascus politicians convened a congress in Haifa in December

17. Porath, *Emergence*, pp. 105–107.
18. Participants included Arif al-Arif, Salim Abd al-Rahman al-Hajj Ibrahim, Rashid al-Hajj Ibrahim, Umar al-Bitar, Jamil al-Shawwa, and Yaqub al-Ghusayn (intelligence reports, Sept. 30, Oct. 4, 14, 1920, ISA, Chief Secretary's Papers, POL/7, 2/163.
19. A gathering of shaykhs, qadis, and muftis in early November appointed a committee to examine this question (high commissioner, dispatch to FO, Nov. 29, 1920, FO 371/5262; high commissioner, dispatch, Jan. 7, 1921, telegram, Jan. 17, 1921, and FO, reply, Jan. 22, FO 371/6390).

1920. They called it the Third Arab Congress in order to stress its continuity with the first (1919) and second (1920) congresses held in Damascus. The membership was now, however, exclusively Palestinian; the total of three dozen delegates were drawn from each administrative district. The congress elected an executive committee—generally known as the Arab Executive—to coordinate political activities between the plenary sessions with the help of a permanent secretariat based in Jerusalem. The Arab Executive was headed by Musa Kazim al-Husayni, with Arif al-Dajani as his deputy. The nine members were middle-aged, respected men from ranking landowning families and included two prominent Christian merchants.[20] The congress passed resolutions that denounced Zionism and maintained that Ottoman regulations should be applied in Palestine because legally it was military occupied territory. But the participants tended to be less critical of the idea of British tutelage per se than they were of the Zionist-inspired policies that were being applied. Nowhere was "southern Syria" mentioned.[21]

Arab politicians also did not object to the participation of four Muslims and three Christians on an advisory council formed by the high commissioner in October 1920. The appointees were prominent citizens, and they carefully avoided claiming to represent the general public. They considered the council a temporary measure, useful as long as the status of Palestine remained uncertain and representative institutions could not be established.[22]

The politicians also supported the high commissioner's ef-

20. Al-Hajj Tawfiq Hamad (Nablus), Abd al-Fattah al-Sadi (Acre), Shaykh Abd al-Latif al-Hajj Ibrahim (Tulkarm), Shaykh Sulayman al-Taji al-Faruqi (Ramlah), Ibrahim Shammas (Greek Orthodox, Jerusalem), Yaqub Bardakash (Christian, Jaffa) (political report, Dec. 1920, FO 371/6374; Musa Kazim Pasha, letter to high commissioner, Dec. 19, 1920, ISA, Chief Secretary's Papers, POL/2221, 2/244; Porath, *Emergence,* pp. 108–109).

21. See section on the national demands at the beginning of this chapter.

22. Members included Ismail al-Husayni (Jerusalem), Shaykh Frayh Abu Middayn (bedouin, Beersheba), Sulayman Abd al-Raziq Tuqan (Nablus), Sulayman Nasif (Christian) (Samuel, report on the first meeting of the advisory council, Oct. 10, 1920; FO 371/5123).

91

forts to reach an agreement with the Muslim dignitaries concerning the organization of their community. A Muslim committee formed in late 1920 even agreed to let the British administration have a say in appointments and financial accounting. During the spring of 1921, however, the community was preoccupied with the controversy over the succession to the post of mufti of Jerusalem: following the death of the mufti Kamil al-Husayni in March 1921, the three Nashashibi-supported candidates outvoted Kamil's brother al-Hajj Amin al-Husayni in the election. The British authorities let al-Hajj Amin assume the post, possibly to placate his family for loss of the mayoralty. Soon after, al-Hajj Amin joined with the nationalist mufti of Haifa, Shaykh Muhammad Murad, in objecting to letting the British have a semisupervisory role over the Muslim committee. A second committee was formed in August 1921, which redrafted the proposals so that the government would not exercise any control over appointments or fund disbursements. The high commissioner agreed to the new proposals and supported the formation of a completely autonomous Supreme Muslim Council to supervise these matters.[23]

In the January 1922 elections for the Supreme Muslim Council, the Nashashibi faction was heavily outvoted by the Husaynis and therefore withdrew from the meeting, leaving al-Hajj Amin to become president.[24] Thus the Husayni-Nashashibi rivalry, already intense over the mayoralty and muftiship of Jerusalem, assumed additional overtones and complexities.

From 1920 to 1923, the Arab Executive worked to unify the politically aware elements in order to bolster its claim to

23. See Elie Kedourie, "Sir Herbert Samuel and the Government of Palestine," *Middle Eastern Studies* 5 (January 1969), and Porath, "al-Hajj Amin," for analyses of the appointment of al-Hajj Amin as mufti and the formation of the Supreme Muslim Council; also Porath, *Emergence,* pp. 188–193.

24. The other members were Abd al-Latif Salah (Nablus), Muhammad Murad (Acre), Said al-Shawwa (Gaza), and Abdallah Dajani (Jaffa) (high commissioner, dispatch to CO, Jan. 20, 1922, CO 733/18).

epresent the Palestine Arabs before the mandatory power
and the League of Nations, as well as to underline its asser-
ion that the entire Arab community rejected the program of
he Zionist movement. Until Britain's position in Palestine
was confirmed formally by the League in 1923, the Arab
leaders sustained their hope that the combined impact of diplomatic missions and political noncooperation would result in
substantial changes in British policy.

The Arab Executive largely succeeded in its efforts to win
popular support. It relied on the local Muslim-Christian societies, the annual congresses, and the permanent secretariat.
Porath has noted that the societies "constituted a basic framework of leaders and activists, who were able whenever necessary to motivate the masses under their influence. This organizational structure suited the traditional social structure
and the accepted status of the local elite."[25] The societies
financed their own activities, sent reports to the secretariat,
and organized petitions and other campaigns on instructions
from Jerusalem. The secretariat, headed by Jamal al-Husayni,
drafted proposals, corresponded with the branch societies,
and, for one year, published a mimeographed newsletter.[26]

The executive committee was expanded to twenty-four
members, with Musa Kazim Pasha reelected each year as
president and head of the delegations to London. Arif al-
Dajani was replaced by Umar al-Bitar as vice-president in
June 1922,[27] however, after Arif Pasha's credibility as a na-

25. Porath, *Emergence,* p. 282. For details on the Muslim-Christian societies in
the various towns, see ibid., pp. 275–284.
26. Ishaq Darwish was the first secretary, but he was soon succeeded by Jamal
al-Husayni, a relative. Copies of the newsletter (August 1921 to July 1922) are on file
in ISA, Arab Documents, file 1722. Correspondence between the districts (particularly Samarah in Tulkarm, Tuqan in Nablus, and Kasma in Galilee and Beisan) and
Jerusalem is on file in ISA, Arab Documents, files 1057–1059, 1072, 1773, 3596, and
3785.
27. This change was made at the special assembly in June 1922. The assembly
first considered electing Shaykh Murad vice-president (acting president while Musa
Kazim Pasha was heading the delegation to London), but he declined. On the
assembly, see political report, June 1922, CO 733/23; political report, July 1922, CO
733/24; Montague David Eder (Zionist Executive) to ZO (London), July 17, 1922;

tionalist leader was undermined by his brother's participation in the Zionist-funded National Muslim Society in Jerusalem. In June 1923, the vice-presidency was shared by Michel Bayruti of Jaffa (a Christian) and al-Hajj Tawfiq al-Hamad of Nablus (a Muslim), who was a close friend of Musa Kazim Pasha. The secretaryship was shared in 1923 by three men and three eight-member permanent committees were established in the fields of administration, economics, and political affairs, thus providing evidence of the increasing organizational complexity of the movement.

Congresses were held in late May 1921 (the fourth), August 1922 (fifth), and June 1923 (sixth), with a special assembly held in June 1922.[28] These congresses were considerably larger than the third congress of December 1920. At least 75 delegates attended the 1922 congress and 115 the 1923 gathering. The available lists of participants indicate that half of the delegates came from regionally and nationally prominent families.[29] Only one Nashashibi participated, however, a further sign of the profound effects of the family schism. About 15 percent of the participants were Christian, primarily merchants and journalists from Jerusalem, Jaffa, and Haifa. No mayors or other government appointees could participate, but several religious leaders were active. The muftis of Tiberias and Haifa served on the Arab Executive, and the latter—

Van Vriesland to Eder, Aug. 16, 1922; Arabic press report, July 21, 1922, all in CZA, Z4/1391/II/a; Jamal al-Husayni, letters to the chief secretary concerning the election of the acting president, June 26, 27, July 2, 1922, ISA, Chief Secretary's Papers, POL/1, 2/158.

28. On the fourth congress: Palestine government report, CO 733/13, and Zionist Executive report, CZA, Z4/1366. On the fifth congress: political report, Aug. 1922, CO 733/25; secretary, Arab Executive, letter to high commissioner, Aug. 30, 1922, ISA, Arab Documents, file 1058; Zionist Executive report, CZA, Z4/1392/II/a. On the sixth congress: chief secretary transmitted reports by the government secretariat and the Zionist Executive (Kisch), June 22, 27, 1923, CO 733/46; political report, June 1923, CO 733/47.

29. The delegates from Nablus to the fourth congress included, for example, members of all the leading families: Abd al-Hadi, Tamimi, Tuqan, Hamad, Salah, Nimr, Anabtawi, Jamal, Darwazah, and Shakaah.

Muhammad Murad—was simultaneously a member of the Supreme Muslim Council.

The fourth congress in May 1921 selected a delegation to go to London to negotiate with the British government. The fifth congress (1922) rejected the constitution proposed by Britain and launched a boycott of the legislative council elections. And the sixth congress (1923) stiffened the rejection of a reconstituted advisory council and proposed further steps toward noncooperation.

Fissures in the United Front

Just as the Arab Executive appeared to have established the bases for a permanent organization, to have extended its membership to include almost all politicians and leading personages, and to have succeeded in its election boycott, its cohesion was shattered. The fissures resulted in part from internal pressures, such as the hesitation of many members to embark on a more militant program of noncooperation against the British, and in part from external causes, in particular the final implementation of the mandate in September 1923. This act doomed the possibility of altering the text of the mandate instrument to delete the pro-Zionist provisions and thrust a crisis upon the Arab Executive.

The potential for divisions along the lines of family and personal antagonisms had been present since 1920, when Raghib al-Nashashibi agreed to replace Musa Kazim al-Husayni as mayor of Jerusalem. The family rivalry was further accentuated when al-Hajj Amin became mufti of Jerusalem and president of the Supreme Muslim Council. Prominent individuals who failed to gain influence in the Arab Executive or Supreme Muslim Council, such as Shaykh Sulayman al-Taji al-Faruqi, or who lost their position in the executive, such as Arif al-Dajani, gravitated toward the opposition camp led by the Nashashibis.[30]

30. Porath, *Emergence*, pp. 210–211.

Broader political issues came into play in 1923, when som
politicians shied away from militant noncooperation. On
group, led by Sulayman Nasif, even considered participatin
in the legislative council elections. Raghib al-Nashashibi, Ari
al-Dajani, and the mayors of Acre, Gaza, and Nablus wer
among those willing to join a reconstituted advisory council.[3]
Differences became more apparent at the sixth congress (Jun
1923). The delegates initially approved Jamal al-Husayni's re
commendation that they immediately stop paying taxes i
order to compel Britain to change its policy. Several larg
landowners attacked this idea because they feared that it woulc
hurt them personally. Nonpayment of taxes would be a mani-
festly illegal act, and the government might impose such stifl
penalties as sequestering property. Led by Sulayman Tuqan of
Nablus, who did not attend the congress, such ranking figures
as al-Hajj Said al-Shawwa (Gaza), al-Hajj Tawfiq Hamad (Nablus), Abd al-Latif Salah (Nablus), and Hafiz Tuqan (Nablus)
succeeded in killing the proposal by referring it back to the
economic committee for further debate.[32]

The Nashashibis and the Jerusalem branch of the Dajanis
felt sufficiently encouraged by these indications of dissident
opinion—and by the impasse reached once the mandate was
brought into force that fall—to launch the Palestine Arab
National party (al-Hizb al-Watani) in November 1923. The
organizers had previously sought financial support from the
Zionist movement's executive committee and had explained
that their political stand would involve opposition to the Supreme Muslim Council and the Arab Executive and willingness to work in cooperation with the government, although
not—in public—with the Zionist movement.[33]

31. See Chapter 8.
32. See references in footnote 27, and particularly political report, June 1923, CO
733/47; chief secretary, dispatches, June 22, 27, 1923, CO 733/46.
33. In late August 1923, Fakhri al-Nashashibi hinted to Kalvarisky that he would
appreciate a contribution of £280–300 to help initiate the party (Kalvarisky, letters to
ZO, London, Aug. 24, 31, 1923, CZA, S25/4379). Hasan Sidqi al-Dajani's discussions with Kisch about the Supreme Muslim Council are in Kisch to ZO (London),
May 23, 1923, CZA, Z4/2421.

The National party's founding congress met in Jerusalem in November 1923. To the chagrin of the organizers, the hundred delegates supported resolutions that denounced Zionism and demanded an elected government. Rather than tempering their demands, they sought to overbid the Arab Executive. In addition, Arif al-Dajani was humiliatingly defeated in his bid for the presidency by Shaykh Sulayman al-Taji al-Faruqi, who had publicly denounced the National Muslim societies for their ties with the Zionists.[34] The Dajanis therefore withdrew from the party, even though Arif and Hasan Sidqi had been elected to its central committee. Raghib al-Nashashibi was a mayor and could not participate overtly in the party. Therefore Fakhri al-Nashashibi was the only one of the original planners to remain on the party's central committee.[35] Kisch and Kalvarisky's hope that the National party would condone the Zionist movement was temporarily stymied.

The National party was slow to gain adherents because it lacked a strong leadership and had no clear raison d'être. Gradually, however, opponents of the Arab Executive and the Supreme Muslim Council gravitated to the party.[36] Its newspaper, *Mirat al-Sharq,* refrained from criticizing Zionism strongly and supported cooperation with the government as the best means to achieve self-rule.[37] The party did not acquire any significant rationale beyond personal animosity until the elections for the Supreme Muslim Council in January 1926 and for the municipal councils in 1927.[38]

The party leaders felt obliged to join forces with the Arab

34. Political report, Nov. 1923, CO 733/52; Kisch to ZO (London), Nov. 15, 1923, CZA, Z4/4112; Kisch to M. Frank, Nov. 12, 1923, CZA, S25/665; Porath, *Emergence,* pp. 222–223.

35. Abdallah Mukhlis was secretary and al-Hajj Idris al-Maghrabi treasurer.

36. Adherents included Shaykh Asad al-Shuqayri (who also formed his own party, the Village Mutual Association, in cooperation with the Madi family in 1926); Said Abu Khadra of Jaffa; Najib al-Nassar, Christian editor of *al-Karmil;* Bulus Shihadi of *Mirat al-Sharq;* and some members of the Zionist-funded Agricultural parties, notably Tawfiq Fahum of Nazareth and Said al-Shawwa of Gaza.

37. Porath, *Emergence,* p. 224.

38. Ibid., p. 226.

Executive on overriding national issues. Both organizations boycotted Lord Balfour during his visit in the spring of 1925, for example, and Shaykh al-Taji of the National party acted as the spokesman for a joint delegation that presented demands to the colonial secretary soon afterward.[39] But several attempts to unite the two groups aborted. At one time, the Arab Executive leaders demanded that the National party dissolve and amalgamate with the Muslim-Christian societies: only after its dissolution would its former members obtain five representatives on the Executive, and Shaykh al-Taji would become vice-president.[40] The National party rejected these terms.

After the National party (by then known as muaradah—oppositionists) won half the seats in the elections for the Supreme Muslim Council[41] and substantial influence in the municipalities,[42] the Arab Executive had to take the oppositionists seriously, especially because the Executive itself was almost moribund at that time. Many of the Muslim-Christian societies had disintegrated, and Jamal al-Husayni lacked enough money to carry on day-to-day operations in the secretariat.[43]

39. Political report, Feb. 1925, CO 733/90; political report, March 1925, CO 733/92; political report, April 1925, CO 733/93; Samuel, dispatch, May 1, 1925, transmitted minutes of the Arabs' meeting with Colonial Secretary Leopold Amery, CO 733/92; Ronald Storrs, *Memoirs: Orientations* (London: Nicholson and Watson, 1937), p. 436, on Balfour's visit.

40. Political report, Dec. 1924, CO 733/88. For further efforts at reunification in 1926, see *Palestine Bulletin,* May 16, July 11, Aug. 5, Sept. 5, 20, 1926.

41. A civil court annulled the election on technical grounds, and the high commissioner appointed an interim council, but he adhered to the fifty-fifty results of the original election, with al-Hajj Amin remaining president (his position was not up for election).

42. The muaradah candidates received all the Jewish votes in the mixed towns—Jerusalem, Haifa, Safad, and Tiberias—which provided the decisive votes for this party. Hasan al-Shukri of the National Muslim Society became mayor of Haifa. In Jaffa, there were no Jewish seats (Tel Aviv had a separate council), and the majlisiyyah (councilites; pro-Husayni) supporters of Mayor Asim al-Said outnumbered the muaradah Dajanis four to three, along with two nonpartisan councilors. For election results see *Palestine Bulletin,* April 4, 10 (Jerusalem), 13 (Safad), 29 (Tiberias), May 16, 22 (Haifa), 25, 29, 31 (Jaffa), 1927. See also Porath, *Emergence,* pp. 238–240.

43. Porath, *Emergence,* p. 243.

In late 1927, indications of new political trends began to appear. Some prominent residents of Jaffa and Gaza formed a Liberal party, through which they criticized the persistent Husayni-Nashashibi cleavage and advocated social reforms.[44] The Liberal party had a significant impact on the Seventh Arab Congress, which convened in July 1928. This congress included young professional delegates, not bound to the elite family structure, and adopted several resolutions along the lines of the Liberal party program.

Reunification

The Seventh Arab Congress of 1928 ended five years of division among the Arab politicians. Disagreements that initially arose over the failure of noncooperation had been perpetuated by the opportunities for personal gain from the 1926–1927 municipal and Muslim Council elections. More fundamentally, many politicians had come to believe that the Arabs' position in Palestine was not as severely threatened as they had initially feared, and therefore they felt they should grasp the available levers of power. Even though, for example, the high point of Jewish immigration during the decade was reached in 1925, the colonial secretary was able to calm Arab anxiety by pointing out that the natural increase in the Arab population exceeded the increase in Jewish population even when Jewish birth and immigration rates were combined. A severe economic depression from 1926 to 1928 caused heavy unemployment in the Jewish community, and Jewish emigration actually exceeded immigration in 1927.

With their fears of Jewish immigration somewhat dimin-

44. Sponsors included Isa al-Isa, the Christian editor of *Filastin* (Jaffa); Fahmi al-Husayni, editor of *Sawt al-Haq* (The Voice of Truth), and his relative Hamdi al-Husayni, a pan-Arab politician and journalist from Gaza (this family was only remotely related to the Jerusalem Husaynis); Alfred Rock, a Catholic from Jaffa; Abd al-Rauf al-Bitar, a municipal councilor in Jaffa and brother of the Arab Executive's Umar al-Bitar; Hilmi and Fawzi Abu Khadra of Jaffa and Gaza; and Hanna Asfur, a lawyer from Haifa (Arabic press report, from *Sawt al-Shaab* [Voice of the People] Nov. 13, 1927, and Kisch to Stein, Jan. 2, 1928, CZA, S25/517; *Palestine Bulletin,* Nov. 16, 21, Dec. 7, 1927, Jan. 4, 1928).

ished, Arab politicians sought to consolidate their influence. They not only contested the municipal and Muslim Council elections, but abandoned their opposition to the establishment of a legislative council. The Arab Executive held private discussions with a British official on this subject in 1926.[45] The British hinted that a legislative council might be formed if the Arabs could reunite their political factions and thus provided a further incentive for the politicians to compose their differences.

By the middle of 1927, the politicians were making serious efforts to convene a congress and revive the Arab Executive as an umbrella organization. But the muaradah and majlis-iyyah camps remained divided, some members of each camp opposing reunification.[46] Various other groups—including the new Liberal party, Christian Arab organs, and a new society of educated Muslim youths—sought representation at the congress and developed their own platforms on special-interest issues.

After months of bargaining, the seventh congress convened from June 20 to 22, 1928.[47] Its platform and the membership of the new executive committee were agreed to beforehand. The congress established seven permanent committees to elaborate and execute the main policy planks. And the new executive was charged with elaborating a general plan to reorganize the national movement in order to end the factional splits.

The key resolution demanded the formation of a representative council and parliamentary government as the means to attain the national goals and fulfill the previous congresses' demands for autonomy. Protests were entered against the granting of the concession to exploit the Dead Sea minerals to a Zionist company and against Britain's allegedly giving Jewish laborers preference over Arabs in public works proj-

45. See Chapter 8.
46. Porath, *Emergence,* pp. 250–251, on divisions within the Muaradah.
47. Palestine Zionist Executive, "Addendum to Political Report," and Kalvarisky, report, CZA, S25/4210; T. R. Feiwel, *No Ease in Zion* (London: Secker and Warburg, 1938), pp. 141–142; Darwazah, I, 59–60; Porath, *Emergence,* pp. 252–254, 289.

ects. The congress demanded a larger government allocation
for education and an autonomous education board and requested the reestablishment of an agricultural bank. On behalf
of the Christian Arabs, the congress defended the rights of the
Orthodox Christian community against actions by its Greek
hierarchy and supported the right of (the predominantly
Christian) Palestinians living abroad to retain their citizenship.

The new Arab Executive had forty-eight members, twelve
of them Christian. By reuniting the majlisiyyah and muaradah factions and by including independents and liberals, it
provided the Arabs with a basis for resuming negotiations
over a legislative council. Its composition reflected the effort
to balance and include all factions. Although Musa Kazim
Pasha retained the presidency, the two vice-presidents—
Tawfiq al-Hajj Abdallah, mayor of Acre, and Yaqub al-
Farraj, deputy mayor of Jerusalem and a leader of the Orthodox community—were supporters of the muaradah. The
three secretaries were Jamal al-Husayni (majlisiyyah), Awni
Abd al-Hadi (liberal, pan-Arab), and Mughannam Ilyas al-
Mughannam (a Protestant lawyer, muaradah).

Although this coalition suffered serious internal strains in
the early 1930s and dissolved in 1934, it served its immediate
purpose in 1928–1930 by representing the Arabs before the
British authorities and pressing them to establish representative institutions. The reunification occurred shortly before
new tensions arose in the Arab community's relations with
the Zionist movement. These tensions began with an incident
at the Wailing Wall in September 1928—only three months
after the Seventh Congress—and built up rapidly that winter
until the violent explosion of August 1929. That outbreak
undermined the Arab Executive's cautious efforts to negotiate for a legislative council and helped activate social forces
that would alter the composition and direction of the Arab
political movement. The mobilization from above of the
1920s gave way to the mobilization from below of the 1930s.

5 / Mobilization from Below, 1929–1939

The Zionist movement regained its momentum late in 1928 as the economic prospects improved in Palestine, Jewish immigration increased, and non-Zionist American Jews joined forces with the Zionist Organization in an enlarged Jewish Agency. These developments lent urgency to the Arab Executive's negotiations with the British administration. Throughout the spring and summer of 1929, the Muslim-Jewish controversy over rights at the Wailing Wall raised religious passions and al-Hajj Amin al-Husayni steered the Muslim institutions toward a more militant course, but the elders of the Arab Executive persisted in negotiating with the chief secretary over the formation of a legislative council.[1] These elders feared that they would lose control over the national movement to younger activists in alliance with religious leaders if they could not achieve some tangible results from their new effort at an accord with the government. In August 1929, violent outbreaks arising from the Wailing Wall dispute put an abrupt end to the Arab-British negotiations, crystallized Zionist opposition to any legislative council, and accelerated mobilization in the Arab community.

In addition, social groups that had previously been inarticulate began to organize in 1929–1930. Over two hundred

1. See Chapter 8 on the council plan; also high commissioner, dispatch to CO, June 18, 1929, CO 733/167/67105. See Chapter 9 on the Wailing Wall outbreak.

Muslim and Christian women from upper- and middle-class urban families assembled in Jerusalem on October 26, 1929, for the First Palestine Arab Women's Congress.[2] The congress elected a fourteen-member executive committee to press its demands on the government and organized itself through committees in several towns. In November a large congress on economic issues was held in Haifa, and two agricultural congresses met in April and June 1930, near Hebron and Haifa, respectively.[3]

The Arab Executive was still able to coordinate these efforts and act as the spokesman before the British authorities. It sponsored a general assembly on October 27, 1929, that brought together over a thousand delegates from Transjordan, Syria, and Lebanon as well as Palestine. The three secretaries of the Executive presented evidence before the commission that inquired into the August 1929 riots and prepared lengthy analyses of government proposals for political and economic reforms. The Executive also attempted to regularize its own fund collection and internal statutes.[4] A Fund of the Arab Nation was established in 1932 to purchase Arab lands so they would not be sold to Jewish companies, but the other organizational recommendations were never implemented.[5]

In March 1930, the Arab Executive dispatched its first delegation to London since 1923. The delegation tried to keep pace with the new public concerns by stressing economic

2. Mogannam, pp. 70–77; Fannie Fern Andrews, *The Holy Land under Mandate,* 2 vols. (Boston: Houghton Mifflin, 1931), II, 206–207. See also Chapter 3.

3. Andrews, II, 207, 209; *Falastin,* English edition, June 28, 1930. See also Chapter 3.

4. Hasan Sidqi al-Dajani submitted to the Executive an outline for the regular collection of contributions from townspeople through local and central financial committees; see his letter, Nov. 7, 1929, ISA, Arab Documents, file 1056.

5. Fuad Salih Saba, auditor for the Arab Executive, drew up a detailed memorandum on the organization of the congress, the Executive, elections to the congress, and the Fund of the Arab Nation. It was circulated to member societies and individuals for comments and then analyzed by a committee appointed by the secretariat. Only the fund proposal was implemented. See his letters, Sept. 2, 1930 (ISA, Arab Documents, file 1056), Sept. 7, 1930 (file 1809), Oct. 9, Nov. 4, 1930 (file 3594).

problems as well as political issues. It adopted a firm line on the issue of self-government and the banning of the sale of land by Arabs to Jews.[6] Both the elderly Musa Kazim al-Husayni and his younger relative, al-Hajj Amin, were members of the delegation, the latter at the insistence of the Arab Executive because he was increasingly asserting his leadership role and challenging the Executive's preeminence and the Executive wanted to make him responsible and accountable.

The delegation failed to win any concessions, but the Arab Executive leaders were encouraged by the international investigation of the conflicting claims to the Wailing Wall in the summer of 1930. They were also mollified by the reports of Sir John Hope Simpson on land problems and by the White Paper of October 1930. The White Paper asserted the need to establish a legislative council and to regulate Jewish immigration and land purchases in accordance with the Arabs' needs as well as those of the Jewish community.

The prime minister's letter to Weizmann of February 13, 1931, which negated the economic and immigration provisions of this White Paper, had a shattering impact on the Arab leaders. The letter increased their bitterness against the British and exacerbated divisions among the politicians. Dubbed the "black letter," it lent weight to the arguments advanced by younger politicians, Muslim activists, and pan-Arabs that Britain was their principal enemy and that they must become more militant. The Arab Executive's negotiating efforts lost their credibility, and those who counseled direct action and noncooperation assumed greater influence, but both approaches continued and coexisted. On the one hand, the politicians petitioned the government to form a legislative council and to increase their influence in municipal government. On the other, they refused to cooperate with administrative advisory committees and held demonstrations against immigration and land sale.

6. See Chapter 7 on the delegation.

Radicalization

The increased militancy that developed in the early 1930s was expressed through youth groups, the pan-Arab Hizb al-Istiqlal, pan-Islamic societies, and clandestine revolutionary cells. An early example was a conference of three hundred young politicians in Nablus (July 31, 1931),[7] which pressured the Arab Executive into adopting an anti-British position. These tendencies crystallized in the Palestine branch of the pan-Arab Independence party (Hizb al-Istiqlal al-Arabiyyah fi Suriyah al-Janubiyyah), formed in August 1932,[8] and the congress of Muslim youths, convened in December 1932.

Awni Abd al-Hadi, a confidant of Emir Faysal in the early 1920s and a secretary of the Arab Executive after 1928, was the driving force behind the Istiqlal party. He was joined by such articulate activists and publicists as Izzat Darwazah and Akram Zuaytir and by the banker Ahmad Hilmi Pasha. At the party's first mass meeting on December 14, 1932, the speakers denounced the British and asserted that complete independence was necessary to end Zionist immigration and land buying. They called for closer ties with the Arab states to enhance the effectiveness of the Palestine national movement.[9] Later, Awni Bey pressured the Arab Executive into opposing Arab participation on government advisory boards. The party activists derided the Executive for its passivity and goaded it into noncooperation and the sponsorship of demonstrations in 1933.

Istiqlal had a core of leaders who encouraged political debate in the newspapers, clubs, and urban political gatherings. The party never attempted to establish a mass base or a network of rural and urban branches; its support came primarily

7. High commissioner to CO, Aug. 17, 19, 1931, CO 733/209/87353.

8. High commissioner to CO, Sept. 16, Oct. 4, 1932, CO 733/219/97105/2; Mogannam, p. 235; ESCO Foundation for Palestine, *Palestine: A Study of Jewish, Arab and British Policies,* 2 vols. (New Haven: Yale University Press, 1947), II, 764; *Palestine Bulletin,* Sept. 11, Oct. 12, 1932.

9. *Palestine Post,* Dec. 11, 16, 1932.

105

from young professionals and government officials. Although King Faysal's death in 1933 disrupted plans to undertake pan-Arab action and contributed to the inactivity of the party for the next year,[10] the Istiqlalists had already influenced political attitudes in Palestine, particularly among the social and literary clubs, the scouts, and the activists in the new Youth Congress.

The Youth Congress was formed in December 1932 as a vehicle to organize criticism of the lack of job opportunities for educated Muslim youths. The Arab Executive was a sponsor of the opening congress, which was chaired by Ahmad Wajib al-Dajani, a young member of a leading Jaffa family.[11] Within a year the Youth Congress came under the control of Yaqub al-Ghusayn, who financed its activities with the revenue from his family's orange groves in the Ramlah district. He turned the congress into a political forum and established ties with boy scout groups, including the Abu Ubayda scouts who patrolled the coast near Tulkarm in 1934 to block ships that were unloading illegal Jewish immigrants.[12] Ghusayn also established links with Catholic Palestinians through the Youth Congress vice-president, Edmond Rock of Jaffa, and contacted the Syrian nationalists through his brother-in-law Jamil al-Mardam, a Syrian leader. Youth Congress activists were prominent in the illegal demonstrations in Jaffa in October 1933: eight of the fifteen men sentenced for leading these demonstrations—including Ghusayn and Rock—were leaders of the Youth Congress.[13]

Just as the Youth Congress was initiated by Muslims who resented their limited opportunities compared to those of

10. Hurewitz, *Struggle,* pp. 62–63.

11. Ahmad Dajani to high commissioner, Dec. 6, 1932, ISA, Chief Secretary's Papers, K/190/32; *Palestine Post,* Nov. 9, 1932; Mogannam, p. 244; ESCO Foundation, II, 766.

12. *Palestine Post,* Jan. 7, Aug. 3, 19, 21, Sept. 4, 1934, July 10, 1935.

13. Ibid., July 4, 1934. The others arrested included two from Istiqlal (Awni Bey and Darwazah) and two from the Arab Executive (Jamal al-Husayni and Shaykh al-Muzaffar). See Chapter 9.

Jews and Christians, so the Young Men's Muslim Associations (YMMA) were created in the late 1920s as a result of resentment against Christian missionary activity and to provide a forum to discuss religious and cultural concerns. Many members were active politically. Although the general conference of the YMMAs resolved that the associations would not interfere in politics, the British administration refused to let government employees, including teachers, join the YMMAs.[14] The YMMAs were relatively independent of the Muslim institutions and the Supreme Muslim Council, but their pan-Islamic and anti-Christian tendencies were supported by such conservative (and anti-Supreme Muslim Council) leaders as Sulayman al-Taji al-Faruqi, former head of the National party and editor of the newspaper *al-Jamiah al-Islamiyyah*.[15]

The Supreme Muslim Council itself had become openly involved in politics in 1929 and 1930, when it sponsored the Committee for the Protection of al-Aqsa and orchestrated the Muslim case presented before the international Wailing Wall commission. After the failure of petition politics in 1930 and the British issuance of the "black letter" in 1931, al-Hajj Amin al-Husayni and his supporters challenged the authority of the Arab Executive. In December 1931, al-Hajj Amin convened a large General Islamic Congress in Jerusalem.[16] A separate Arab congress, held directly afterward, took advantage of the presence of a large number of Arabs from abroad to formulate an Arab Covenant, which stressed the themes of unity, independence, and anticolonialism. Al-Hajj Amin was emerging as a political leader whose influence was not confined to Palestine but commanded respect from political and religious figures throughout the Muslim world.

Clandestine societies were also formed during this time. The most important group was led by Shaykh Izz al-Din

14. *Falastin,* English edition, June 28, 1930, p. 2.
15. Porath, *Emergence,* p. 301.
16. See Chapter 6 on this congress.

al-Qassam in Haifa.[17] Shaykh al-Qassam, a graduate of al-
Azhar University in Cairo, had fought the French in Syria in
1919–1920 and moved to Haifa soon after the fall of Faysal's
regime. He preached in the Istiqlal mosque, taught in a Muslim school, visited the villages around Haifa to handle personal grievances before the *sharia* courts, and headed the
Muslim Society in Haifa. Through these contacts Shaykh al-
Qassam could gain political adherents among youths, farmers, and workers living in Haifa's slums. He formed secret
cells as the nuclei for an armed revolt. He claimed that the
politicians of the Arab Executive were insufficiently militant,
and he criticized the Supreme Muslim Council for spending
money to restore mosques rather than to purchase weapons.
He also opposed the random violence of 1929, although he
expected the poor farmers to rise spontaneously once he
raised the call for revolt. Shaykh al-Qassam built his support
on a blend of personal devotion to the Muslim mystical
leader and contemporary national and social objectives. He
and his supporters challenged both the social outlook and the
political maneuvers of the Arab elite.

These quasi-political organizations mobilized people who
had not previously been directly involved in the national
movement. Their challenge spurred the Arab Executive to
greater activism. The emerging groups were suspicious of the
landowning elite and were irritated at the bickering within
the elite, epitomized by the Husayni-Nashashibi rivalry. The
cleavage they caused divided the politicians' energies at a time
when united action was sorely needed to counter the increasing Jewish immigration and land purchases.

Raghib al-Nashashibi had sought to counter the effects of
al-Hajj Amin's General Islamic Congress of December 1931
by convening his own Congress of the Palestine Muslim Na-

17. Subhi Yasin, *al-Thawrah al-Arabiyyah al-Kubra fi Filastin, 1936–1939* (The
Great Arab Revolt in Palestine, 1936–1939) (rev. ed., Cairo: Dar al-Katib, 1967), pp.
30–39. See Chapter 9 on the Qassamites.

tion in Jerusalem at the end of the same month.[18] The thousand Palestinian Muslim delegates declared their opposition to the current leadership of the Supreme Muslim Council. Its executive committee, composed of two delegates from each district and headed by Raghib Bey and Muhammad Nimr al-Nabulsi, provided the organizational framework for Raghib Bey in his plans to contest elections to the Supreme Muslim Council, which were expected in 1932.[19] Although the council elections were never held, the committee formed the nucleus of the political party that Raghib Bey established in 1934.

A Grand National Meeting of all the political groups held in March 1933 was the scene of intense backbiting between the Husayni and Nashashibi factions, which angered the other participants and weakened the force of its resolutions.[20] By late 1933, the Arab Executive was at the point of disintegration, undermined by family rivalries and radicalizing pressures. Such older leaders as Musa Kazim Pasha hesitated to confront the British government openly, but were unable to devise a strategy that could alter British policy. They drifted with the political currents, lending the name of the Arab Executive to the demonstrations and political noncooperation organized by youth groups and the Istiqlal activists.

After the octogenarian Musa Kazim Pasha died in March 1934, the Arab Executive disintegrated swiftly. It was formally dissolved in August 1934, in the midst of the campaign for municipal council elections.[21] The Executive had decided in its final August meeting to permit the formation of politi-

18. High commissioner, dispatch to CO, Jan. 30, 1932, CO 733/222/97208; ESCO Foundation, II, 763.
19. These elections were canceled by the high commissioner after he made satisfactory financial and auditing arrangements with al-Hajj Amin. See correspondence in CO 733/222/97208; high commissioner, dispatch to CO, Sept. 17, 1932, chief secretary, dispatch to CO, Oct. 27, 1932, CO 733/213/97033.
20. Chief secretary to CO, April 1, 1933, CO 733/239/17356/4; Mogannam, p. 93; ESCO Foundation, II, 773; *Palestine Post,* Feb. 26, 27, March 29, 31, 1933.
21. *Palestine Post,* Aug. 6, 1934. Upon Musa Kazim Pasha's death, Yaqub al-Farraj (age sixty) became acting president until its dissolution in August.

cal parties and to convene a general congress in 1935 to elect a new Arab Executive, but no congress was held. The politicians were preoccupied with establishing political parties and testing their strength: no umbrella organ could be established until their relative weight was known and until overwhelming external pressures would compel them to reunite.

The Proliferation of Political Parties

Four political parties were organized in 1934–1935 in addition to the Youth Congress and Istiqlal, but these four were organized by members of the political elite to serve as their power bases. Although essentially elite factions, the National Defense party of the Nashashibis and the Palestine Arab party of the Husaynis could mobilize grass-roots support through the *hamulah* structure. The Reform party and the National Bloc served only as local bases for individual politicians, Dr. Husayn Fakhri al-Khalidi and Abd al-Latif Salah, respectively.

The National Defense party was formed at a general meeting on December 2, 1934, which selected a twelve-man executive committee, nominally responsible to a thirty-five-member central committee.[22] Because he had lost his position as mayor two months earlier, Raghib al-Nashashibi could assume the presidency of the party. Although its support came primarily from the mayors and elite of the larger towns, Fakhri al-Nashashibi secured the allegiance of the Jaffa branch of the Palestine Arab Workers Society, and the party reached the peasantry through the family networks of the

22. Yaqub al-Farraj (Greek Orthodox leader) became vice-president; Mughannam al-Mughannam (Protestant) and Hasan Sidqi al-Dajani shared the secretaryship; al-Hajj Nimr al-Nabulsi was treasurer. Nabulsi had been associated with Raghib Bey at the 1931 Congress of the Palestine Muslim Nation; Dajani and Farraj had worked with Raghib Bey on the Jerusalem municipal council. The mayors of Nablus (Sulayman Tuqan), Jaffa (Asim al-Said), and Ramlah (Shaykh Mustafa al-Khayri), municipal councilors in Gaza and Jaffa (such as Adil al-Shawwa and Umar al-Bitar), and a member of the Supreme Muslim Council (Abd al-Rahman al-Taji) supported the party. Asad al-Shuqayri, mufti of Acre, and Isa al-Isa, Greek Orthodox editor of *Filastin*, also tended to support it. See *Palestine Post*, Nov. 5, Dec. 3, 1934, March 25, 1935; Hurewitz, *Struggle*, pp. 61–62; Mogannam, pp. 236–239; ESCO Foundation, II, 776–777.

Nashashibis, Dajanis (Jerusalem), Tuqans (Nablus), and Nabulsis (Nablus). The party was cautious concerning political and social issues. It accepted the offer of a legislative council in 1935–1936, for example, and criticized the activism of the scouts and Youth Congress as "disruptive" and "irresponsible." The party's leaders undoubtedly feared upheavals in the social status quo as much as they feared the British and Zionists. They also realized that the Palestine Arabs had few diplomatic and economic weapons to use against the British and Zionists and hoped that the tactic of conciliation—rather than confrontation—would at least influence the British favorably. And they maintained close relations with Emir Abdallah of Transjordan in anticipation that his backing would strengthen external support for the Palestinian cause and, in particular, to bolster their own influence within Palestine.

The Husaynis countered the Nashashibi move by establishing the Palestine Arab party in March 1935.[23] Several activists from the Arab Executive supported the party, and the leaders maintained close contact with the scouts' movement, the Youth Congress, and the workers' societies in Jerusalem and Haifa. In the mid-1930s the party fluctuated between cooperating and competing with the Istiqlal party, although it never adopted the latter's pan-Arab position.

Al-Hajj Amin al-Husayni did not assume the leadership of the Palestine Arab party because he did not want to jeopardize his official post. His relative, Jamal al-Husayni, already a seasoned politician, having been secretary to the Arab Executive, became the party's president. The party supported the basic national demands and criticized reformist measures, such as the proposal of a legislative council. Nevertheless, its

---

23. Alfred Rock was vice-president and Emile al-Ghuri, secretary. Both were Roman Catholics, the former a prominent Jaffa citrus grower, the latter a young journalist. Former Arab Executive supporters included the Dajanis of Jaffa, Abdallah Samarah of Tulkarm, and Yaqub Bardakash of Jaffa (Internal regulations of the party, April 23, 1935, in ISA, Arab Documents, file 3098; *Palestine Post,* March 28, Sept. 17, 1935; Hurewitz, *Struggle,* p. 61; Mogannam, pp. 241–242; ESCO Foundation, II, 776).

leaders continued to hope that nonviolent pressure tactics could induce the British government to alter its policies before the Zionist movement became too powerful.

The Reform party and the National Bloc were formed by politicians who did not want to fall under the influence of either the Husayni or the Nashashibi camp. Dr. Husayn Fakhri al-Khalidi defeated Raghib al-Nashashibi in the election for mayor of Jerusalem in September 1934. He had been the senior medical officer in the Department of Health and a member of the executive of the Nashashibi's Congress of the Palestine Muslim Nation. Raghib Bey charged that Khalidi had been "bought" by the Husaynis in the election campaign and summarily "excommunicated" him from his congress. Khalidi, anxious to avoid domination by the Husaynis, responded by forming his own party at a meeting in Ramallah in June 1935. As mayor of Jerusalem, Khalidi felt that he should not lead the party, and therefore it acquired a collegial leadership.[24] The party attracted the support of several mayors and retired civil servants because of the respect accorded Khalidi and his family. Tacit support came from some Arab government officials and teachers. The party accepted the legislative council proposal as a useful intermediate step, realizing the importance of augmenting Arab influence vis-à-vis the British administration. The party also emphasized the need to maintain national unity to counter Zionism, and it adopted a cautiously reformist social program.

Abd al-Latif Salah had greater national ambitions than Khalidi. He aspired to build the National Bloc, formed in 1935 in Nablus, into a vehicle to increase his personal stand-

24. Khalidi shared the post of secretary with Mahmud Abu Khadra (former mayor of Gaza) and Shibli Jamal (Christian). It was supported by the mayors of Gaza (Fahmi al-Husayni), Bethlehem (Isa Bandak), and Acre (Tawfiq Abdallah) and by retired civil servants such as Muhammad Ishaq al-Budayri (a former judge). Khalidi's brother Ahmad Samih was a college principal and YMMA official; Shaykh Khalil al-Khalidi was president of the Supreme Sharia Court in Jerusalem; Mustafa al-Khalidi was a judge on the Supreme Court (*Palestine Post,* June 24, 26, 1935; Hurewitz, *Struggle,* p. 62; Mogannam, pp. 243–244; ESCO Foundation, II, 779).

ing.[25] Salah had supported the Husaynis in the early 1920s when he served on the Supreme Muslim Council, but he had broken with them after he was defeated for reelection in 1926. In 1933, Salah played a mediating role between the Husayni and Nashashibi factions at the Grand National Meeting. His own position on political tactics fluctuated: at one time he supported the idea of a legislative council in the hope of gaining a seat on it, but at other times he backed the demand for noncooperation made by the young politicians in the hope of gaining their support. These shifts hurt his credibility, and he was never able to make the National Bloc an important force within Nablus. That major town continued to be dominated by the Tuqan and Nabulsi families, who supported the Nashashibi's National Defense party.

By mid-1935, six political parties had been established in the Arab community. The national movement had been so fractionalized that the Arab politicians could not take any concerted action against either the British or the Zionists. As Jewish immigration reached its peak, the Histadrut increased its militant actions, land acquisition by the Zionist companies accelerated, and the buildup of the Haganah forces was no longer secret, the Arab party leaders came under strong pressure from the clubs and press to reestablish a united front. They were also under pressure from the high commissioner to select spokesmen with whom he could discuss proposals for a legislative council and land legislation. In November 1935, the leaders of all the parties except Istiqlal, which insisted on noncooperation, agreed to meet with the high commissioner to discuss these proposals.[26]

By then, however, a crisis atmosphere had gripped the country. The discovery in October of crates of arms and ammunition at the Jaffa port, addressed to a resident of Tel Aviv, inflamed the Arabs, who feared that the arms were

25. High commissioner to CO, April 22, 1936, CO 733/193/75102; Hurewitz, *Struggle,* p. 62; Mogannam, p. 242; ESCO Foundation, II, 780.
26. See Chapter 8 on the legislative council proposal; Hurewitz, *Struggle,* p. 63.

intended for the Haganah. Economic dislocations stemming from the Italo-Ethiopian War sharply affected Palestine. As unemployment mounted, Histadrut's picketing against Jewish companies who hired Arabs in factories or orange groves exacerbated Arab fears for their livelihood. The government's approval of the grant of the Huleh valley development concession to a Zionist company raised fears of large-scale displacement of villagers. These tensions peaked after the "martyrdom" of Shaykh al-Qassam in late November, during his brief attempt to raise the standard of revolt in the mountains near Haifa. His funeral turned into a mass outpouring of religious and national emotions. The political leaders found that the public would not let them limit their discussions with the British to the issue of a legislative council, but demanded that they include requests for restrictions on immigration, land legislation, and arms control.[27]

The atmosphere degenerated further in early 1936, partly in reaction to political crises in Egypt and Syria and partly because of the growing debate over Palestine's future. Politicians eulogized Shaykh al-Qassam at a memorial service attended by four thousand people.[28] The leaders of Istiqlal denounced cooperation with the British, even in a legislative council. But other politicians began to view the legislative council proposal as a last-ditch means to salvage the situation and contain the militancy of the Arab public. These politicians tried to form a delegation to present their case in London, but they were unable to agree among themselves on the composition of the delegation.[29]

On the night of April 15, members of the Ikhwan al-

27. For reports on the atmosphere in late 1935, see high commissioner, telegram, Dec. 5, dispatch, Dec. 7, telegram, Dec. 23, 1935, CO 733/278/75156; *Palestine Post*, Oct. 22, Nov. 1, 11, 26, Dec. 4, 1935.

28. Ahmad al-Imam, secretary, Haifa Muslim Society, letters to Jamal al-Husayni, Dec. 3, 31, 1935, ISA, Arab Documents, file 3098; *Palestine Post*, Jan. 5, 1936.

29. *Palestine Post*, April 16–23, 1936; high commissioner to CO, April 2, 23, 1936 (CO 733/307/75438), April 11, 21, 1936 (CO 733/307/75348), Feb. 13, 1936 (CO 733/297/75157). See also Chapter 7.

Qassam held up cars on a highway, robbing the Arab travelers and killing two Jews. Members of the Jewish community retaliated by killing some Arabs who lived near Petah Tiqvah and by holding a mass funeral procession in Tel Aviv. Arab politicians in Nablus and Jaffa responded by calling for a general strike. These leaders were anxious to avoid any further violence and felt that an orderly strike would be the best way to underline Arab grievances and compel the British to redress them. Disgusted at Chaim Weizmann's charge that the forces of civilization were struggling against the forces of barbarism and the desert,[30] Sulayman Tuqan, the powerful mayor of Nablus, immediately called a large meeting of the leaders of thirty villages to lend his support to the strike, and professionals and merchants also rallied behind it.

The Arab Higher Committee

On April 25, the six political parties formed a Committee of Ten to coordinate the local strike committees. The committee soon became known as the Arab Higher Committee (al-Lajnah al-Arabiyyah al-Ulyah). Al-Hajj Amin al-Husayni was selected as president, thus identifying him publicly as the preeminent leader of the national movement. Hitherto he had sheltered behind his religious office, but now he had to assume responsibility for his actions.[31] Awni Abd al-Hadi of Istiqlal became secretary; this was the key organizational and propaganda post. Ahmad Hilmi Pasha, another Istiqlalist and the president of the Arab Bank, acquired the treasurer's slot.

---

30. Weizmann's address to the First World Congress of Jewish Physicians, Tel Aviv, April 23, 1936, quoted in high commissioner, dispatch, April 29, 1936, CO 733/297/75156; Barbara Kalkas, "The Revolt of 1936: A Chronicle of Events," in Abu-Lughod, ed., *Transformation*, pp. 243–244.

31. Some strikers sympathetic to the Nashashibis proposed Sulayman Tuqan as committee president, but most felt that he was not dynamic enough nor sufficiently influential outside his district. They also wanted al-Hajj Amin to make an open break with the British and stop sheltering behind his office (interview with Aziz Shihadeh, Ramallah, May 22, 1971).

The heads of the various political parties comprised the rest of the committee.[32]

The position of secretary changed hands four times during the strike. The British arrested Awni Bey on June 7 because the high commissioner viewed him as the committee's most effective organizer.[33] He was replaced by Muin al-Madi of Istiqlal, until he went to Iraq on a propaganda mission. Izzat Darwazah, also of Istiqlal, then became secretary, but he, too, was detained, on June 20. The committee then chose a young Christian auditor, Fuad Salih Saba,[34] to become secretary. Saba remained in office until the Arab Higher Committee itself was banned in October 1937.

The Arab Higher Committee sought to achieve a united front, but it was divided between those who supported the economic-political strike as an instrument of moral pressure on the British government and those who viewed the strike as a revolutionary act in which violence, as well as civil disobedience, would play a necessary part. The former tended to come from the Nashashibi adherents and the latter from the Husayni faction and Istiqlalists.[35]

On a day-to-day level, the strike was directed by the local national committees, committees to enforce the road-traffic strike, national guard units, labor societies, the Jaffa boatmen's association, Muslim and Christian sports clubs, Arab boy scouts, and the women's committees. It was loosely coordinated by the Arab Higher Committee, but the committee's influence was limited. British officials believed that "its

32. The other committee members were Raghib al-Nashashibi and Yaqub al-Farraj of the National Defense party, Jamal al-Husayni and Alfred Rock of the Palestine Arab party, Dr. Husayn Fakhri al-Khalidi of the Reform party, Abd al-Latif Salah of the National Bloc, and Yaqub al-Ghusayn of the Youth Congress (high commissioner, telegram, April 26, 1936, CO 733/310/75528; his telegram May 5, 1936, CO 733/297/75156).

33. High commissioner, dispatch, June 8, 1936, CO 733/310/75528.

34. High commissioner, telegram, May 18, 1936, CO 733/311/75528/6; *Palestine Post,* June 8–11, 18, 21, July 10, 1936.

35. Fakhri al-Nashashibi apparently joined the latter in contacting guerrilla groups and Fawzi al-Qawuqji (interview with Izzat Darwazah, Damascus, May 14, 1971; *Palestine Post,* Aug. 3, 1936).

function is to deal with broad questions of policy and is not directly concerned with [the] organization of strikes."[36] Because thousands of people were on strike in the towns and vegetable and fruit hawkers were prevented from selling their wares in the city streets, the national committees established central stores to distribute grain, rice, and sugar and made payments in cash or bread to many strikers.[37] The women's committees collected and distributed goods and funds for the poorest families. Merchants paid a special tax to the local committees in order to receive permission to transport goods from the ports to the central towns.

On May 7, the national committees held a congress at which the delegates called for civil disobedience and elaborated plans to refuse to pay taxes and stop the functioning of the municipalities.[38] The port workers in Jaffa closed down that port and on May 12, the Arab Chamber of Commerce joined the strike. The Arab mayors, meeting in Ramallah on May 31, supported an indefinite municipal strike, although most of the mayors would have preferred to hold only a one- or two-day symbolic strike for fear that the British administration would take over the municipalities. In fact, only six municipal councils actually carried out their strike pledge.[39] Arab government officials also came under heavy pressure to

36. High commissioner, telegram, May 23, 1936, CO 733/310/75528; for information on the local groups see his telegram, July 3, 1936, on women's relief work, CO 733/313/75528/33, and his dispatch, Sept. 12, 1936, CO 733/311/75528/6; Zionist intelligence report on Arab national committees in the Southern District, July 9, 1936, CZA, S25/2968.

37. In mid-July, it was reported that Jerusalem shopkeepers received 500 mils (half a pound) a week and two loaves of bread a day; in Jaffa, the ration was only a daily portion of flour (*Palestine Post,* July 13, 1936).

38. The proposal to withhold taxes was originally made by the leaders of the Motor Transport Strike Committee, Hasan Sidqi al-Dajani and Salah Abdu, on May 1.

39. The pro-Zionist major of Haifa (Hasan Shukri) was "sick" at the time of the May 31 meeting and left soon after for a "vacation" in Beirut. Yehoshua Porath told me that the six councils that struck (Nablus, Ramlah, Lydda, Tulkarm, Hebron, and Jaffa) were all sympathetic to the Nashashibis and wanted to embarrass Dr. Khalidi, mayor of Jerusalem, who did not strike because the British would have replaced him by the Jewish vice-mayor, Daniel Auster.

strike, which they circumvented by contributing a tenth of their salaries to the strike fund.[40] By the end of June, however, the strikers' pressure had become so intense that the high commissioner permitted the government advocate, Musa al-Alami, to circulate a memorial among the senior officials. The memorial, which was signed by 137 officials, argued that if the government did not accept the strikers' precondition and suspend immigration, peace could not be restored.[41] Twelve hundred second-division Arab officials added their signatures to the appeal in August.

The Supreme Muslim Council closed down its schools and curtailed its nonreligious functions, keeping open only the poor-relief services, *shari'a* courts, and mosques. A statement by the colonial secretary implying that the council did not support the strike because some Muslim institutions continued to operate prompted officials of the *shari'a* courts to publish a memorial backing the strike and pushed al-Hajj Amin to the brink of proclaiming a *jihad* (holy war).[42]

Because most organizing took place at the local levels and the government prohibited the national committees from holding another general congress after the one on May 7, the main role of the Arab Higher Committee was to issue policy statements concerning the strike and hold discussions with Arab officials from abroad who sought to mediate between the Palestinians and the British. The most sustained mediation effort came in late August, when Nuri al-Said, foreign minister of Iraq, visited Jerusalem.[43] By then the British government had announced that it would send a high-level Royal Commission to Palestine to investigate the causes of and find remedies for the disturbances. Nuri al-Said sought to win British support for the suspension of Jewish immigration during the Royal Commission's deliberations, in return for

40. High commissioner, telegram, May 4, 1936, CO 733/307/75438/1.
41. The memorial is contained in CO 733/313/75528/37.
42. Al-Hajj Amin's letter to the colonial secretary, enclosed in high commissioner, telegram, June 17, see also July 1, 1936, CO 733/297/75156 pt. 3.
43. See Chapter 6.

which the Arabs would end the strike. The colonial secretary rejected this proposal—which the high commissioner had supported—and Nuri Pasha's effort collapsed.

The colonial secretary then decided to break the strike by force. Faced with this threat, many members of the Arab Higher Committee feared, on the one hand, that their political movement would be destroyed and, on the other, that the expanding guerrilla forces would get out of their own control. The committee persuaded the strikers to accept a face-saving formula by which the Arab kings proposed that the strike end and the Arabs present their case to the Royal Commission. The Arab Higher Committee was not allowed to convene a congress of the national committees either to discuss Nuri Pasha's mediation or to decide whether to end the strike. Therefore it had to dispatch its members to the various towns in order to learn the views of the local activists and obtain their support.[44]

Although the strike ended on October 12, the national committees and national guard units were not dissolved. They spearheaded the ensuing campaign to boycott the Jewish community. Raghib al-Nashashibi wanted the Arab Higher Committee itself to disband, so that he could regain his autonomy of action, but he acquiesced to the committee's decision to remain united as long as the Royal Commission was in Palestine.[45] He also was a member of the special committee that amassed the evidence to be presented before the Royal Commission, along with Awni Abd al-Hadi, Jamal al-Husayni, and Fuad Saba.[46]

The Arab Higher Committee was thereafter stymied and embarrassed by its own decision to boycott the Royal Commission, a decision taken when the British announced the continuation of Jewish immigration simultaneously with

44. The congresses had been scheduled for August 20 and September 17; see *Palestine Post,* Aug. 18, 27, 29, Sept. 14, 16, Oct. 11, 1936.
45. *Palestine Post,* Oct. 23, 1936.
46. Confidential conversation of E. S. (Elias Sasson) with J. F. (Joseph Francis, journalist), Oct. 26, 1936, CZA, S25/3051.

their announcement of the commission's departure. The last-minute reversal of this noncooperation position, in early January 1937, enabled the Arab politicians to present their case before the commission, rather than be left unheard. By the spring of 1937, however, the Arab Higher Committee was virtually moribund, its members at odds with each other and their contact with the local committees almost abandoned.

Rumors began to circulate that the Royal Commission would recommend partition, perhaps carving a Jewish state out of the coastal area between Tel Aviv and Haifa and in the Esdraelon valley, the main areas of Jewish settlement. But the commission's recommendation, issued July 7, 1937, accorded a much larger area to the Jewish state and placed several Arab towns within a British enclave, thereby reducing sharply the Arab-controlled zone.

Raghib al-Nashashibi and Yaqub al-Farraj had withdrawn from the Arab Higher Committee only four days before the report was issued. They, like many others, had expected that the Jewish state would cover only a relatively small area, and therefore might be acceptable to the Arabs. Raghib Bey aspired to become the prime minister in a state that would combine the Arab portion of Palestine with Transjordan, under Emir Abdallah's rule. Since Raghib Bey lacked enough public support to outweigh the Husaynis and the young politicians, he felt that this would be his one opportunity to gain a ruling position. But his gamble failed. The Royal Commission report dealt a severe blow even to Raghib Bey's supporters. Although he was no longer a member of the Arab Higher Committee, he felt compelled to follow its lead in protesting against the partition plan and proposing the formation of a unitary state covering all of Palestine.[47] But both Raghib Bey and Emir Abdallah still privately hoped that the

47. *Palestine Post,* July 4, 12, 22, 1937; high commissioner, dispatch, July 24, 1937, transmitted Raghib Bey's memorandum of July 11 rejecting the partition proposal, CO 733/351/75718/6; Hurewitz, *Struggle,* pp. 78–80.

British would implement a partition plan along more acceptable lines so that they could salvage their own positions.

Leadership in Exile

By February 1937, the colonial secretary had accepted the Zionist leaders' view that al-Hajj Amin al-Husayni was the chief fomenter not only of political opposition but also of urban terrorist groups and that he should be deported as soon as the British could find a legitimate reason.[48] Al-Hajj Amin's verbally militant response to the partition recommendation, his call for support from the Arab rulers, and reports in the London *Times* that Arab "moderates" were afraid to speak in favor of partition because of his alleged terrorist activities seemed to provide such a pretext. The British authorities decided to arrest him on July 17, 1937, during a meeting of the Arab Higher Committee.[49] But the police bungled the attempt, and al-Hajj Amin took sanctuary in al-Haram al-Sharif, a holy place where the police would not dare to intrude.

By late July, the British officials in Palestine realized that Arab opposition to partition was far more widespread than they originally estimated and that no "moderate" opinion willing to accept the partition plan existed. Although initially stunned by the Royal Commission's proposal, people soon reacted by dispatching angry petitions to the government. The district commissioner for Galilee reported:

> That the Arab population of Galilee should ever be reconciled to the scheme is clearly too much to hope. Their reaction . . . was one of blank amazement. Many of the more responsible and influential landowners and rural magnates have retired into an ostrich-like position of holding the report to be impos-

48. Chief secretary, telegram, Feb. 27, 1937, colonial secretary, comments on it, March 4, CO 733/326/75023/2.
49. Colonial secretary, telegram, July 14, 1937 (the same date as the *Times* article), requested that al-Hajj Amin be deported; high commissioner, telegram on the failure to arrest him, July 19, 1937, CO 733/352/75718/9.

sible and therefore not worth discussion. . . . Christians, Muslims, fellahin and landowners are probably more united in their rejection of the proposal than they have ever been before. Their common feeling . . . is that they have been betrayed and that they will be forced to leave their lands and perish in some unknown desert.[50]

The residents of northern Palestine, including Galilee, had been relatively quiet during the strike. But, according to the partition plan, Galilee would fall entirely within the Jewish state, and its 250,000 Arabs would be forced to leave. Local groups, the Association of Arab Citrus Growers, and the Arab Women's Committee submitted lengthy memoranda and passionate appeals to the government, describing their plight and their sense of outrage at this "reward" for not joining the strike. New local committees, independent of the Arab Higher Committee, sprang up in many towns. Some stated that "they proposed to fight their own battles without any assistance from the Higher Committee,"[51] and others merely ignored its role. Even though the committee no longer served as an organizing center within Palestine, it continued its propaganda efforts abroad. It sent missions to Iraq and Geneva in August and promoted a pan-Arab congress in Bludan, Syria, in early September.[52]

When violence broke out in the countryside during the summer and urban terrorism resumed, the colonial secretary continued to revile al-Hajj Amin as the "black-hearted villain" masterminding the troubles.[53] An excuse to remove him was provided by the assassination on September 26 of the new district commissioner of the Galilee, whom many Arabs expected to supervise the transfer of that district to

50. Lewis Y. Andrews, acting district commissioner, monthly report for July, enclosed in high commissioner, dispatch, Aug. 5, 1937, CO 733/351/75718/6. Ironically, Andrews was assassinated in September.

51. Ibid.

52. See Chapter 6 on the Bludan Congress.

53. Ormsby-Gore (colonial secretary) letter, to acting high commissioner, Sept. 8, 1937, CO 733/352/75718/9.

Jewish rule. Although the assassination was carried out by members of the clandestine Ikhwan al-Qassam, the British began interning local politicians in Galilee the next day. The colonial secretary then ordered the deportation of al-Hajj Amin and the entire Arab Higher Committee on October 1 and banned all the national committees as well.[54] Only the members of the National Defense party were exempt from the dragnet, an exemption that earned them greater public resentment and charges of collusion with the British authorities.

The British had intended to eliminate the control of al-Hajj Amin and others whom it viewed as "extremist," but in fact these men escaped the dragnet and only four members of the Arab Higher Committee—Ahmad Hilmi Pasha, Fuad Saba, Husayn Fakhri al-Khalidi, and Yaqub al-Ghusayn—were deported to the Seychelles Islands in the Indian Ocean.[55] Al-Hajj Amin and Jamal al-Husayni escaped to Lebanon and Syria, respectively. Awni Abd al-Hadi, Alfred Rock, Izzat Darwazah, and Abd al-Latif Salah were already abroad on various diplomatic missions and avoided arrest by staying outside Palestine. Al-Hajj Amin rapidly consolidated his control over these politicians, even though he lived under French surveillance near Beirut. His stature within Palestine, which had diminished after the 1936 strike, was considerably enhanced by his exile.

Al-Hajj Amin could not exercise day-to-day control over the rebel groups that formed inside Palestine. Izzat Darwazah, living in Damascus, served as the main contact to whom the guerrilla leaders came for financial and military aid.[56] A Syrian politician, Nabih al-Azmah, who had lived in exile in Palestine for many years, headed the Committees for the

54. The members of the Jerusalem national committee had been detained on August 15.
55. Rashid al-Hajj Ibrahim was also deported to the Seychelles. Although not a member of the Arab Higher Committee, he was active in Istiqlal and managed the Haifa branch of the Arab Bank.
56. Yasin, *al-Thawrah,* pp. 61–62; interview with Izzat Darwazah, Damascus, May 14, 1971. See Chapter 9 on military coordination during the revolt.

Defense of Palestine, which raised funds in Arab and Muslim countries and among Arab communities in Africa and North and South America.

Jamal al-Husayni and Awni Abd al-Hadi became ambassadors for the revolt. Al-Hajj Amin appears to have played these two men off against each other in order to profit from their missions without becoming dependent on either one. Awni Bey was instrumental in convening the Inter-Parliamentary Congress in Cairo in October 1938, and Jamal Effendi headed the Palestinian delegation to the London conference in February 1939.[57]

Most of the local-level politicians within Palestine had been detained in late 1937, resulting in a serious leadership vacuum in the towns. The most influential roles were assumed by the guerrilla commanders, who controlled the rural areas by mid-1938 and, for short periods, dominated the towns. By contrast, during the 1936 strike, political leadership was wielded by the urban politicians and supplemented by scattered guerrilla bands. The new situation had important social and political implications because the poor peasantry were asserting themselves against the landowning elite. Ill-educated village fighters placed doctors, judges, lawyers, and writers in distinctly subordinate roles. For a brief period, the populace challenged the political dominance of this elite.

Despite the efforts of the nominal commander in chief, the various guerrilla leaders never coordinated their efforts and frequently clashed with each other. These disputes among families and over territorial control diverted energies from the rebellion.[58] The commander in chief, Abd al-Rahim al-Hajj Muhammad, was challenged by Arif Abd al-Raziq, who came from a rival family in Tulkarm. Abd al-Raziq was willing to perform political assassinations at al-Hajj Amin's bidding and to collect funds within Palestine to send to the exiled politicians in Beirut, actions Abd al-Rahim denounced

57. See Chapter 6 on the congress and Chapters 6 and 7 on the London conference.
58. See Chapter 9 on the various commanders; Shimoni, p. 393.

.nd tried to prevent.[59] The political assassinations peaked
with a spate of attacks against the Nashashibis and their supporters in late 1938, by which time Raghib Bey, Sulayman
Tuqan, and members of the Bitar family of Jaffa were living
in self-imposed exile in Cairo or Beirut. They did not return
to Palestine until the early summer of 1939, after negotiations
in London had ended and calm had returned.

Despite the degeneration of the Husayni-Nashashibi rivalry
into outright assassination, pressure from the Arab states induced al-Hajj Amin to let two Nashashibi representatives join
the Palestinian delegation to the London conference in February 1939. This act restored the national front, at least on
paper. Two independent Palestinian intellectuals—Musa al-
Alami and George Antonius—also joined the delegation and
played prominent roles at the London conference. Musa al-
Alami, son of a mayor of Jerusalem, had been the government advocate and was private secretary to the high commissioner in 1932–1933. He was instrumental in persuading the
British government to convene the conference and to release
the four politicians who had been deported to the Seychelles
as a sign of its serious intentions.[60] Musa al-Alami was also
the brother-in-law of Jamal al-Husayni and therefore had
close ties to the leading politicians. Yet he had maintained his
outspoken and independent views and was respected by the
British administration. George Antonius was a former official
in the Education Department and author of the major inter-
pretative study *The Arab Awakening,* which analyzed the
roots of Arab nationalism and the contradictory promises
made by the British in World War I. Antonius served as
secretary to the Arab delegations at the London conference,
coordinating the position papers and scheduling meetings. He

59. Intelligence summary, Oct. 18, 1938, enclosed in high commissioner, dispatch, Oct. 19, 1938, CO 733/359/75021; letter from Hasan Salamah (military commander in Lydda) to Abd al-Qadir al-Husayni (military commander in Hebron-
Jerusalem), Dec. 1938, intercepted by the British and quoted in the London *Times,*
Jan. 18, 1939.
60. Furlonge, pp. 117–125. See Chapters 6 and 7.

also was a key member of the committee that analyzed the 1915–1916 Husayn-McMahon correspondence, and he remained in London through April 1939 to hold private discussions with British officials in the hope of reaching an acceptable compromise.[61]

But al-Hajj Amin al-Husayni—whom the British banned from attending the conference—had the last word. Britain's act of outlawing him, stripping him of the presidency of the Supreme Muslim Council and the Arab Higher Committee, and forcing him into exile had enhanced his stature as a national leader and a symbol of resistance. After he rejected the British White Paper of May 1939 that followed the London conference, no Arab politician could accept it openly without risking his own position in the national movement.

Within Palestine, the structure of political life had disintegrated by mid-1939. The prominent political figures were either exiled or discredited, and local politicans were still detained. Rudimentary attempts by some of the guerrilla leaders to build a counter government had been crushed. The residents of the towns and villages were exhausted and bewildered.

The new White Paper withdrew the hated partition plan and held out the possibility that the Arab community would retain its majority status in Palestine. To that extent the rebellion had succeeded, but the price paid for the seeming victory had been exceedingly high. The Arabs' chance to seize a real victory from the one offered on paper was limited, if not entirely destroyed.

The national movement that began with petitions and selective noncooperation in the early 1920s had led, as its demands were blocked and its aspirations thwarted, to a bitter revolt in the late 1930s. As long as Britain was determined to

61. Antonius, letters to Walter S. Rogers, Feb. 15, April 6, 1939, St. Antony's College, Private Paper Collection; notes on talk between Antonius and Shuckburgh (CO), April 17, 1939, CO 733/387/75872/38; Sir Miles Lampson (Cairo) transmitted memorandum from Antonius, June 3, 1939, CO 733/408/75872/18.

old onto Palestine, the revolt could not succeed. The situation by 1939 posed serious dilemmas for the nationalists and
contributed to inward-turning and rancor among the leaders.
Those who relied on diplomatic pressure achieved limited
results, but the rebels also failed, leaving the Arab community, at the close of 1939, without either an active political
leadership or a sense of national direction.

PART III /

THE POLITICS OF

FRUSTRATION

6 / Appeals to Arab and Muslim Countries

Nationalist movements focused on their internal grievances and concentrated their political efforts against the colonial power, but they also recognized the importance of
gathering support for their cause from peoples and rulers
outside the colony. The most obvious sources of support
were members of the same ethnic group or religion, who
were likely to sympathize with the movement's aims and to
volunteer diplomatic and material aid. Neighboring countries might provide a sanctuary for political exiles and rebels
during an insurrection.

Such assistance had serious limitations. The members of
the similar ethnic or religious group might themselves be
subject to colonial rule and therefore unable to aid another
nationalist movement. Even if they were not fully preoccupied with their own problems, they might be able to offer
only moral support to others. Moreover, nationalists might
find that receiving support from one foreign ruler would
alienate his rival and entangle them in political controversies
unrelated to their own cause. Most seriously, for movements
that were challenged by another nationalist movement within
the same colony, the latter movement would also appeal to
its potential supporters abroad, using the same means to influence the international actors and affect the policy of the
colonial authorities.

The Palestine Arab politicians sent missions to Egypt,

Arabia, Iraq, Iran, and India, as well as to the neighboring states of Transjordan, Lebanon, and Syria. These missions argued that the problems facing Palestine were part of a broad challenge to the Islamic and Arab worlds. They urged the leaders to raise these issues before the British government and the League of Nations and to provide the Palestinians with material support. By the 1930s, the Palestine nationalists won the support of most Muslim leaders and Arab politicians, although its manifestations varied considerably and they found that acquiring the support of one ruler sometimes meant alienating another. The gravitation of the Nashashibis to Emir Abdallah of Transjordan, for example, exacerbated internal divisions within the national movement.

The major problem, however, was that the rulers whose aid the Palestinians sought lacked adequate diplomatic leverage against the British and other European powers. Few held membership in the League of Nations, and even the small number of independent Arab states were dependent militarily on Britain or France. Only in the late 1930s did the Nazi threat cause the British to seek allies in the Arab world and thus become attentive to the Arab rulers' concern about Palestine and allow them to play an active role in the negotiations over its fate. In the final analysis, although the Palestine Arabs' effort to appeal to Arab and Muslim countries was strikingly successful in arousing sympathy, it could not be politically decisive.

Appeals to Rulers

When the Arab politicians in Palestine turned their attention in late 1918 and 1919 to the Arab government in Damascus headed by Emir Faysal, they hoped that the formation of a federation with Syria would overcome the dangers inherent in the Balfour Declaration and limit the impact of Jewish immigration. Their support for Faysal was entirely self-interested; it depended upon his upholding the Arab case in

Palestine and vanished as soon as he lost control of Damascus. But Faysal was a doubtful ally. He had been willing to parley with Weizmann in 1918 and 1919 in the hope of obtaining diplomatic and financial aid against French designs on Syria.[1] Weizmann recognized that a Jewish Palestine required sympathetic relations with the surrounding Arab countries and considered Faysal the one public figure he could approach. Faysal, in turn, hoped for Zionist financial aid and diplomatic backing.[2]

Faysal's agreement with Weizmann of January 3, 1919, was predicated on the fulfillment of Arab aspirations in Syria.[3] But he soon came under heavy pressure from politicians at home who opposed all aspects of Zionism. The All-Palestine Congress in late January 1919 and the Nadi Filastin in Damascus pressed the anti-Zionist case on him. Thus his views on Zionism had hardened by the autumn of 1919, when he returned to Europe and discovered that Weizmann was not willing to back him diplomatically by asking the French government to drop its insistence on ruling Syria.[4] Irritated that Weizmann was not keeping what he perceived to be his part of the bargain and fearing imminent loss of his kingdom to the French, Faysal gave a detailed interview in the *Jewish Chronicle* (October 3, 1919) in which he emphasized that Palestine must remain part of an Arab empire. The Jewish community should enjoy regulated immigration, "free use of the Hebrew language," "equal rights with the Arabs," "full control of Jewish schools," and "the means of establishing there a Jewish cultural centre." Asserting that this was the meaning of Zionism as Weiz-

---

1. Clayton (CPO) to FO, June 12, July 1, 1918, FO 371/3398/27647/105824 and 123904; C. Weizmann, pp. 234–235.
2. Clayton to FO, Oct. 27, 1918, transmitting message from Eder to Weizmann about Faysal's request for a loan and financial advisers, FO 371/3398/27647/178952.
3. Aaron Klieman, *Foundations of British Policy in the Arab World: The Cairo Conference of 1921* (Baltimore: Johns Hopkins Press, 1971), p. 34; Antonius, pp. 437–439, provides the text of the Faysal-Weizmann agreement.
4. Colonel Cornwallis, London, report, Sept. 25, 1919, FO 371/4183/2117/134093.

mann had explained it to him,[5] Faysal adhered to this interpretation through the spring of 1920. The French occupied Damascus in July of that year and Faysal fled into exile, ending all possibility that an Arab federation would unite Palestine with Syria and Lebanon. The politicians in Palestine quickly reorganized their movement on a purely Palestinian basis, dropping all references to Palestine as "southern Syria" from their political vocabulary.[6]

Nevertheless, they sought support from Sherif Husayn of Mecca, Faysal's father, who had initiated the Arab revolt in 1916 and could state authoritatively whether Palestine was included in the zone that had been promised independence in his correspondence with McMahon. In 1921, Husayn began to negotiate a treaty with the British to obtain sorely needed financial aid so that he could consolidate his rule in the Hijaz and fend off his powerful rival, Ibn Saud. The British government was anxious that the accord include Husayn's acceptance of the treaties of Versailles and Sèvres because he would thereby acknowledge the mandatory system and the application of the Balfour Declaration to Palestine. At first, Husayn agreed to accept the legitimacy of Britain's "special position" in Palestine, Iraq, and Transjordan, which were distant from his own territory; but he balked at accepting the existing boundaries of the Hijaz with Najd and Asir.[7]

The Palestinian leaders became alarmed at Sherif Husayn's stance and inserted themselves into the negotiations, which resumed in London the next year. Husayn sent his special representative, Naji al-Asil, to London with a draft treaty

5. See Lord Curzon, minute, Oct. 9, 1919, on the interview and Herbert Samuel, protest against it, FO 371/4183/2117/137796. See also Faysal to Edmund Allenby, April 27, 1920, enclosed in Allenby telegram to Curzon, May 13, 1920, which states, "All that I have admitted is to safeguard rights of Jews in that country as much as rights of indigenous Arab inhabitants are safeguarded and to allow same rights and privileges" (FO 371/5035).

6. Porath, *Emergence,* pp. 103, 110–112.

7. Yehoshua Porath, "The Palestinians and the Negotiations for the British-Hijazi Treaty, 1920–1925," *Asian and African Studies,* 8 (1972), 26; for somewhat different interpretations of the course of the negotiations see Klieman, pp. 121–122, 223, and Antonius, pp. 332–334.

that included a reference to Britain's "special position" in Palestine. The second Palestinian delegation to London persuaded Asil to omit this article,[8] but the British negotiators insisted that the clause be reinstated. Although the draft treaty was initialed in April 1923, Husayn issued his own version in mid-May. His version asserted that Britain would not only support Arab independence but would also help the Arabs unite their countries, including Palestine. The Palestinians' reaction of delight turned to dismay when the British released the initialed draft.

The local Muslim-Christian societies then pressed the Arab Executive to convene the Sixth Arab Congress that June to protest Husayn's sellout. A cable from Husayn requesting the delegates to retain confidence in him only provoked greater criticism by the delegates and accelerated their efforts to organize another delegation to London that would monitor Asil's negotiations.[9] That autumn Asil held firm to the Palestinians' demand for a clause supporting a "native representative government" in Palestine.[10]

Palestinian pressure on Husayn peaked in early 1924. Although Husayn was willing to talk to Zionist leaders who visited him in Amman at that time,[11] he found himself increasingly beholden to the Palestine Arabs, who were the only Arabs to acknowledge his claim to the caliphate. The Palestine issue became the final obstacle in his negotiations

---

8. Porath, "Palestinians," pp. 28–34.

9. The three members of the delegation were Amin al-Tamimi, Musa Kazim al-Husayni, and Wadi al-Bustani. See political report, May 1923, CO 733/46; political report, June 1923, CO 733/47; Arab Executive, report to the sixth congress, June 16, 1923, ISA, Arab Documents, file 1026; Porath, *Emergence,* pp. 179–182; Porath, "Palestinians," pp. 34–38; Wedi F. Boustany, *The Palestine Mandate: Invalid and Impractical* (Beirut: American Press, 1936), p. 54.

10. Musa Kazim Pasha's letters to the Arab Executive and Husayn are in ISA, Arab Documents, file 1541; also Amin al-Tamimi to secretary, Arab Executive, Sept. 16, 1923, and to Musa Kazim Pasha, Oct. 29, 1923, in ibid.; see Porath, "Palestinians," pp. 38–42.

11. Political report, Jan. 1924, CO 733/65; political report, Feb. 1924, CO 733/66; correspondence in ISA, Arab Documents, file 3589; Kisch, letter to ZO, Jan. 24, 1924, CZA, Z4/2421.

with London. But his hold on the Hijaz was increasingly precarious. Ibn Saud was poised to invade, and Husayn lacked the military strength to resist him. Husayn was forced to abdicate in late September, and all need for the treaty vanished with his demise.

The Palestinians' victory was double-edged. They had prevented Husayn from acquiescing to British pressure to repudiate the argument that Palestine lay within the area promised independence by the McMahon-Husayn correspondence. And yet the lack of a British-Hijazi treaty meant that Husayn could not receive military and financial aid from Britain and thus weakened his internal position. Moreover, his demise diminished the possibility of an Iraq-Transjordan-Hijaz axis to which Palestine might become linked. In balance, the Palestinian leadership considered their moral victory—retaining the favorable interpretation of the McMahon-Husayn correspondence—to be the more important result. Porath wrote, "They were concerned with driving Zionism from Palestine, and the question of Arab unity as a goal in its own right did not impel them to take any steps toward advancing or realizing this end."[12]

During the early 1920s, Palestine Arabs also looked for support to Turkey, where Mustafa Kemal was consolidating his rule. He forced the European powers to renegotiate the 1920 Treaty of Sèvres that had laid down the legal basis for the mandatory system. The Arabs hoped that the new peace conference, convened in Lausanne, would reassess the mandatory system itself. Their hope had been encouraged by the Turkish National Pact, which espoused the principle of self-determination for the former provinces of the Ottoman Empire. Within Palestine, there was a strong current of support for Islamic Turkey against the Christian European powers, despite bitter memories of Ottoman rule during the war.

The Arab Executive sent a three-man delegation to Istan-

12. Porath, *Emergence,* p. 182.

bul in November 1922, where one of the delegates, Shaykh Abd al-Qadir al-Muzaffar, remained until early 1923. The two other members—Musa Kazim al-Husayni and Amin al-Tamimi—traveled to Lausanne, where they tried without success to appear before the conference and to persuade the Turkish delegates to uphold their cause. But the Turkish negotiators were preoccupied with their own national requirements and agreed to drop the issue of the mandated territories in order to secure their own needs. The Palestinian delegation left empty-handed.[13] Despite this failure, support for Mustafa Kemal within Palestine remained high until 1924, when he alienated many devout Muslims by abolishing the caliphate.[14]

Islamic Appeals

Simultaneously and on a continuing basis, Palestinian politicians emphasized the importance of Palestine to Muslims around the world. They stressed the responsibility of all Muslims to maintain al-Haram al-Sharif in Jerusalem, which contained al-Aqsa mosque and the Dome of the Rock. They established ties with religious and political groups in non-Arab as well as Arab countries. This effort culminated in the World Islamic Congress convened by al-Hajj Amin al-Husayni in Jerusalem in late 1931.

The Supreme Muslim Council that had been formed in 1922 displayed its concern for its central role by undertaking repairs of the Haram area, long neglected by the Ottoman rulers. The first stage of repairs was completed by August 1928. One British official noted a "remarkable psychological change" among the mosque's custodians: they "have become alive to their responsibilities and opportunities; a more appreciative outlook regarding it has become manifest among the more educated Muslims. . . . This revival, both spiritual and material, . . . indicates the stirring of a new feeling in the

13. Ibid., pp. 162–166; Political report, Jan. 1923, CO 733/42.
14. Porath, *Emergence,* p. 161.

Muslims of this country."[15] Many of the funds to restore the sanctuary came from Muslims abroad.[16] Al-Hajj Amin al-Husayni, president of the council, used the fund drive to heighten Muslim concern for Palestine and to enhance his own stature. He headed delegations to Egypt in 1923 and to Iraq, Kuwait, Bahrain, and southern Iran in 1924,[17] appealing to Shii as well as to Sunni Muslims. He also attended pan-Islamic congresses in Cairo and Mecca in 1926.[18]

The delegation to Mecca during the hajj of 1922 argued that the sanctuary was threatened by Zionist designs:

> The Islamic Palestine Nation that has been guarding al-Aqsa Mosque and Holy Rock ever since 1300 years declares to the Muslim world that the Holy Places are in great danger on account of the horrible Zionist aggressions.
>
> We as faithful watchful guards . . . have devoted ourselves to its defence. The Egyptian, Hijazian, Turk, Persian, Afghan, Hindu, Javite or any other Muslim in the East or West has the same right as we. . . . The Zionist Committee, which is endeavouring to establish Jewish rule in Palestine and to rob al-Aqsa from the Muslims on the plea that it [was] built on the ruins of Solomon's Temple, aims at making Palestine a base of Jewish influence over the [Arabian] peninsula, and the whole East.[19]

The delegation convened a Pan-Arab congress during the hajj as well as distributing literature and contacting pilgrims throughout the Muslim world. Although subsequent delega-

15. Chief secretary, dispatch to CO, Aug. 30, 1928, CO 733/160/57527.

16. King Fuad of Egypt sent £10,000; Ibn Saud also sent a contribution. By late 1924 contributions totaled £70,000 and reached almost £95,000 by mid-1928 (political report, Sept. 1924, CO 733/74; chief secretary, dispatch, Aug. 30, 1928, quoting al-Hajj Amin, CO 733/160/57527).

17. He was accompanied by Rashid al-Hajj Ibrahim in Haifa and Amin al-Tamimi of the Supreme Muslim Council in 1924 (political report, March 1924, CO 733/67; political report, April 1924, CO 733/68).

18. *Palestine Bulletin,* May 25, July 18, 1926.

19. The delegation included Shaykh Abd al-Qadir al-Muzaffar, Rafiq al-Tamimi, and Amin Nur Allah of Haifa. Declaration quoted was attached to political report, July 1922, CO 733/24. A report on the trip is in political report, Aug. 1922, CO 733/25, and seven letters from the delegation's secretary, Adib Abu Dabbah of Jaffa, are in ISA, Arab Documents, file 1721. See also Porath, *Emergence,* pp. 262–265.

tions attended the hajj in 1923 and 1924,[20] the British insisted that they abstain from political activities. Some British officials therefore objected to including a leading politician—Jamal al-Husayni, secretary of the Arab Executive—in the Supreme Muslim Council's delegation to India in late 1923,[21] where it was the guest of the Khilafat Committee.

The delegation found itself caught between its relationship with Sherif Husayn and its desire for broad support in the Islamic world. The Indian Muslims denounced Husayn for weakening Muslim unity by breaking with the Ottoman Empire during the war.[22] But the Palestinians still needed Husayn's support; hampered by association with him, the delegation failed to collect much money, although the Khilafat Committee continued to support the Palestinians at various Islamic forums and diplomatic conferences.[23] Its leader, Muhammad Ali, was buried in al-Haram al-Sharif in January 1931, symbolizing the centrality of Jerusalem even to non-Arab Muslims.

During the crisis over the Wailing Wall in 1929–1930, al-Hajj Amin was able to enlist the support of prominent Muslim figures behind the Palestine cause. In June and July 1930, these scholars and politicians argued before the international commission, meeting in Jerusalem, that the Muslims of Palestine

20. The muftis of Haifa (Shaykh Muhammad al-Murad) and Gaza (Muhammad al-Husayni) led the 1923 delegation (political report, June 1923, CO 733/47; high commissioner, telegram, Sept. 26, 1923, CO 733/49). Al-Hajj Said al-Shawwa, Gaza's representative on the Supreme Muslim Council, accompanied the 1924 delegation.
21. India Office, complaints, CO 733/56; Samuel, minute on his talk with al-Hajj Amin, Sept. 21, 1923, al-Hajj Amin, letter to Samuel, Sept. 30, and Musa Kazim Pasha's letter to chief secretary informing him that Khalil Sakakini would replace Jamal al-Husayni as secretary of the Arab Executive during the latter's absence, Oct. 4, ISA, Chief Secretary's Papers, 2/184, POL/151/W.
22. The delegation obtained nearly £7,000 from the Nizam of Hyderabad, its only sizable contribution. See political report, Dec. 1923, CO 733/63; al-Hajj Amin to secretariat, Palestine government, March 3, 1924, ISA, Chief Secretary's Papers, 2/184, POL/151/W; Porath, "Al-Hajj Amin," pp. 153–155.
23. *Palestine Bulletin,* July 28, 1926, quoting a Khilafat leader at the Islamic conference in Mecca; al-Hajj Amin, discussion with Indian Muslim delegation en route to London, in Cairo, see high commissioner to O. G. R. Williams (CO), Oct. 22, 1930, CO 733/179/77013, pt. 5.

were merely the custodians of al-Haram al-Sharif on behalf of all Muslims.[24] They maintained that jeopardizing the Palestine Muslims' rights would have repercussions around the Islamic world.

The pinnacle of al-Hajj Amin's efforts came at his World Islamic Congress of December 1931,[25] which was financed largely by the Khilafat Committee of India. The 130 delegates came from all the Muslim countries except Turkey. The congress almost foundered because of the Egyptian and Saudi rulers' rival claims to become caliph and their fear that al-Hajj Amin sought that position for himself. But al-Hajj Amin succeeded in bringing together a wide array of Muslim groups, not only official delegations and *ulama,* but also Shii societies and members of the Young Men's Muslim Associations and other lay groups. The congress issued resolutions condemning Zionism, the mandatory system, colonialism, French policy in Morocco, Italian actions in Libya, and the Soviet Union's antireligious measures. It also resolved to establish a university of al-Aqsa in Jerusalem, but this decision was denounced by the *ulama* of al-Azhar University in Cairo, who wanted to retain their central role in religious education, and was greeted with concern by Christian Arabs in Palestine, who feared that a revival of Islam would damage their status.

Although the congress established a central bureau in Jerusalem under Sayyid Ziya ad-Din Tabatabai, the exiled Persian premier, none of its plans came to fruition.[26] The bureau's most significant gesture was the prestigious delegation it sent to Mecca in 1934, headed by al-Hajj Amin. This delegation mediated between Saudi Arabia and Yemen during their

---

24. *Falastin,* English edition, June 28, 1930, p. 2.
25. The congress established a twenty-five-member executive committee, under al-Hajj Amin. The treasurer was Muhammad Allubah Pasha, an Egyptian Wafdist. See H. A. R. Gibb, "The Islamic Congress at Jerusalem in December 1931," in *Survey of International Affairs 1934* (London: Oxford University Press, 1935), pp. 99–109.
26. Ibid., p. 108; George Antonius, annual report for 1933–1934, Sept. 10, 1934, to the Institute of Current World Affairs, New York, in Antonius Papers, St. Antony's College, Private Paper Collection; on al-Hajj Amin and Muhammad Allubah's overland fund-raising trip to India, see *Palestine Post,* May 9, June 26, Nov. 19, 1933.

border war. Their conflict was viewed as a blow to Islamic unity and thus warranted intervention by concerned Muslims.[27] Although the delegation's influence on the peace terms was unclear, it enhanced al-Hajj Amin's international stature and created goodwill upon which he could capitalize when the Palestinians sought Saudi and Yemeni support in the late 1930s.

Support in the Arab World

These years of preparation won the Palestinians—and in particular al-Hajj Amin—support by Muslim leaders in Saudi Arabia, Yemen, Iraq, Egypt, and even Iran and India. Concurrently, Palestinian leaders cultivated nongovernment support in these countries, particularly through middle-class Muslim and secular associations. In the early 1920s, these groups were preoccupied with their own struggles against the British and French and had little time or energy to devote to assisting each other. By the end of the decade, however, significant political concessions had been won by all the countries adjoining Palestine. Egypt acquired semi-independent status in 1922; Lebanon won a constitution in 1926; and the Syrian Druze revolt of 1925–1927 led to a draft constitution in 1928, which was promulgated in 1930. In Iraq, Faysal was crowned king in 1921 and, by 1930, an amended treaty of alliance with Britain prepared the way for Iraq's joining the League of Nations in 1932. Even Emir Abdallah of Transjordan reached an agreement with Britain in 1928 that led to the promulgation of an organic law and elections in 1929. In contrast, the constitutional situation in Palestine remained unchanged and Jewish-Arab tensions were growing.

Members of the elite in Palestine and Syria shared close personal ties. Many families were intermarried. Damascus had been their political and cultural center before World War

27. Gibb, pp. 109, 319; *Palestine Post*, July 12, 1934, describes the reception accorded al-Hajj Amin on his return to Palestine from Mecca.

I, and memories of their solidarity in 1918–1920 lingered on. Palestinians demonstrated their support for Syrian independence in 1926 by holding a general strike to protest the visit to Jerusalem of the French high commissioner for Lebanon and Syria.[28] Some Palestinian youths joined the Syrian revolt in the mid-1920s,[29] and Palestine served as a sanctuary for many Syrian political exiles. Syrians also expressed their sympathy for Palestinian causes. Violent demonstrations were staged against Lord Balfour when he visited Damascus in 1925, and appeals to aid Arab victims of the August 1929 riots were circulated in Syria. But Palestinian politicians always suspected that the Syrian nationalists would put their own needs before those of the Palestinians and were sharply critical of the parleying between the Zionist leadership and a group of Syrian exiles (known as the Syro-Palestinian Committee) in Cairo and Geneva in the early 1920s. This committee was willing to recognize the Jewish national home on condition that the Zionist movement assist Syria to obtain independence.[30]

The first pan-Arab gathering was held in 1931 in Jerusalem, immediately after the convening of al-Hajj Amin's World Islamic Congress. The one-day Arab congress issued an Arab Covenant that reasserted the indivisibility and unity of the Arab lands and emphasized the need for the Arab nation to combat all forms of colonialism.[31] The members decided to convene a pan-Arab congress in Baghdad the following autumn. The anti-imperialist and pan-Arab tone of the Arab Covenant reflected the influence of the Istiqlalist Awni Abd al-Hadi, rather than that of al-Hajj Amin, even though the congress was convened under the latter's auspices.

Awni Bey had maintained close ties with Faysal in Iraq and, even after Faysal's death in September 1933 caused the

28. *Palestine Bulletin,* March 31, 1926.
29. Ibid., Jan. 27, Feb. 2, Nov. 1, 1926.
30. Porath, *Emergence,* pp. 112–114.
31. Gibb, p. 107n.

cancellation of the pan-Arab congress scheduled for Baghdad, Awni Bey retained his ties with the Iraqi regime, whose leaders continued to promote pan-Arabism. They sought a confederation of Iraq, Transjordan, and Palestine that would permit some continued Jewish immigration but would not risk an eventual Jewish majority. Since such a confederation would enhance the stature of the Iraqi branch of the Hashimite family, it was opposed by the head of the Transjordanian branch, Emir Abdallah, as well as by the rival Saudi ruler (who had ousted Faysal's father from the Hijaz) and the antimonarchial Syrian politicians. Thus, although Arab leaders supported Arab unity in theory, their personal ambitions were the principal impetus behind promoting—or blocking—particular schemes. The British and French governments opposed any such plans, and so they necessarily remained purely theoretical.

Emir Abdallah was the one leader with clear ambitions vis-à-vis Palestine, but his negotiations with Zionist groups in the early 1930s to sell or lease land in Transjordan to Jewish immigrants[32] caused his relations with the Palestinian nationalists—especially al-Hajj Amin—to degenerate into open antagonism. Although Abdallah tried to redeem his nationalist standing by supporting Palestinian protests against illegal Jewish immigration and by reaffirming that the wartime pledges to the Arabs were prior to and "more clear" than the Balfour Declaration,[33] he allied himself increasingly with the relatively pro-British Nashashibi camp within Palestine. Abdallah even intervened in Palestinian domestic affairs by proposing to the British that al-Hajj Amin be replaced as

32. Percy Cox (British resident, Amman), dispatch to CO on negotiations involving Zionist land agents and Circassian landowners, May 16, 1931, CO 733/199/87072 pt. 3; high commissioner objected to the arrangements on the grounds that the mandate specified that the Balfour Declaration was not to apply to Transjordan, see his talk with Weizmann, March 12, 1934, CO 733/257/37356; see A. Cohen, pp. 252–255, on Abdallah's negotiations in 1933; ESCO Foundation, II, 766–777.
33. Abdallah, letter to the high commissioner, July 25, 1934, CO 733/251/37250/2; also his letter, Oct. 18, 1933, CO 733/239/17356/1.

president of the Supreme Muslim Council by Shaykh Asad al-Shuqayri, the Husaynis' bitter enemy.[34] The alliance was cemented in 1937, when Abdallah urged the Arabs to accept the partition proposal on the assumption that the Arab zone would merge with his emirate and Raghib al-Nashashibi would obtain a leading role in his cabinet.

Support in the Late 1930s

During the general strike of 1936, the efforts to involve the Arab and Muslim worlds in the Palestine issue bore fruit at both the public and government levels. Syrians and Iraqis demonstrated to protest British policy in Palestine, and they raised funds for the Palestinians. The first anti-Jewish riots broke out in Baghdad, Damascus, and even Cairo: the substantial Jewish communities in these cities began to be linked in the public mind with actions by their coreligionists in Palestine. Fawzi al-Qawuqji, the exiled Syrian guerrilla leader who had formed guerrilla units in late 1935 to use against the French in Syria, diverted his three-hundred-man force to Palestine, where he operated from the middle of August to November 1936 alongside the Palestinian guerrilla forces.

At the government level, both Abdallah and Iraqi Foreign Minister Nuri al-Said attempted to mediate between the Arab strikers and the British authorities. Because of Abdallah's strained relations with both the Husaynis and the pro-Iraqi Istiqlalists, he wielded little influence over the Arab Higher Committee, and his appeals to end the strike had little effect.[35] Nuri Pasha, however, commanded considerable prestige among Palestinian leaders and was viewed as an astute politician by British officials. His memorandum of August 17, which proposed that the strikers stop their violence be-

34. Cox, Amman, to S. Moody, CO, London, on talk with Abdallah, Feb. 11, 1937, CO 733/326/75023/2.
35. Norman Anthony Rose, "The Arab Rulers and Palestine, 1936: The British Reaction," *Journal of Modern History*, 44 (June 1972), 319; Kalkas in Abu-Lughod, ed., *Transformation*, pp. 256–258.

fore the British suspend immigration and open negotiations with them, formed the basis for his discussions of August 20–24 in Palestine with the high commissioner and the Arab Higher Committee.[36] On August 30 the committee issued a proclamation accepting Nuri Pasha's mediation plan. But the British yielded to pressure from Zionist leaders to repudiate his mediation and refuse to suspend immigration, even temporarily. On September 2 the government decided to crush the Arab strike by whatever force was necessary.[37]

At first the Arab Higher Committee reacted by accelerating its efforts to win the Arab leaders' support for a position that immigration must be suspended until the upcoming Royal Commission issued its recommendations.[38] By late September, however, the Foreign Office had advised its consuls in the Arab states that Britain would not make any such prior commitments and that the disturbances must end unconditionally, adding that the Arab rulers would be permitted to make representations before the Royal Commission on behalf of the Palestinians.[39] Hard pressed to maintain the strike, the Arab Higher Committee decided to grasp at this straw. It drafted a statement that urged the Palestinians to end the strike and to have confidence in British justice and the findings of the Royal Commission. The statement was sent to and signed by the kings of Saudi Arabia, Iraq, Yemen, and Transjordan and was received back by the Arab Higher Committee on October 8–9.[40] It was promptly endorsed by the local committees, and the strike ended on October 12. Only the Egyptian government declined to adhere to the

36. Rose, "Arab Rulers," p. 220; Kalkas in Abu-Lughod, ed., *Transformation,* pp. 259–260; high commissioner, dispatch on Nuri Pasha's discussions, Aug. 21, 1936, and telegram, Sept. 1, supporting his efforts, CO 733/297/75156, pt. 4.

37. Rose, "Arab Rulers," p. 223; Kalkas in Abu-Lughod, ed., *Transformation,* pp. 266–268; colonial secretary, dispatch to high commissioner, Sept. 1, 1936, rejecting Nuri Pasha's mediation, commenting on his talk with Weizmann, and relaying the cabinet's decision to crush the strike, CO 733/297/75156, pt. 4.

38. Rose, "Arab Rulers," p. 218.

39. Ibid., pp. 226–227.

40. Ibid., p. 228; Kalkas in Abu-Lughod, ed., *Transformation,* pp. 269–271; Hurewitz, *Struggle,* p. 71.

appeal, apparently on the grounds that the Palestinians should stick to their demand that immigration be suspended and not merely trust the "good faith" of the British.[41]

The Arab Higher Committee resorted to the same stratagem in late December, when it sought to end its boycott of the Royal Commission. Three Istiqlal activists, including Awni Abd al-Hadi, journeyed to Iraq and Saudi Arabia. They returned on January 5, 1937, with the kings' request to lift the boycott and present the Palestine case to the commission.[42]

Palestinian politicians hoped that, in return for these appeals, the kings would exert pressure on the British government to resolve the fundamental issues in Palestine in a manner favorable to the Arabs. But the Arab rulers lacked leverage. They could submit proposals to the British government, as the Iraqi, Saudi, Yemeni, and Transjordanian rulers did in 1936 and 1937.[43] Public demonstrations in Arab cities could arouse the specter of widespread hostility to Britain and the undermining of its strategic position in the Arab and Muslim worlds.[44] A few could address the League of Nations, which Iraq joined in 1932 and Egypt in 1937. But France dominated Syria and Lebanon, and Britain still retained a powerful military and financial hold over Iraq, Transjordan, and Egypt. These countries had negligible military capacity and little diplomatic influence in Europe. When, for example, in July 1937, an Iraqi diplomat at the League supported the Palestinians' stand against partition, League members criticized the audacity of a supposed client of Britain speaking out in such a manner.[45] The Egyptian government was more cautious in its approach and waited until the September session of the

41. Sir Miles Lampson, Cairo, telegram to FO quoting Egyptian Prime Minister Mustafa al-Nahhas Pasha, Nov. 9, 1936, CO 733/320/75550/27.

42. *Palestine Post,* Dec. 10, 11, 13, 20, 22, 27, 31, 1936, Jan. 3, 4, 7, 1937.

43. Note, for example, the Iraqi and Saudi formulas submitted to the Royal Commission in February 1937, attached to CO 733/341/75528/44.

44. Note Foreign Minister Eden's letter to the colonial secretary, Jan. 20, 1937, cited in Chapter 2, n. 45.

45. Carstairs (British representative in Geneva) to CO, Aug. 10, 1937, CO 733/341/75528/44.

league's assembly to protest the partition plan. Iraqi and Syrian denunciations were, of course, also occasioned by their rivalry with Abdallah, whose emirate would benefit from the partition plan.[46]

In an effort to broaden support among Arab politicians, the Arab Higher Committee planned a National Arab Congress to be held in Bludan, Syria, in early September 1937. Al-Hajj Amin visited Damascus in late June to make preliminary contacts,[47] and Muin al-Madi remained there to carry through the arrangements in coordination with Nabih al-Azmah, a Syrian who had recently returned from years of exile in Palestine. When the partition plan was announced in July, the convening of the congress became more urgent. The organizers hoped it would undertake such practical measures as fund raising and diplomatic campaigns on behalf of the Palestinians. Some even wanted it to sponsor a guerrilla force to oppose partition.

Some four hundred delegates attended the Bludan congress of September 8–10.[48] Forty percent were Syrian, a third Palestinian, a quarter Lebanese or Jordanian, and a scattering Iraqi and Egyptian. Virtually all were opponents of their own regimes and had been involved in efforts to form committees to support the Palestine cause. Leaders of all the Palestinian political parties were present, except for al-Hajj Amin al-Husayni, who remained in Jerusalem for fear that the British would prevent him from returning to Palestine if he left the sanctuary of al-Haram al-Sharif. Al-Hajj Amin was elected honorary president of the congress and Naji al-Suwaydi, a former prime minister of Iraq, be-

46. Chief secretary, July 10, 1937, transmitted the Arab Higher Committee's July 8 appeal to the Arab states, asking them to denounce the partition plan, CO 733/351/75718/6; Hurewitz, *Struggle*, p. 90.

47. Gilbert MacKereth (British consul, Damascus), dispatch, July 5, 1937, CO 733/326/75023/2.

48. MacKereth, reports to FO, Sept. 11, 14, 1937, and chief secretary, dispatch to CO, Sept. 25, 1937, CO 733/353/75718/85. See also Hurewitz, *Struggle*, pp. 88–89.

came president.[49] The congress also elected an executive committee composed of the members of the Arab Higher Committee plus one representative for each Arab party from outside Palestine. It formed three working committees: the political committee, chaired by a leader of the Egyptian Young Men's Association; the financial and economic committee, chaired by the president of the Beirut chamber of commerce; and the propaganda committee under a leader of the Damascus National Bloc party.[50] The committees hammered out lengthy reports that were adopted by the congress as a whole.

The political committee called for the abolition of the mandate and the Balfour Declaration and the prohibition of Jewish immigration and land purchase. It proposed that Britain conclude a treaty that would grant Palestine independence as an Arab country where the Jews would be a respected minority. It hinted that the Arab world would have to oppose Britain if British policy did not change, but urged political action through legitimate means. The financial and economic committee outlined measures to regularize fund collection through local Defense of Palestine committees and called for a trade boycott of the Jewish community. The propaganda committee noted the Arabs' failure to make their case known throughout the world and proposed measures to expand their information network.

Although the resolutions formally committed a wide range of Arab politicians to the Palestine cause, and the executive committee made non-Palestinians, for the first time, responsible actors in the conflict, the resolutions did not go beyond previous Palestinian demands, and many of the Palestinian

49. Muhammad Allubah of Egypt and Bishop Aghnatios Hurayti (Greek Orthodox bishop of Hama and Aleppo) shared the vice-presidency. Riyadh al-Sulh, of the Syro-Palestine committee in Geneva, was supervisor.
50. These were Abd al-Hamid Said, Umar al-Dauq, and Fakhri Barudi, respectively. Palestinians active on the political committee included Muin al-Madi and Amin al-Tamimi; the economic committee included Raghib al-Dajani, Rashid al-Hajj Ibrahim, and Fuad Saba; the propaganda committee included Wadi al-Bustani and Isa al-Isa.

participants were disappointed at the outcome. A group of a hundred Syrian and Palestinian delegates convened a secret meeting after the congress to discuss means to foment disturbances inside Palestine, including arms smuggling and attacks on Arabs who cooperated with the British.[51] Yaqub al-Ghusayn, head of the Youth Congress and an in-law of Syrian Prime Minister Jamil al-Mardam, was apparently a leading figure at this meeting.

The Bludan congress marked the rapid rise in Arab concern for the Palestine conflict, but its plans to form Defense of Palestine committees and to regularize fund collection were hardly under way when the British crackdown on October 1 precipitated a broadly based revolt inside Palestine. The revolt itself greatly accelerated Arab support efforts. Nabih al-Azmah coordinated the Defense of Palestine committees from Damascus, where he was joined by Palestinian exiles. Funds were collected from Arab communities in North and South America and from Muslims in the Gold Coast and India, as well as from Arab countries. The funds were earmarked for refugee relief, although much of the money was undoubtedly spent on supplies for the guerrillas.[52] Few non-Palestinians participated in the actual fighting, but Syria became a vital sanctuary for political exiles and guerrilla fighters and a conduit for arms and other supplies. Abdallah, however, tried to prevent the guerrillas from crossing through Transjordan.

A second pan-Arab gathering, in October 1938, coincided with the peak of guerrilla operations in Palestine. Initiated primarily by Awni Abd al-Hadi and the Egyptian leader Muhammad Allubah Pasha (a vice-president of the Bludan congress), the Cairo World Inter-Parliamentary Congress of the

51. Memorandum on the secret meeting, Annex 6 of MacKereth dispatch, Sept. 14, 1937, CO 733/353/75718/85.
52. *Palestine Post,* Aug. 8, Sept. 10, 1938; MacKereth, dispatches on contributions, Jan. 5, May 31, 1939, and his letter to the Gold Coast, March 9, 1939, CO 733/408/75872/23.

Arab and Muslim Countries for the Defense of Palestine[53] brought together twenty-five hundred delegates from a dozen countries. Only sixty were parliamentary deputies. Most were youths and students, who worked closely with the Defense of Palestine committees. The governments of Transjordan and Saudi Arabia would not allow any delegates to attend, however, and the Egyptian Wafd party (at that time in opposition) boycotted the congress, illustrating again how inter-Arab and internal politics could intrude on joint action. Awni Bey, Jamal al-Husayni, and Alfred Rock represented the Arab Higher Committee.

The resolutions were similar to those of the Bludan congress. The participants rejected the Balfour Declaration and partition plan and called for an end to Jewish immigration, the release of political prisoners, and the establishment of a national government with a representative parliament that would conclude a treaty with Britain. The Palestinian representatives were disappointed that the resolutions were not stronger. Awni Bey had hoped that the congress would call for political union of the Arab states. Al-Hajj Amin had hoped for financial commitments to support the revolt. Tension between Awni Bey and Jamal al-Husayni erupted when Jamal Effendi blocked Awni Bey's effort to persuade the congress to pass a resolution calling for an end to the disturbances so that the British could impose a favorable settlement. Jamal Effendi was suspicious of taking such a unilateral step without obtaining prior pledges from Britain because similar hopes had been dashed only two years before. He felt that additional gains could be won from the revolt, whereas Awni Bey felt that the revolt had already shown the depth of Palestine Arab feeling and that the time had come to turn to a diplomatic resolution based on broad pan-Arab support for the Palestinians' demands.

---

53. High commissioner, dispatch, Nov. 3, 1938, CO 733/359/75021; *Palestine Post,* Aug. 8, 1938; Hurewitz, *Struggle,* p. 89; Elizabeth Monroe, *Britain's Moment in the Middle East* (Baltimore: Johns Hopkins Press, 1963), pp. 122–123.

The congress' one tangible result was consonant with Awni Bey's view. A delegation was sent to London in November, led by Muhammad Allubah, to urge Britain to reconsider its policies. It was joined by Izzat Tannus, the Palestinian director of the Arab Center in London, and by Musa al-Alami, brother-in-law of Jamal al-Husayni.[54] Britain was becoming amenable to Arab arguments and was looking for a diplomatic means to resolve the conflict, which had compelled it to transfer substantial forces from Europe to Palestine. During the delegation's stay in London, Britain published the Woodhead Partition Committee report and a White Paper that effectively canceled the partition plan and proposed convening a conference that would include representatives of the Jewish Agency, the Arab states, and the Palestine Arabs.

The London Conference

Officials from Egypt, Iraq, Saudi Arabia, Transjordan, and Yemen were invited to the conference, held at St. James Palace from early February until mid-March 1939.[55] The British felt that the Arab statesmen would help to moderate the Palestine delegation's position and, through informal discussions with the Zionist leaders, would seek a viable compromise. Before the conference, the delegations assembled in Cairo and outlined a common program and approach. Although they adopted the Palestinian stance that Britain should recognize Palestine's right to independence, with minority guarantees to the Jewish community, they also sought a British-Palestinian accord. During the conference, the Yemeni Prince Sayf al-Islam al-Husayn persuaded the British to establish a subcommittee to examine the Husayn-McMahon pledges, in order to remove that nagging question from the plenary dis-

54. Four non-Palestinian Arabs served on the delegation, in addition to Allubah, and the three participants from the Arab Higher Committee were appointed to it but were not permitted to enter England. See Furlonge, pp. 120–123, for an account of Alami's efforts in London that never mentions the delegation's role.

55. For an overview of the conference see Hurewitz, *Struggle,* pp. 95–100, and Chapter 7.

cussions.[56] Ali Mahir, chief of the royal cabinet in Egypt, then proposed that another subcommittee discuss minority guarantees in an independent Palestine Arab state. But the colonial secretary insisted that he could not accept the idea of an *Arab* state or a state permitting the Arabs a majority voice in the government, although he supported the idea of an independent *Palestine* state. Therefore he would not let the subject be handled by such a subcommittee.[57]

Three of the most influential Arab participants—Tawfiq al-Suwaydi (deputy foreign minister of Iraq), Ali Mahir of Egypt, and Fuad Hamza (deputy foreign minister of Saudi Arabia)—met privately with Zionist delegates on three occasions. But these discussions did little to dispel mutual fears and may have actually increased the Arabs' suspicion of Zionist aims. At the first meeting,[58] Ali Mahir stressed that the basic point at issue was the fact that the Balfour Declaration had granted an exceptional position to the Jews. Tawfiq al-Suwaydi emphasized that continued large-scale immigration would cause more serious disturbances and a greater estrangement between the two peoples. David Ben Gurion immediately took issue with Mahir, and the American rabbi Stephen Wise insisted that any Jew who wanted to settle in Palestine should be allowed to immigrate.

At the final meeting, Chaim Weizmann reiterated the position that the Jewish national home's right to grow by immigration must remain unimpaired, and Ben Gurion suggested that all of Palestine become a Jewish state, federated with the surrounding Arab states. Ali Mahir implored the Zionist leaders to recognize the reality of the existence of an Arab people in Palestine and urged that a slowdown of immigration might secure peace. Fuad Hamza angrily dismissed Ben Gurion's call for accelerated immigration and a Jewish state,

56. Proposal made at the sixth meeting, Feb. 15, 1939, and approved at the seventh meeting, Feb. 16, FO 371/23224.

57. Proposal made at the seventh meeting, Feb. 16, 1939, and rejected at the eighth meeting, Feb. 18, ibid.

58. Minutes of the first informal meeting, Feb. 23, 1939, FO 371/23225.

cautioning him that the purpose of their current discussions was to search for ways to restore peace, not to exacerbate the conflict.[59]

From the British perspective, these informal talks were counterproductive because they failed to bridge the Arab-Zionist gap and exposed three influential Arabs to the militancy of key Zionist leaders. But the Arab states' delegates still searched for Arab-British reconciliation. They urged the British to place a time limit on the period of transition to independence, so that the Palestine Arabs need not fear Jewish obstructionism and the Jewish community would have an incentive to reach an agreement with these Arabs.[60] These efforts continued after the conference formally closed.[61] The British White Paper of May 1939 incorporated some of the Arabs' suggestions, such as the requirement that any Jewish immigration after a five-year period would require Arab approval and the qualified promise of independence after ten years. But the plan remained unacceptable to most members of the Arab Higher Committee[62] and therefore to the Arab states, gaining only Abdallah's support. Nuri Pasha of Iraq continued to search for face-saving formulas to provide the Palestinians with tangible evidence of Britain's goodwill.[63]

The London conference, at which the Arab rulers were not only sympathetic bystanders to the Palestine cause but active participants in its fate, was the culmination of efforts to tie

59. Minutes of the third informal meeting, March 7, 1939, FO 371/23228.

60. Comments by Suwaydi and Mahir at the last meeting, March 17, 1939, FO 371/23231.

61. The Egyptian ambassador in London, Hassan Nashat, was involved, along with Nuri al-Said and George Antonius. Proposals by Nashat to colonial secretary, March 24, 1939, and Antonius, talk with Butler (FO), March 30, FO 371/23232.

62. Porath lists six members who rejected the White Paper: al-Hajj Amin al-Husayni, Jamal al-Husayni, Fuad Saba, Dr. al-Khalidi, Izzat Darwazah, and Alfred Rock. Four wanted to cooperate with the British on the basis of the White Paper: Awni Abd al-Hadi, Ahmad Hilmi, Yaqub al-Ghusayn, and Abd al-Latif al-Salah. Yehoshua Porath, *The Palestinian Arab National Movement, 1929–1939* (London: Frank Cass, 1977), p. 292.

63. Newton (Baghdad), telegram to FO, July 18, 1939, FO 371/23238; Furlonge, pp. 126–128.

the Palestine case to wider Arab concerns and to assert its centrality to the Muslim world. The Palestinian appeals—through the al-Aqsa fund drive, the World Islamic Congress, and Bludan congress, the Defense of Palestine committees, and the Cairo Inter-Parliamentary Congress—reached political activists and the educated publics, as well as the rulers. Although the rulers' appeals in 1936 and their participation in the London conference of 1939 could not provide decisive support for the Palestinians, the Arab rulers' explicit commitment to the struggle was a significant victory for the Palestinian movement in its effort to expand its base of support and to acquire diplomatic leverage vis-à-vis the British.

7 / Diplomacy in Geneva and London

Although appeals to similar ethnic groups broadened the base of support for nationalist movements and increased their diplomatic leverage, their main efforts were necessarily directed toward the colonial ruler and, secondarily, the international community. Support from major powers, or even recognition of the movement by the international organization, could result in material and moral pressure on the colonial power. In the Middle East after World War II, Britain and the United States pressured France to withdraw from Lebanon and Syria. In the 1950s, nationalists from the Maghrib used the United Nations to advance their cause. Between World Wars I and II, however, the League of Nations was dominated by European powers who had vested interests in the colonial system. The Wilsonian concept of self-determination was applied to the Balkans after World War I, but not to the Arab provinces of the Ottoman Empire, which were placed under mandatory regimes. The Zionist movement was sanctioned by the League of Nations, but its members criticized Britain for according independence to Iraq and Egypt.

The Palestine Arab politicians quickly recognized the limitations inherent in the League, but they felt that if they did not present their case, they would appear to have failed by default. As early as 1926, the Bethlehem newspaper *Sawt al-Shaab* (Voice of the People) argued that the Arabs must send memorandums to the Permanent Mandates Commission even though they could not expect help from the League, "a mere association of imperialistic powers."[1] But the Palestinians had no direct access to the League. Although the Arab Executive sent yearly memorandums to the Permanent Mandates Commission from 1924 to 1934[2] and sent occasional representatives to Geneva,[3] it lacked the funds to send regular representatives there or to establish a permanent lobby. In any case, nongovernment lobbyists were not allowed to address the PMC or the Council of the League. Moreover, questions of fundamental principle concerning the mandatory system and the form of government in the mandated territory lay outside the purview of the PMC.[4] After the British banned the Arab Higher Committee in late 1937, the government ceased forwarding the petitions of the principal Arab leaders to the PMC for its information.

The nationalists' principal demands and efforts were directed toward the British rulers. Britain proved willing to negotiate over fundamental issues of self-rule with the political leadership of Egypt, Iraq, and Transjordan, but refused to discuss the basic issues in the terms voiced by the Palestine Arabs, namely, the legality of a policy based on the Balfour Declaration and the right of the Palestine Arabs to self-determination. Rather, Britain sought to limit discussion to such specific grievances as excessive Jewish immigration and land buying or the need to establish a legislative council.

Faced with this refusal to discuss the first premises of British policy, Palestinian politicians vacillated between insistence on raising fundamental issues and willingness to discuss particular areas of disagreement. It was never clear which

1. Quoted in *Palestine Bulletin,* May 4, 1926; see also Musa al-Alami, letter to Eastwood, received May 25, 1939, concerning a last-ditch effort to be heard by the League, CO 733/408/75872/30, pt. 1.
2. The 1924 memorandum is cited in political report, Sept. 1924, CO 733/74. The 1934 one is in ISA, Arab Documents, file 1724.
3. The first delegation stopped in Geneva in the fall of 1921; Awni Abd al-Hadi went there in 1930; and several others lobbied there in the late 1930s.
4. Chapter 2 describes the limitations on the PMC's role.

pproach—if either—would be effective. These contrasting
pproaches were articulated in the fall of 1936, when the
Arab Higher Committee was considering how to present its
views to the Royal Commission. Raghib al-Nashashibi
argued that the Arabs would only antagonize the British
commissioners if they again questioned the Balfour Declara-
ion and the mandate. He maintained that the only produc-
ive approach would be to emphasize that the Arabs sought
o cooperate with the British and that they hoped to reach an
agreement to stop immigration, prohibit land sale, and form
a national government in order to improve the Arabs' economic and political conditions.[5] The Husaynis countered
with the argument that this approach would begin a bargaining process in which the Arabs would compromise their
principles and obtain diluted results, such as a few meaningless restrictions on immigration and land sale or a legislative
council lacking real power. They felt that the Arabs must
reassert their fundamental opposition to Zionism, reaffirm
their view that Palestine was included in the area promised
independence by the McMahon-Husayn correspondence, and
point out the contradictions between British practice in Palestine and article 22 of the Covenant of the League of Nations.
They argued that Britain could still revise its policy in Palestine so that the Arabs could achieve independence.[6]

The Arab politicians' attitudes toward establishing a legislative council also reflected this ambivalence. Such a council
could be the first step toward independence, but it could also
signal Arab capitulation to the Balfour Declaration and hasten
the advent of Jewish rule. The statements of the Arab Executive's four delegations to London and their arguments before

5. This confidential strategy session was reported to the Zionists by J. F. (Joseph
Francis) in a talk with E. S. (Elias Sasson); see the latter's memo of Oct. 26, 1936,
CZA, S25/3051.

6. A third viewpoint was presented by Awni Abd al-Hadi and other Istiqlalists
who argued against the Arabs' petitioning the British and felt they should insist on
direct negotiations to obtain independence (ibid.). See also Awni Bey's letter to high
commissioner, Dec. 18, 1936, CO 733/343/75550/9A30.

British officials and commissions were similarly ambivalent. The desire for some tangible gains, even an advisory council or token land legislation, tempted the politicians, but the price of such an agreement—acquiescence to the Balfour Declaration—was always too high.

The Arabs' position was weakened in part by uncertainty about the best tactics and by their own internal fissures, but most of all by their inherently weak bargaining position vis à-vis the British. Even after violent disturbances and the active involvement of Arab rulers impelled the British toward serious modifications in their policy, imperial strategy and preparations for the imminent war against the Axis powers still dictated British actions.

The First Delegation, 1921–1922

In the opening years of British rule, the Arab Executive placed top priority on presenting its views before the British government on the assumption that the British would change their policies once they understood the reality of the Arabs' situation and demands. The British military administration had prohibited the departure of a delegation to the Paris peace conference in March 1919 and prevented the Palestinians from sending a delegation in the spring of 1920.[7] The first opportunity to present their views arose during the Cairo conference of March 1921, when the Arab Executive sent a six-man delegation to Cairo, headed by its president, Musa Kazim al-Husayni. Colonial Secretary Winston Churchill was preoccupied with British problems in Iraq and Transjordan and only received the Palestinian delegates briefly, on March 22.[8] Nevertheless, when Churchill came to Jerusalem soon after, he held a discussion with the Arab Executive and with the Zionist Commission on March 28. The Executive presented him with a memorandum that critiqued the Balfour Declaration on legal and historical grounds and detailed the moral and economic

7. Porath, *Emergence,* pp. 103, 124.
8. Political report, March 1921, CO 733/2.

angers its implementation would create. The memorandum called for the abolition of the principle of the Jewish national home, a halt to Jewish immigration and to further legislation until a national government could be formed, and the subsequent unification of Palestine with the neighboring Arab states.

Churchill replied in an equally blunt fashion, stating that he would not repudiate the Balfour Declaration. He asserted that Britain's right to rule Palestine was based on military conquest and urged the Arabs to give the Zionists a fair chance, as the British would not tolerate their "trampling down" the Arabs. Finally, he declared: "The present form of government will continue for many years, and step by step we shall develop representative institutions leading up to full self-government. All of us here to-day will have passed away from the earth and also our children and our children's children before it is fully achieved."[9]

Shocked at the total opposition between their views and those of Churchill, the Executive leaders decided to send a delegation directly to London, as Egyptian politicians had urged in March. Parliament was also scheduled to discuss the mandatory system in May. The diplomatic effort was accelerated by violence in Jaffa in early May 1921.[10] The Fourth Arab Congress resolved in early June to send a delegation that would stay in London as long as needed to reach an agreement with the government. Disagreements over membership in the delegation delayed its departure until July 19. In the end, its membership was almost identical with that of the delegation to Cairo in March.[11] Its style has been aptly described by Aaron Klieman:

9. Ibid. Klieman, pp. 127–128, comments on the meeting and, pp. 259–273, provides the complete text of the statements by the Arab Executive and Churchill.

10. See Chapter 9 and Porath, *Emergence,* pp. 137–138.

11. Ibid., pp. 137–139. The delegates were Musa Kazim Pasha, Tawfiq Hamad, Muin al-Madi, Ibrahim Shammas, Amin al-Tamimi, and Shibli Jamal (secretary). Fuad Saad, a Francophile Catholic from Haifa, was also elected, and Ruhi Abd al-Hadi was chosen as a second secretary. Neither actually accompanied the delegation because Saad protested the exclusion of Bishop Hajjar from it and Ruhi Bey accepted a government post (high commissioner, dispatch, July 2, 1921, CO 733/4).

While the Arab delegation remained extreme in its demands—
insisting upon abrogation of the Balfour pledge, an end to
Jewish immigration, and the beginning of representative government—it was moderate in terms of its approach. Sharing
fully in the need to resent and to oppose the idea of transform-
ing Palestine into a home for the Jews, the delegation saw its
role in striving through diplomacy, political pressure, and
propaganda rather than by force and bloodshed.[12]

But the initial meetings with Churchill in August 1921
merely repeated the two sides' positions and increased the
Arabs' fears on key points. Churchill, for example, proposed that the delegation talk to Weizmann in order to reach
an accommodation and to find out the plans being made to
develop Palestine's economy. Affronted by this suggestion,
secretary Shibli al-Jamal replied that the delegation had
come to talk to the government, not the Zionists.[13] Most
important, the delegation was not reassured on the question
of an eventual Jewish majority: the Colonial Office minutes
reported that on August 22, Churchill said "it would be
many years before the Jews would be in a majority in
Palestine."[14]

The delegation did, however, discuss ideas for a legislative
council with one member of the Colonial Office, Hubert
Young. But Churchill stressed that no legislative council
would be allowed to control the government or check Jewish
immigration, and its laws would have to fall within the
framework of the mandate.[15] Not surprisingly, the delega-

12. Klieman, p. 191.
13. The delegation apparently contacted the Zionist Organization and learned
that Weizmann insisted that any Arab–Zionist agreement conform to the Balfour
Declaration (ibid., p. 193); Hubert Young, memorandum to Churchill, Aug. 22,
1921, enclosing the delegation's letter to Churchill, Aug. 18, CO 733/14.
14. Minutes of Churchill-delegation talk, Aug. 22, 1921, CO 733/14. See also
Young (CO), conversation with Zionist officials (Howard Sacher and S. Landman)
as reported in the latters' minutes, Aug. 23, 1921, CZA, Z4/2512.
15. High commissioner, telegram, Aug. 21, 1921, minutes on Churchill-
delegation talk, Aug. 22, CO 733/14; Young, talk with delegation, Aug. 23, 1921,
CO 733/16.

tion rejected the council proposals in their letter to Churchill on September 1.[16]

Having reached an impasse, the delegation and the Colonial Office marked time for the next two months. Some members of the delegation traveled to Geneva in September for the session of the League's Council and for the Syro-Palestinian Congress,[17] while others attempted to develop contacts among members of Parliament. The Colonial Office wanted the delegation to return to Palestine, as Sir John Shuckburgh made clear in his conference with them on September 15.[18] But the high commissioner, Sir Herbert Samuel, did not want the delegation to return empty-handed, particularly because the potentially explosive anniversary of the Balfour Declaration was approaching on November 2.

The delegation sent a somewhat more conciliatory letter to Churchill in late October,[19] and the Colonial Office decided to capitalize upon an earlier hint from the delegation that they might meet the Zionists at the Colonial Office to hear a British policy statement, although they continued to refuse to negotiate with the Zionists.[20] An initial arrangement for Churchill to deliver such a policy statement before a joint gathering of the delegation and Weizmann on November 26 was changed at the last minute to the convening of a general discussion chaired by Shuckburgh on November 29.[21] During the two-hour meeting, Weizmann presented a conciliatory position, declaring that, through mutual goodwill, the two nations could build a prosperous and happy country, but the delegation must realize that the principles of the draft

16. Delegation, letter to Churchill, Sept. 1, 1921, CO 733/16.
17. Porath, *Emergence,* p. 117.
18. Minutes of Shuckburgh-delegation meeting, CO 733/15; Shuckburgh, minute, Oct. 2, on Samuel's telegram, Sept. 29, 1921, CO 733/6.
19. See CO 733/16 and Porath, *Emergence,* p. 142.
20. Shuckburgh, memorandum to cabinet, Nov. 1921, CO 733/15; the hints were dropped in the delegation's letter to Churchill, Aug. 18, see Young, memorandum to Churchill, Aug. 22, 1921, CO 733/14.
21. Shuckburgh, letter to delegation, Nov. 12, 1921, CO 733/16; Shuckburgh, note on Churchill's change of mind, Nov. 22, 1921, CO 733/15.

mandate were unalterable.[22] Musa Kazim al-Husayni replied that the draft was unacceptable to the Arabs because it granted special rights to the Jewish community. He asserted that a clear interpretation of the Balfour Declaration was required before further discussions could be held.[23] Weizmann agreed to discuss questions of Jewish immigration and constitutional provisions to safeguard the Arab position in Palestine, reaffirming that the Zionists did not want to dominate the Arab community, and the Arab delegates agreed to present their views on the draft constitution Shuckburgh would shortly submit to them.

Beneath this conciliatory façade, however, lay irreconcilable differences. Weizmann and Shuckburgh felt that the Arabs would acquiesce in the mandate if it were a *chose jugée*,[24] and therefore the most important task was to hasten the League's ratification of the mandate while they kept the Arab delegation dangling until its funds ran out or its constituents repudiated it.[25] The Arab delegates remained dissatisfied with the draft constitution,[26] but moderated their demands somewhat: in particular, they did not demand the immediate formation of a national government.

In February 1922, Shuckburgh again sought to break off discussions, using the excuse that the delegation might have leaked the text of the draft constitution to a pro-Arab news-

22. Reports of the meeting are in Mills, summary and comments, CO 537/855, Shuckburgh, minute, ibid., Weizmann, letter to Shuckburgh, Dec. 1, 1921, CO 733/16, and Weizmann, private letter to Chief Secretary Deedes, Dec. 13, 1921, transmitted by Deedes to Shuckburgh, Dec. 22, 1921, CO 537/854.

23. Shuckburgh attempted to interject a conciliatory position stressing that, even though the draft mandate could not be changed, another interpretation of the Balfour Declaration might reduce the uncertainty that had bred fear and hostility among the Arabs.

24. Shuckburgh, memorandum to cabinet, Nov. 1921, CO 733/15; Weizmann to Shuckburgh, Dec. 1, 1921, CO 733/16.

25. Mills, comments, CO 537/855, quoted in Klieman, pp. 196–197.

26. In a letter to Churchill, February 4, 1922, they stated that they were anxious to form a legislative assembly on a largely elective basis that would control matters vital to the public interest, such as immigration. They argued that economic absorptive capacity should not be the only principle guiding immigration policy (CO 733/36).

paper, the *Morning Post*. But strong denials by the delegation—and further urging from Samuel that the government continue discussions—led to resumed contact.[27] In the revised draft constitution of March 1, the Colonial Office proposed that an advisory immigration board be established to include Arab representatives. But the delegation rejected this proposal, too, and reiterated that the principle of the Jewish national home was unacceptable as the basis for negotiations.[28]

Samuel's concern to keep the delegation in London until the end of the religious holidays, which had touched off violence in 1920,[29] prompted Shuckburgh to write again to the delegation in early April.[30] But no further moves came until Samuel arrived in London in late May and urged Churchill to make an authoritative policy statement clarifying the meaning of the Jewish national home and announcing the establishment of a legislative council. Churchill let Samuel draft such a policy memorandum, which he then sent to both the Zionist Organization and the Arab delegation. Samuel hoped that the delegation would be reassured enough to return home and continue discussions there, even if the delegation could not formally approve the memorandum.[31] The Zionist Organization accepted the statement, realizing that their rejection might jeopardize the promulgation of the mandate.

The statement, known as the Churchill White Paper, reaffirmed the Balfour Declaration but asserted that the Arab community would not be subordinated to the Jewish com-

27. Shuckburgh, minute, Feb. 7, 1922, CO 733/33; *Morning Post* editor to CO, Feb. 9, delegation to Churchill, Feb. 10, and CO reply, Feb. 24, in CO 733/36.

28. CO to delegation, enclosing draft constitution, March 1, 1922; delegation reply, March 16, ibid., reprinted in Cmd. 1700, *Correspondence with the Palestine Arab Delegation and the Zionist Organization* (London: HMSO, 1922).

29. Shuckburgh, minute, April 1, 1922, CO 733/36.

30. Shuckburgh to delegation, April 11, 1922, in Cmd. 1700.

31. Samuel, memorandum to Shuckburgh, May 18, 1922, CO 733/34; Churchill's agreement to the memorandum, May 27; the memorandum was sent by Shuckburgh to Weizmann May 27 and handed by Samuel to the delegation May 30. The delegation's refusal arrived on June 17, the ZO's acceptance on June 18 (Cmd. 1700).

munity. It laid down the principle of economic absorptive capacity to regulate immigration, emphasized that the Zionist Executive would have only an advisory role vis-à-vis the Palestine government, and proposed that the legislative council should regulate immigration in consultation with the British administration. On paper these were substantial modifications of British policy, but they did not preclude an eventual Jewish majority and they offered the Arabs no levers of power by which to prevent that eventuality.[32] Some members of the delegation—in particular Muin al-Madi, Ibrahim Shammas, and Shibli al-Jamal—wanted to accept the legislative council,[33] but the majority rejected the White Paper, partly on principle, partly because of pressure from supporters in Palestine, and partly from their hope for a more drastic change in British policy if a new government came to power in London.

Despite its failure to obtain an agreement, the delegation had made inroads into British policy. The Jewish national home had been defined, the government had substituted an elected legislative council for a nominated one,[34] and the possibility of the Arabs advising the government on immigration policy had been introduced. Most encouraging to the delegation, the House of Lords had just rejected the draft mandate as incompatible with British pledges to the Palestinians and opposed to the wishes of the majority of the population. These were no mean achievements, and they encouraged the Arab politicians to believe that further diplomatic efforts and stronger political arguments could win them even more significant concessions.

32. Cmd. 1700; Hurewitz, *Struggle*, p. 22. An additional point of contention between the British and the delegation continued to be whether Palestine was included in the area promised independence by the McMahon-Husayn correspondence.

33. Porath, *Emergence*, pp. 145–146.

34. Young, minute on talk with Sulayman Nasif, London, Aug. 7, 1922, CO 733/35.

The Delegations of 1922–1923

The dispatch of a second delegation, only three months later, was prompted by the opening of Turkish-Allied negotiations in Lausanne. Although the delegation failed to influence these talks, the delegates traveled on to London in late December. They hoped that the new Conservative government would repudiate Churchill's policy toward Palestine, since several Conservative members of Parliament had strongly criticized Churchill's policy while they were in opposition. But the new colonial secretary stressed to the three delegates—Musa Kazim Pasha, Amin al-Tamimi, and Shibli Jamal—that this policy would not be altered.[35] The government even rejected Samuel's suggestion that the delegation be invited to join in announcing the legislative council elections scheduled for February for fear that the delegation would only denounce the elections and strengthen the boycott effort.[36] Despite the impasse, the delegation won a few results in Parliament and the press. The publication of excerpts from the McMahon-Husayn correspondence by the *Daily Mail* strengthened the Arabs' case and prompted the House of Lords to pass a second motion criticizing the draft mandate.

The Arab boycott of the legislative council elections also achieved results that summer, when the government formed a special Cabinet Committee on Palestine, whose decisions were approved by the cabinet on July 31. The military services, Foreign Office, India Office, and Colonial Office all submitted their views concerning the political and strategic importance of Palestine and the policy alternatives that would meet the conflicting pressures on Britain from the Zionists and Arabs.

35. Minutes of meeting between the delegation and the duke of Devonshire, Jan. 11, 1923, CO 733/54. Porath, *Emergence,* p. 168, gives as the main reasons for adhering to the policy "the convenience of continuing a policy which had already been formulated and the recognition that the Balfour Declaration was an explicit commitment which had received international approval, and which could not be abandoned without risking a loss to Britain's prestige and status as a world power."
36. Samuel, telegram to CO, Jan. 27, 1923, and minutes, CO 733/41.

In the end, the only concrete proposal was to form an Arab Agency, whose members would be appointed by the high commissioner. This agency would advise the local British administration in a fashion similar to the Zionist Executive, but would lack any formal status in the mandate instrument.[37]

Before this proposal was outlined, the Arab Executive had decided to send a third delegation to London. This decision was prompted by the establishment of the cabinet committee and by the renewal of British-Hijazi negotiations in London. Musa Kazim Pasha and Amin al-Tamimi were joined on the delegation by the Maronite lawyer Wadi al-Bustani. They arrived on June 22, but neither they nor the Zionist Organization were allowed to present their views before the cabinet committee. Instead, they had to submit them in writing. Samuel felt that this delegation was more hard-line than the previous ones and urged the government to keep it at arms length.[38] Thus the delegation was not even informed that it could not address the committee until August 1, the day after the cabinet approved the committee's recommendations. And these recommendations were never conveyed to the delegation.[39] Nor was the delegation ever able to arrange an interview with the colonial secretary to air its grievances.[40] The government easily outmaneuvered the Arab delegation, and it had hardly returned home before the mandate came into force in late September. All hopes of altering its terms were dashed.

37. Cabinet committee report, CO 733/58.
38. Shuckburgh, minute, July 16, 1923, CO 733/54.
39. Delegation, letters to Devonshire, July 24, 30, 1923, CO replies, July 28, Aug. 1, CO 733/58.
40. The delegation returned to Palestine in mid-September, after issuing critical statements to the press and sending a long memorandum to the prime minister. They rejected the Arab Executive's proposal that they visit America during the fall to build up support among emigrant Arab communities and then spend the winter in London. See delegation, letter to CO, Aug. 22, 1923, reply, Aug. 28, CO 733/58, and in ISA, Arab Documents, file 1541; press statement, Aug. 15, 1923, in al-Kayyali, ed. *Wathaiq*, pp. 75–77, and ISA, Arab Documents, file 2425; delegation, telegram to Jamal al-Husayni (Jerusalem), July 24, 1923, ISA, Arab Documents, file 2480; delegation, memorandum to prime minister, CO 733/59; political report, Aug. 1923, CO 733/49; Arab Executive, telegram to delegation, Sept. 3, 1923, reply, Sept. 9, ISA, Arab Documents, file 1541; political report, Sept. 1923, CO 733/50.

The rest of the 1920s witnessed a hiatus in diplomatic efforts. The attempt to obtain a fundamental revision in British policy had failed, Arab politicians were divided over the appropriate means to attain their national objectives, and fears of an eventual Jewish majority were somewhat reduced. But the conflict over the Wailing Wall that burst in August 1929 brought their fears to the fore again.

The Delegation of 1930

Violence over the Wailing Wall made the Arab Executive leaders concerned that their efforts to persuade the British government to make a second attempt to establish a legislative council might not succeed because of the Zionist leaders' increasing opposition to forming any such council. They were also becoming aware of the extent to which important economic resources had been permanently alienated to the Jewish community. Their decision to send another delegation to London to present their case was supported by the high commissioner, Sir John Chancellor, who felt that such a delegation could serve as a safety valve for the Arabs and emphasize to London the seriousness of their grievances.

The delegation was preceded by an exploratory trip of Jamal al-Husayni, who discussed the idea of a legislative council with the colonial secretary, Lord Passfield, on November 19, 1929.[41] Jamal Effendi returned to Palestine optimistic about the possibility of negotiations.

The fourth delegation, which arrived in March, was composed of six of the most authoritative spokesmen for the principal political factions that had reunited at the seventh

41. Al-Hajj Amin sent Jamal Effendi on behalf of the Supreme Muslim Council to discuss plans for a special commission to examine the Wailing Wall issue. He also published an article in the *Daily Mail* and distributed a printed pamphlet on the Arab case to members of Parliament. Jamal Effendi, letter to Lord Passfield, Nov. 14, 1929, A. Edgcumbe (private secretary), reply, Nov. 21; minutes of Jamal Effendi-Passfield talk, Nov. 19; Arabic press summary, Dec. 20, police appreciation summaries, Nov. 2, 16, 23, 1929, CO 733/178/67500; pamphlet, minutes, CO detailed rebuttal in ibid.; *Daily Mail,* Nov. 22, 1929; interview with Jamal Effendi, Beirut, May 8, 1971.

congress, held in 1928: Musa Kazim al-Husayni (by then eighty-two years old), Jamal al-Husayni, al-Hajj Amin al-Husayni, Raghib al-Nashashibi, Awni Abd al-Hadi, and Alfred Rock. Al-Hajj Amin tried to wrest the presidency of the delegation from his relative Musa Kazim Pasha. When he failed, he sought to withdraw entirely from the delegation, on the excuse that he had to remain in Palestine to prepare the Muslim case before the international Wailing Wall Commission.[42] But the Arab Executive insisted that al-Hajj Amin participate so that he could not disrupt any agreement or cause trouble for them back at home.

After two sessions with the prime minister and discussions with the Colonial Office, the delegation found little common ground with the British. They left abruptly in mid-May 1930, after less than two months' presence. The all-inclusive membership of the delegation may have been a factor in its failure: the members could agree on the maximum demands, but internal rivalries precluded their modifying these in light of British objections. The delegation as a whole, for example, reiterated the demand for a national Palestinian government with British technical advisers, whereas Jamal al-Husayni, in his private discussion in December, had been receptive to the idea of a legislative council that would include government officials as well as elected representatives and would not wield ultimate authority.

The delegation also demanded an end to Jewish immigration until the national government had been formed, an immediate increase in Arab participation in the higher civil service, the stoppage of land sales from Arabs to Jews, and the reestablishment of an agricultural bank. There was some room for discussion of the economic issues. The British offered to investigate the land situation, to obtain technical advice on the feasibility of an agricultural bank, and to promulgate interim legislation that would safeguard cultivators'

---

42. Porath, *Emergence*, p. 271, and *Palestinian Movement*, p. 110.

interests. The delegation did not oppose these inquiries, but argued that previous investigations had always concluded that the government's support of Zionism was at the root of Palestine's difficulties. Moreover, a recent study had indicated that there was no more land available for immigrants. The delegation therefore maintained that the government was merely delaying action by sending further experts. The delegation issued an angry cable upon its departure: "Whereas we are convinced that continuation in usurping our rights in favour of Zionist policy means our extirpation as nation and consequent disappearance from our country and [the] question for us is one of life or death we believe our people will fight this policy with all non-violent means."[43]

In fact, Britain was under severe pressure from the Zionist leaders not to pass any restrictive land legislation. Despite the government's desire to delay such legislation, it sent Sir John Hope Simpson to Palestine that summer to undertake a hasty survey of the land problem. He found that serious landlessness was attributable as much to the usurious rural credit system and consequent indebtedness as to the Zionists' land buying. The latter, however, was more visible and had greater political repercussions.[44]

The cumulative effect of these commissions, the Arab diplomatic efforts, and the British policy reassessment was seen in the White Paper of October 1930, which stated that Britain had a dual obligation to both the Arab and Jewish communities.[45] This was an important change in emphasis from the 1922 White Paper that gave priority to Jewish interests. The

43. Delegation, telegram to Arab Executive, May 12, 1930, quoted in high commissioner, telegram to CO, May 14, 1930, CO 733/187/77105 (also quoted in Kayyali, ed., *Wathaiq*, pp. 172–173); CO, notes on the discussions with the delegation, CO 733/185/77072 pt. 3; high commissioner, telegrams, May 10, 14, and dispatch, April 5, 1930, CO 733/187/77105.

44. Great Britain. Parliamentary Papers, Cmd. 3692, *Report on Immigration, Land Settlement and Development by Sir John Hope Simpson . . .* (London: HMSO, 1930). For a scathing criticism of Hope Simpson and the high commissioner, see Pinhas Ofer, "The Role of the High Commissioner in British Policy in Palestine: Sir John Chancellor, 1928–1931" (Ph.D. dissertation, University of London, 1971).

45. Cmd. 3692.

White Paper of 1930 concluded that, because the establishment of a Jewish national home must not harm the non-Jewish population, restrictions must now be made on immigration and land sale and that a legislative council must be introduced in due course to satisfy the legitimate aspirations of the Arab community.

Although Arab politicians doubted that the British would actually implement any of these recommendations, they privately welcomed the Passfield White Paper, even though they could not support in public any policy based on the Balfour Declaration. Jamal al-Husayni returned to London in late 1930, in part to determine whether the British would stick by the White Paper despite the storm of protest that had broken out among the Zionists and their parliamentary supporters. The government was already involved in secret discussions with Zionist leaders to modify the terms of the White Paper, but the Colonial Office reassured Jamal Effendi that the government would stand firm. He returned to Palestine in a hopeful frame of mind.[46]

The "black letter" of February 1931, delivered by the prime minister to Weizmann, therefore had a particularly devasting effect on Arab political attitudes. It negated the economic and immigration restrictions outlined in the White Paper and confirmed all the 1930 delegation's fears that the "Arab case will not justly be solved by British Government influenced by Zionists."[47] The recent commissions seemed merely devices to postpone action, and the government had proved incapable of resisting Zionist pressure on the key issues of immigration and racial exclusiveness.

One of the few political cards remaining in the Arabs' hands was noncooperation. To protest the "black letter," the

46. Jamal Effendi also talked to the Indian Muslim delegates to the India Round Table Conference and repeated Muslim arguments concerning the Wailing Wall to the CO; Shuckburgh, note to T. D. Shiels, Dec. 15, 1930; Shuckburgh to Chancellor, Jan. 8, 1931, and Chancellor, reply, Jan. 16, and minutes, CO 733/178/67500.

47. Delegation, telegram to Arab Executive, May 12, 1930, quoted in high commissioner, telegram to CO, May 14, 1930, CO 733/187/77105.

Arab Executive boycotted the investigations by the new director of development, who was appointed under its aegis.[48] By late 1932, Arabs resigned from government advisory committees and in 1933, Arab politicians boycotted both the visiting colonial secretary and the commission sent to investigate the October 1933 demonstrations.[49]

Since few Arab political leaders ever traveled to London, the policy of noncooperation drastically reduced their contact with the British authorities.[50] The Arab Executive had planned to establish a permanent bureau in London, but it never raised enough funds to support the project and had to depend on sporadic missions and the efforts of sympathetic organizations and individuals in Britain.[51] Only in 1935 did Alfred Rock, a leading citrus merchant in Jaffa and a member of the new Palestine Arab party, attempt to establish an Arab Center in London.[52] It was initially staffed by British citizens who had served as officials, missionaries, or teachers in Palestine.[53]

The parliamentary debates of early 1936 made clear the extent that British public opinion was ignorant of Arab attitudes and problems and influenced only by the Zionist per-

48. Arabic press report quoted *al-Hayat,* Aug. 18 on the Arab Executive's decision to boycott the development director, Aug. 16, 1931, CO 733/ 211/87402, also in Kayyali, ed., *Wathaiq,* p. 236. Chancellor, telegram, Aug. 19, 1931, CO 733/ 209/87353. The Arab Executive had also considered boycotting the Shaw Commission of 1929 because of its restricted terms of reference; Margaret Farquaharson (National Political League, London), letters to Jamal al-Husayni, Sept. 24, Oct. 3, 1929, Arab Executive, letter to the chairman of the commission, Oct. 3, 1929, ISA, Arab Documents, file 3505.

49. The Arab Executive voted no confidence in the Murison Commission of Inquiry on November 17 and declared a boycott on December 7. Twenty-seven Arabs gave evidence before the commission, but only one was not connected with the government or security forces (commission, report, Jan. 1934, CO 733/239/ 17356/4).

50. See high commissioner to O. G. R. Williams (CO), Oct. 19, 1933, accompanying a letter of introduction for Awni Abd al-Hadi to the CO, CO 733/239/17356.

51. Early plans for a bureau were made in 1923, see political report, May 1923, CO 733/46, and political report, June 1923, CO 733/47.

52. Hurewitz, *Struggle,* p. 85; "Who's Who" at the London Conference, 1939, FO 371/23227.

53. The center was headed by Colonel S. F. Newcombe.

spective. The Arab party leaders agreed to the high commissioner's proposal to send an all-party delegation to London to present their case for the establishment of a legislative council. The British cabinet shared the high commissioner's hope that this delegation would serve as a safety valve and prevent, or at least delay, a violent explosion.[54] But the cabinet admitted it could do little to accommodate the Arabs.

The heads of the Arab political parties could not agree among themselves on the composition of the delegation, even after three weeks of bargaining.[55] In any event, the start of the general strike made it impolitic to leave for London, as the party heads informed the high commissioner on April 22.[56] Almost no Arab representatives were in London during the strike. Two minor politicians tried to present their case before the Colonial Office and press,[57] and Jamal al-Husayni and Izzat Tannus also came to London in the summer of 1936 and the spring of 1937.[58] Although they planned to remain in London through the summer to lobby for acceptance of the anticipated Royal Commission report if it came up with an

54. High commissioner, telegram, March 28, 1936, proposed sending a delegation, CO 733/293/75102; cabinet approval, April 1, in CAB 25 and CO 733/307/75438/1; colonial secretary expressed skepticism in dispatch to high commissioner, March 31, reply, April 1, ibid.; Williams (CO), memorandum, April 24, on the points that the delegation might raise, CO 733/297/75156.

55. Some wanted the party heads to constitute the delegates, even though the parties headed by Jamal al-Husayni and Awni Abd al-Hadi had not accepted the legislative council proposal. Jamal Effendi preferred retaining the 1930 delegation's structure, with Dr. Husayn Fakhri al-Khalidi substituted for the late Musa Kazim Pasha (high commissioner, dispatch, April 28, 1936, CO 733/307/75438/1; intelligence report, April 18, 1936, in high commissioner, dispatch, April 26, CO 733/310/75528).

56. Enclosed in high commissioner, dispatch, April 28, 1936, CO 733/307/75438/1.

57. Shibli Jamal (Reform party) and Emile al-Ghuri (Palestine Arab party). Notes on their talk with Archer Cust, June 28, 1936, CO 733/302/75288; and Ghuri's discussion with Williams (CO), Sept. 9, 1936, CO 733/297/75156, pt. 5.

58. The Arab Higher Committee had decided to sponsor a delegation, but each member had to provide his own funds. The Palestine Arab party financed Jamal Effendi and Tannus (high commissioner, telegram, April 6, 1937, CO 733/340/75438).

acceptable partition plan,[59] they had to hasten home in July when the report proved unacceptable.

After October 1937, the Arab Higher Committee was banned in Palestine and its members were denied admittance to England.[60] But Tannus returned to London in November to head the Arab Center, which published several pamphlets denouncing British military actions in Palestine and issued statements to the press to counter government pronouncements.[61] These efforts had no discernible impact on British public opinion.

Within Palestine, Arab politicians had boycotted most of the hearings of the Royal Commission.[62] They also boycotted the Woodhead Partition Commission in 1938, whose investigations were based on the recommendations of the Royal Commission. The outlawing of the Arab Higher Committee had ended direct contact with the British authorities in Jerusalem, and the subsequent rebellion made bargaining over the details of British policy irrelevant. The most fundamental issues had to be placed on the table for negotiations, and yet the outlawing of the Arab Higher Committee, the flight of al-Hajj Amin to Lebanon, and the countrywide revolt made all sides more intractable and created a virtually unbridgeable gulf between the Arab and Zionist positions.

59. Chief secretary to Cosmo Parkinson (CO), July 8, 1937, enclosing intercepted letter from Jamal al-Husayni (London) to al-Hajj Amin al-Husayni (Jerusalem), late June, CO 733/351/75718/3.

60. Abd al-Latif Salah managed to enter England, remaining unnoticed until he requested an interview with the prime minister in September 1938 (Salah to prime minister, Sept. 26, 1938, CO 733/372/75156/94). See also correspondence between Newcombe (Arab Center) and CO on admitting Tannus (permitted) and Awni Abd al-Hadi (forbidden), Nov. 1937, CO 733/355/75744; correspondence between various British consuls and CO on admitting other Arab Higher Committee members, 1938, CO 733/383/75744.

61. Frances Newton, *Punitive Measures in Palestine* and *Searchlight on Palestine,* for example.

62. The testimony of several Arab Higher Committee members is presented in Kayyali, ed., *Wathaiq,* pp. 463–599.

The London Conference

When the Woodhead Commission concluded that no partition plan was feasible, Britain had to admit that neither the mandate nor the surgical partition were tenable arrangements. The devastating implications of this realization were obscured by the government's decision to convene a conference that would resolve the issue of the future status of Palestine. The conference would include representatives of the Jewish Agency, five independent Arab states, and the Palestine Arabs. The Palestinian politicians refused to sit at the same conference table as the Jewish Agency representatives because this would confer legitimacy upon them. Many of the Zionist leaders, in turn, objected to sitting with Arabs who had headed the rebellion.[63]

The Palestine Arab delegates were selected by the outlawed Arab Higher Committee. After a vigorous campaign by Fakhri al-Nashashibi to have members of the National Defense party included in the delegation—his efforts being supported by both the British and Nuri al-Said of Iraq—al-Hajj Amin permitted that party to provide two members of the Palestinian delegation.[64] The British government maintained its ban on al-Hajj Amin, although other members of the Arab Higher Committee were permitted to come to London. Al-Hajj Amin circumvented the ban by issuing a resolution that, although he was head of the delegation, he would "voluntarily" remain in Beirut and authorize Jamal al-Husayni to preside. Jamal Effendi was joined by Awni Abd al-Hadi, Musa al-Alami, George Antonius, Husayn Fakhri al-Khalidi, Alfred Rock, Amin al-Tamimi, and the two leaders of the National Defense party, Raghib al-

---

63. Hurewitz, *Struggle*, p. 96.
64. See colonial secretary, talks with the Palestine Arab delegation, Feb. 2, 1939, and with National Defense party members, Feb. 6, FO 371/23223; Hurewitz, *Struggle*, pp. 97–98; correspondence between Lampson (Cairo) and FO and between high commissioner and CO over the issue, CO 733/406/75872/11.

Nashashibi and Yaqub al-Farraj. Yaqub al-Ghusayn and Fuad Saba served as secretaries.[65]

Presenting the Arab consensus at the second meeting between the British and Arab delegates, Jamal al-Husayni argued that it "is the case of a population, who are by nature peaceful and hospitable, trying to preserve the integrity of their country and to prevent the land to which they are deeply attached from being forcibly converted into a national home for another people."[66] He reiterated the national demands: independence, abrogation of the mandate and the Balfour Declaration, conclusion of a treaty between Britain and the sovereign Arab state of Palestine, and an end to all Jewish immigration and the sale of land to Jews. He concluded: "The Arabs are prepared to negotiate, in a conciliatory spirit, the conditions upon which reasonable British interests shall be safeguarded; to approve the necessary guarantees for the preservation of, and right of access to, all Holy Places, and for the protection of all legitimate rights of the Jewish and other minorities in Palestine."

The demands were far beyond anything that the British could grant the Arabs of Palestine, but they were not in excess of what other Arab states had obtained from the British. In fact, throughout the conference the Arab delegates tried to win the colonial secretary's support for the principle of an *Arab* state in which minority rights would be accorded to the Jewish community.[67] But he would commit himself only to the idea of an independent *Palestine* state and to the

65. Members who did not go, in addition to al-Hajj Amin, were Ahmad Hilmi and Izzat Darwazah. Abd al-Latif Salah was already in London but declined to participate in the conference. See Salah, letters to colonial secretary, Jan. 29, Feb. 5, 1939, reply by Harry C. Luke (CO), Feb. 10, CO 733/406/75872/11; interview with Darwazah, Damascus, May 14, 1971; Porath, *Palestinian Movement,* pp. 282–283.

66. Minutes of second session, Feb. 9, 1939, FO 371/23223.

67. See statements by Raghib al-Nashashibi, Jamal al-Husayni, and colonial secretary, in minutes of eighth session, Feb. 18, 1939, FO 371/23224; also informal discussion between British and Arab states' delegates, Feb. 17, 1939, FO 371/23225.

general assurance that the British would neither agree to a Jewish state nor continue the mandate indefinitely.[68]

Nevertheless, the Palestine Arabs did win important concessions. In the initial discussions, the colonial secretary proposed that a round table conference be convened the next autumn, adding delegates from the United States, the Council of the League of Nations, and the British Opposition party to the present delegations. This conference would frame a constitution, and the conference would be followed by an approximately ten-year transition period. Britain alone would decide on the termination of that transition, although Arab and Jewish representatives would be consulted.[69] After a month's debate, the colonial secretary began to modify this idea and to outline constitutional alternatives.[70] Jamal al-Husayni expressed a preference for a unitary state with a one-chamber legislature based on proportional representation, that is, one Jew to two Arabs. An ordinary majority would suffice for most bills, but a majority of both Arab and Jewish delegates would be required for special issues, even though he realized that this might cause deadlocks on certain points. Although the final White Paper did not outline a constitution, it did specify that Palestinians would be put in charge of government departments when peace was restored and that, after five years, a body representing the Palestinian people and the British government would review the constitutional arrangements and recommend the form of an independent state. Moreover, the British agreed to place a time limit on the transition period, specifying ten years.[71]

68. Minutes of seventh session, Feb. 16, 1939, FO 371/23224; and see Chapter 6.
69. British meeting with Arab states' delegates, Feb. 19, 1939, FO 371/23225; Jamal Effendi's objections, minutes of twelfth session, March 1, 1939, FO 371/23226.
70. Minutes of first session of committee on policy, March 2, 1939, and minutes of second session, March 4, 1939, FO 371/23227.
71. Minutes of third (March 6) and fourth (March 7) sessions of committee on policy, ibid. The ten-year time limit was qualified by a clause stating that, if it appeared to the British government that independence should be postponed, the Palestine people, the League Council, and neighboring Arab states would be invited to cooperate in framing further plans.

Important modifications were also made concerning immigration policy. At first, the colonial secretary maintained that, after the Jewish community reached 35–40 percent of the total population during the next decade, Britain itself would decide if immigration should continue, merely consulting the Arab and Jewish representatives.[72] In contrast, the draft presented on March 15 gave the last word on the subject to the Palestine Arabs, after an initial seventy-five thousand immigrants would arrive during the next five years.[73] The colonial secretary commented, "Hitherto the Arabs of Palestine had feared the indefinite continuance of immigration which might lead eventually to a Jewish majority. It would now rest with them to decide whether the Jewish population of Palestine" should exceed one-third of the total population. He felt that this limitation would serve as an incentive for the Jewish community to cooperate with the Arabs and suggested that they might modify their *avodah ivrit* policy in return for receiving immigration permits.[74] Although the Arab delegates objected to such a large quota for the initial five years, the arrangement went a long way toward meeting their demands.

One interesting sidelight of the conference was the special Arab-British committee that examined the McMahon-Husayn correspondence. Its final report, which was adopted by the conferees,[75] clarified the controversy and published the authoritative texts for the first time, but failed to reach an agreement over the issue of whether Palestine was included or excluded from the area promised independence.

The London conference was the culmination of Arab efforts to negotiate with Britain. Their negotiating stance had changed little over the two decades; their demands remained out of all proportion to the movement's strength. The Arabs challenged the basic premise of British policy—the legitimacy

72. British meeting with Arab states' delegates, Feb. 19, 1939, FO 371/23225.
73. Minutes of thirteenth session, March 15, 1939, FO 371/23230.
74. Minutes of fourteenth (last) session, March 17, 1939, FO 371/23231.
75. Ibid.

of the Balfour Declaration. No British government was willing to abrogate this policy, although it might reinterpret and modify aspects of the application of the Balfour Declaration. As long as there were no international pressures on Britain to modify this policy and as long as Britain was not challenged militarily in the Middle East, the government could adhere to its position despite the inherent contradictions. But after Palestine exploded into rebellion in the late 1930s, forcing Britain to divert troops to that territory at the very time that Britain's position in Europe and the eastern Mediterranean appeared less secure and the danger of a European war loomed, the government sought to resolve the contradictions, uncertain whether to impose partition or to attempt to establish a unitary, binational state. Meanwhile, Arab demands and Zionist counterdemands hardened and the possibility of accepting interim measures, such as a legislative council, vanished. The 1939 White Paper was issued under the shadow of imminent world war, but Britain probably could not have enforced its terms over the opposition of the Jewish community and with only partial and grudging acquiescence by the Palestine Arabs.

8 / Proposals for a
Legislative Council

Nationalist movements had to face the fundamental question of whether to accept offers of a limited constitutional role presented by the colonial power. In some colonies, such an offer could be a first step toward independence, even if the proffered legislative council contained a majority of official members.[1] In settler colonies, however, a council could be a step toward submergence and a further consolidation of the European settlers' power. Acceptance by the indigenous nationalist movement would tacitly legitimize the presence of these settlers and the colonial power's policy of encouraging European settlement. As the Europeans' numbers grew, so would their role in the council. Furthermore, when the council had only an advisory role, the members could not alter government policies, even those directly inimical to their interests.

This problem arose in Palestine after the British dismantled the Ottoman institutions that had allowed the Arab elite an influential role and tried to frame their own organs. These plans necessarily rested on the mandate, which included the Balfour Declaration. By accepting British institutions, the Arab politicians would automatically accept the declaration, which was anathema to them. But, by rejecting them, they would appear recalcitrant and might lose an opportunity to influence policy making within Palestine.

1. William Ivor Jennings, *The Approach to Self-Government* (Cambridge: Cambridge University Press, 1956).

Election Boycott

The first Arab delegation to London discussed the idea of a legislative council with the Colonial Office in early 1922. The British proposed a body with twelve elected members and eleven government officials. The eleven elected members would be apportioned among eight Muslims, two Christians, and two Jews. A special committee on immigration, chaired by the chief secretary, would comprise the elected members of the council, but could only offer advice to the government.

The Arab Executive argued that the ten Arab members of the council would be outnumbered by the combined votes of the government officials and the Jewish representatives, who, they felt, would vote together on major issues concerning the Jewish national home. One proclamation asserted:

> This Legislative Council [is] a means by which the [Arab] nation will execute [its own] death sentence. . . . By accepting it there will be clear proof of its acceptance of the Mandate and of the present Zionist policy. . . . This council has not the powers of Legislative Councils, but rather it is fettered with the wish of the High Commissioner who executes whatever he wishes of its decisions and neglects whatever he wishes. It has not the power of supervision over the Government.[2]

The Arab Executive also felt that the immigration committee, lacking executive powers, would "have nothing to do but to agree to the number of immigrants who shall enter the country in order to destroy its people nationally and economically."[3]

During this period, the League of Nations still had not ratified the mandate, and the Arab Executive hoped to alter its terms. Accepting a legislative council at such a time would appear an act of capitulation, especially since the council

2. Proclamation signed by Jamal al-Husayni, secretary, Arab Executive, Feb. 3, 1923, enclosed in political report, Feb. 1923, CO 733/43.
3. Proclamation published in *al-Sabah*, Sept. 1, 1922, enclosed in political report, Sept. 1922, CO 733/26.

could not discuss proposals that ran counter to the Jewish national home policy, the very policy that the Arab delegations were trying to alter. The Executive sought to prove by a nonviolent boycott of the elections for the legislative council that Arab opposition to the mandatory system was serious and to persuade London to eliminate the special prerogatives accorded to the Zionist movement. The initial decision to boycott the two-tiered elections was made by the Executive on August 31, 1922, and another call was issued on February 3, 1923, when the government announced the dates for the election of secondary electors.

For a short time in early February some prominent politicians considered running for office, but they were dissuaded by the risk of being labeled as traitors and losing their influence.[4] Sulayman Nasif, an Anglophile member of the advisory council, and some other notables tried to persuade the high commissioner to modify the terms of the legislative council to accord the Arabs a majority vote and to limit Jewish immigration to a maximum of five to six thousand yearly.[5] But the high commissioner, Sir Herbert Samuel, was unwilling to alter the constitutional arrangements on the eve of the elections and merely proposed that Nasif use his suggestions as the basis for his election platform and, once elected, lobby to alter the system. Since Samuel had already indicated that he totally opposed most of their proposals, the politicians felt that it was useless to contest the elections.

The boycott effort relied on a variety of social pressures, organized through the religious institutions and political clubs, and exerted by vigorous propaganda, pamphlets, and newspaper editorials. Assemblies were held in every district, usually in mosques, at which participants would take oaths to

4. Samaria district governor, report, noting the attitudes of such moderates as Sulayman Tuqan of Nablus; political report, March 1923, CO 733/44.
5. Nasif was joined by Kamil al-Dajani (Jaffa), Tamimi (Nablus), Muin al-Madi (Haifa), and others. For details of their proposals see high commissioner to CO, Feb. 11, 15, 1923, CO 733/42, and high commissioner, minute on his discussion with them, Feb. 16, 1923, ISA, Chief Secretary's Papers, POL/452, 2/242.

boycott the elections.[6] *Imams* and *khatibs* (preachers) also lectured their Friday congregations on the importance of unity and perseverance and threatened voters with excommunication. Village *mukhtars* (headmen) pledged that their villages would support the boycott. During the elections, Arab Executive spokesmen urged potential candidates to step down, and poll watchers tried to persuade prospective voters not to submit their ballots. After the elections concluded, effective pressure was placed on the few secondary electors to withdraw their candidacy before the final stage of elections could be held.

Shaykh Abd al-Qadir al-Muzaffar, a member of the Arab Executive and the delegation to the Hijaz, was a principal speaker and organizer, orating at al-Aqsa mosque in Jerusalem as well as at assemblies sponsored by the Muslim-Christian societies. His style blended religious and political themes:

> Today will the East from one end to the other pride itself in you and boast of your unity . . . and of your heroic defence of the Holy Cause. In your unanimity to boycott the elections . . . lies the greatest proof of your capability of freedom which you claim and of independence for which you strive. Today will the Muslims and Christians in the four corners of the world boast of the Palestine Arabs who have excellently performed the guardianship of the Holy Places and stood like a lion in the face of those who covet their country.[7]

Only in one instance did the government find enough evidence of coercion to prosecute the boycotters. The heads of the Nablus Muslim-Christian Society and four village leaders were charged with intimidating a nearby village after a candidate had been nominated from that village. Only one person

6. Porath, *Emergence,* pp. 149 and 153.
7. Proclamation, March 12, 1923, published in *al-Sabah,* enclosed in political report, March 1923, CO 733/44. See also proclamation by vice-president Umar al-Bitar, April 15, 1923, enclosed in political report, April 1923, CO 733/45; Porath, *Emergence,* p. 154.

was actually fined for coercion,[8] but members of the Zionist-funded National Muslim societies who participated in the elections were undoubtedly harassed by the boycotters: candidates from Ramlah and Gaza "disappeared" during the election and subsequently withdrew their candidacies.[9] A candidate in Hebron complained to the Zionist Commission that youths had uprooted his cauliflowers and that he lacked the funds and government support necessary to overcome the Muslim-Christian Society's opposition.[10]

Although all seventy-nine Jewish and eight Druze secondary electors had been chosen by the time the period of nomination ended in March, less than 20 percent of the Arab electors had been selected. Hasan Shukri fielded a slate in Haifa. Shaykh Asad al-Shuqayri encouraged participation in Acre. And some voting occurred in Ramlah, Tiberias, and Nazareth.[11] Elsewhere, however, the boycott was virtually complete and the Arab Executive could claim an overwhelming victory for its tactic.

The election boycott emphasized that the Arab leadership would not participate in a constitutional system based on the premises of the Balfour Declaration and that it could carry the general public along with it. This stand did not, however, entail full noncooperation with the British administration in Palestine. There was considerable ambivalence in the leadership's attitudes: many of the elite could have cooperated com-

8. Those charged from Nablus were Tawfiq Hamad, Izzat Darwazah, and Abd al-Qadir al-Yusif Abd al-Hadi (political report, March 1923, CO 733/44; high commissioner, dispatch, June 15, 1923, CO 733/46).

9. Ibrahim Abdin (Ramlah) to Dr. Nissim Malul, Feb. 17, 1923, Kamil al-Mubashir (Gaza) to Malul, Feb. 15, Eisenberg (Rehovoth), letter, Feb. 27, Kamil al-Mubashir, letter, Feb. 23, CZA, S25/518; political report, March 1923, CO 733/44; Porath, *Emergence,* p. 153.

10. Murshid Shahin (Hebron) to Malul, undated letter, CZA, S25/518.

11. Kisch to Glicken (Tiberias), March 9, 1923, CZA, S25/518; Northern District governor, report, March 10, 1923, ISA, Chief Secretary's Papers, POL/452, 2/242. Porath, *Emergence,* p. 156, provides exact numbers of those elected. Kalvarisky claimed that those Arabs elected "were mostly elected through the influence of the National Moslem Clubs and our Political Department," in a letter to the Political Department in London of the ZO, April 12, 1923, CZA, Z4/1392/II/b.

fortably with the British if the shadow of the Balfour Declaration had not intruded. Respected Arab gentlemen did participate on the advisory council from October 1920 until it was disbanded in February 1923. They maintained that they were not representing their community officially but were speaking in their individual capacities and helping to promote administrative policies beneficial to the general public. Fifty prominent Arabs also accepted invitations from the high commissioner to form a Muslim Christian Consultative Committee in August 1921. The committee was intended to discuss nonpolitical matters, such as educational policy and taxes. At the very first session, however, Samuel injected a highly political discussion concerning the form of a constitution, and virtually all the invitees boycotted the second session. The committee never convened again.

Arab Executive leaders, including Jamal al-Husayni, Shaykh al-Muzaffar, and Awni Abd al-Hadi, made an effort to differentiate between political and nonpolitical issues when they met with Samuel in February 1923 to discuss their proposal for an elected body to control education, even though this was at the height of the election boycott campaign.[12] They indicated willingness to cooperate with the government on administrative issues that were not related to the constitution and fundamental policy. In a later meeting with Samuel, the Arab Executive welcomed the holding of elections for the municipal councils, which had not taken place since the beginning of the British occupation.[13]

The election boycott caused Samuel to decide not to attempt to form the legislative council, but he also rejected the view expressed by a member of the Colonial Office that he should carry on "as a naked autocracy."[14] Instead, he decided

12. High commissioner, report on their talk Feb. 6, 1923, dispatch, Feb. 9, 1923, CO 733/42.

13. High commissioner, talk with Arab Executive, March 20, dispatch, March 28, 1923, CO 733/43.

14. Moody, minute, March 23, on high commissioner, telegram of March 21, 1923, ibid.

to reconstitute the advisory council, and he canvassed ten prominent Arabs to gain assurances that they would participate. Formal invitations were issued on May 8, and all had accepted by May 29, when he announced publicly that the council would be formed.[15] The Arab Executive had informally agreed to the plan, but their support was undermined when the high commissioner linked the council's formation to the repudiated constitution. His announcement implied that the constitution was merely suspended; he stated that the two Jewish members of the advisory council would "be nominated after consultation with the Jewish National Council and 79 Jewish secondary electors."[16] The Arab Executive, reversing its neutral stand, immediately called upon the ten Arab nominees to withdraw.[17] Despite the government's efforts to reassure the nominees that the council's status would be no different from that of the first advisory council, all but three withdrew their names.[18]

The basic position of the Arab Executive was expressed in an appeal issued by the vice-president Umar al-Bitar, asserting that the nation can "perceive the small traps put for it" and knows "that this council has been formed according to one of the clauses of the rejected constitution." Participation meant "participation in the imposition of the yoke of Zion-

15. High commissioner, telegram, April 11, 1923, reply, April 16, ibid.
16. Announcement, May 29, 1923, Great Britain, Parliamentary Papers, Cmd. 1889, *Papers Relating to the Elections for the Palestine Legislative Council* (London: HMSO, 1923).
17. Arab Executive, proclamation, May 30, 1923, enclosed in political report, May 1923, CO 733/46.
18. Only the mayor of Acre (Abd al-Fattah al-Saadi), Sulayman Nasif, and Arif al-Dajani maintained their acceptance. Those who resigned were Sulayman Tuqan, Ismail al-Husayni, Amin Abd al-Hadi, Antun Jallad, Mahmud Abu Khadra (Gaza mayor), Raghib al-Nashashibi (Jerusalem mayor), and Shaykh Frayh Abu Middayn (bedouin representative) (letter from the nominees to chief secretary, June 12, 1923, following their meeting with him on June 10, attached to political report, June 1923, CO 733/47; CO to high commissioner, June 15, 1923, CO 733/45; chief secretary, telegrams in August, CO 733/48; chief secretary, telegram, Sept. 7, 1923, CO 733/49). Kalvarisky and Kisch tried to prevent the nominees from withdrawing; see Kalvarisky to Political Department, ZO, June 11, 26, 1923, CZA, Z4/2421.

ism on the necks of the nation." The appeal concluded, "This is the last arrow in the quiver of political Zionism. . . . Success by virtue of solidarity, sacrifice and loyalty [is] at hand."[19]

The Arab Executive still hoped to alter the mandate: the third delegation had just left for London, and the House of Lords had supported Arab criticisms of the mandate. The negotiating position was undercut, however, by the cabinet committee's refusal to consider revisions in British policy and by the formal enactment of the mandate in September. Despite these actions, the Executive continued to refuse any constitution that would required the Arab community to recognize the legitimacy of the Jewish national home.

The British made one further offer. The cabinet committee proposed that an "Arab agency" be formed in order to "redress the alleged preference to the Jews, by offering similar or analogous advantages to the Arabs."[20] But the Arab agency would be a local body, not an international one; its position would not be formalized in the mandate; and it would not have the financial backing and colonizing purpose of the Jewish agency. Its members would not be freely selected by the Arab community, as the Jewish agency's members could be by their constituents, but would be chosen by the high commissioner. Although it would provide the Palestine administration with advice on immigration and administrative matters, it would be a pale reflection of the Jewish agency. Moreover, its establishment appeared to mean that the Arab community—almost 90 percent of the population—should have no greater role than the Jewish community. Above all, it clearly meant accepting the premises of the Balfour Declaration. Therefore, as Samuel admitted, the proposal surely would be rejected not only by the Arab Executive but also by those who had supported

19. Attached to political report, July 1923, CO 733/48.
20. Cabinet meeting, July 31, 1923, CAB 43(23), extract in CO 733/58.

and participated in the advisory council.[21] Musa Kazim al-Husayni summed up the Arab response:

> The Arab inhabitants of Palestine have received such proposal with great surprise. . . . [They have already rejected the legislative and advisory councils] which have a wider jurisdiction than that of the Agency. The Arab owners of the country cannot see their way to accept a proposal which tends to place them on the same footing with the alien Jews. In addition, the name of Arab Agency would make them feel they are strangers in their own country.[22]

The Arab politicians and the London government had reached an impasse. The Arabs expected that their solid rejection of these offers would finally induce the British to offer them genuine political concessions that would accord the Arabs a meaningful role in Palestine. Instead, the cabinet decided that Palestine should be ruled solely by the all-British executive and advisory councils—the "naked autocracy" proposed the previous spring.[23] The Colonial Office decided to wait until a "moderate" Arab party might arise that would accept the mandate and would itself propose a legislative council. Thus the British were unwilling to face the inherent contradictions in their Palestine policy and wishfully waited for Arab opposition to subside.

Arab Initiatives

Now that fundamental revisions in the framework of British rule were precluded, the Arab Executive had to reassess its attitude toward the issue of negotiating on fundamental issues

21. The high commissioner met with twenty-six Arab notables on October 11, 1923, to present the proposal and receive their formal rejection of it. (He had already met unofficially with them on October 5.) Some of the correspondence was published in Great Britain, Parliamentary Papers, Cmd. 1989, *Proposed Formation of an Arab Agency, Correspondence with High Commissioner for Palestine* (London: HMSO, 1923); see CO 733/50 for additional dispatches.

22. High commissioner, dispatch, Nov. 23, 1923, enclosing Musa Kazim Pasha's letter, Nov. 9, CO 733/51.

23. High commissioner, private letter to Shuckburgh (CO), Oct. 12, 1923, and colonial secretary, dispatch to high commissioner, Nov. 9, 1923, CO 733/50.

as against seeking limited concessions. The leaders admitted that the Arab community was seriously disadvantaged by the lack of institutions through which its views and needs could be expressed to the British officials. The Jewish community had regular access to these officials, but Arab contact remained ad hoc. As the fear of Jewish immigration diminished in the mid-1920s, many Arab leaders revised their attitude toward a legislative council and adopted the position that it could, after all, serve as a first step toward self-government rather than toward domination by the Zionist movement.

Sulayman Nasif revived his idea of forming a legislative council with an Arab majority but with a sufficient number of nominated members to reassure the British that it would retain a "moderate" tone.[24] More important, Jamal al-Husayni held informal discussions with Chaim Kalvarisky in late 1924 in which he proposed a two-chamber legislature, the upper house resembling that proposed in 1922 and the lower house elected by proportional representation. The upper house would have to concur on all resolutions passed by the lower house.[25]

The Arab Executive made a formal initiative in 1926. Joined by the leaders of the National party and Muin al-Madi's Village Mutual Association, the Executive opened discussions with the assistant chief secretary, Eric Mills.[26] The initial Arab memorandum asserted that the Arab community had always sought to cooperate with the Palestine government but had been prevented from doing so by the provisions of the mandate that called for the establishment of a Jewish national home. It advocated eventual replacement of the mandate by treaty relations, as had occurred in Iraq. As an interim mea-

---

24. Chief secretary, minute, on his talk with Nasif, June 1, 1924, ISA, Chief Secretary's Papers, POL/452, 2/242.

25. Kisch, report to ZO, London, Nov. 7, 1924, CZA, Z4/2421.

26. Participants included Izzat Darwazah, Rashid al-Hajj Ibrahim, Muin al-Madi, and Bulus Shihadi, with Musa Kazim Pasha and Raghib Bey kept informed of the discussions (Darwazah, I, 58, 271–281; unsigned letter to Kisch, July 23, 1926, CZA, S25/665; *Palestine Bulletin*, Aug. 13, 22, 31, Sept. 1, 6, 16, 1926). Porath, *Emergence*, pp. 245–246, adds Rafiq al-Tamimi.

sure, Palestinians would head the administration, with British advisers, and a bicameral legislature would be formed. No British officials would have seats in either house. The upper house would be divided equally between nominated members and elected delegates, and the entire lower house would be elected on the basis of proportional representation. The lower house could introduce financial bills, question the government, and regulate immigration, taking into consideration not only the economic situation but also the social, health, moral, political, and religious needs of the Arab population.

The proposal was far from acceptable to the British authorities. Mills's counterproposal reasserted the centrality of the Balfour Declaration. He accepted the idea of a lower house based on proportional representation but insisted on sharply limiting its powers. He proposed that the upper house have an equal number of officials and nominated non-officials. Palestinians might advise the British officials, but could not replace them.

The Arab politicians accepted Mills's arrangements for the upper house but were keenly disappointed at the other conditions. The new high commissioner, Lord Plumer, was unenthusiastic about Mills's discussions and wanted to delay indefinitely consideration of a legislative council. He preferred to hold elections for municipal councils before considering plans for a legislature. Plumer would not forward the Arabs' proposals to the colonial secretary, and Mills had to break off the talks in mid-August. But he hinted that negotiations might resume if the Arabs reunited their factions in a clearly representative framework.[27]

Although Mills's statement was intended to end the talks, it actually provided an important impetus toward the establishment of a broadly based Arab Executive two years later.[28]

27. Chief Secretary Symes supported Mills's efforts; see his letter to Plumer, April 1, 1928, CO 733/155/57316, and his proposal of July 1, 1925, attached to CO file by Shuckburgh, May 24, 1929, CO 733/167/67105.
28. Porath, *Emergence*, p. 246.

As soon as Plumer's successor, Sir John Chancellor, reached Palestine in December 1927, the Arab Executive submitted a long memorandum that criticized "taxation without representation."[29] According to the British minutes, Awni Abd al-Hadi urged: "The real request they now made was to enter into negotiations and by being reasonable and meeting halfway, come to some agreement. It could not be denied that they had a right to some sort of legislative powers. . . . Of those countries that had previously been a part of Turkey, Palestine was the only country without some sort of representative or legislative body."[30]

Chancellor believed that the nationalist movement should find an outlet in a constitutional forum before its drive became too strong and militant to be contained. Therefore he replied that he recognized Britain's obligation "to promote local autonomy in Palestine." But he stressed that the government had to maintain its international obligations and that it hesitated "to expose itself again to a rebuff" from the Arabs, as had happened in 1922–1923. Chancellor's cautiously positive response was not supported by the Colonial Office, which reacted anxiously to the idea of renewing constitutional discussions.[31] Chancellor and the Arab Executive were both preoccupied in the spring of 1929 with the growing tensions over the Wailing Wall, but they resumed talks on a constitution in May.

Chancellor had to balance the opposition of the Zionist leaders to a legislative council against the danger of denying the Arabs any influence over policy. He therefore proposed that the members of the council be initially appointed by the

29. Memorandum enclosed in Chancellor, dispatch to CO, Jan. 15, 1929, CO 733/167/67105.
30. Minutes of the meeting in ibid.
31. Shuckburgh, head of the Middle East Department, feared "a great fight over the question" by the Zionists and their supporters in Parliament. Undersecretary William Ormsby-Gore asserted that Palestine required "detached, impartial, firm and rather autocratic government" (minutes on Chancellor's dispatch, ibid.).

British, so as to "reassure Jewish apprehension."[32] Nonetheless it would be called a legislative council and would have an unofficial majority of one. A standing committee on immigration would be established, similar to that proposed in 1922. Both Musa Kazim al-Husayni and Raghib al-Nashashibi, with whom Chief Secretary Sir Harry Luke discussed the plan, supported these provisions. During three weeks of private talks, they drew up a tentative list of nominees, which included several of the 1923 nominees and Musa Kazim Pasha.[33] Their willingness to accept even this weak proposal arose from their growing fear of the militancy of young nationalists and the supporters of al-Hajj Amin al-Husayni. They hoped that securing a commitment to a council would strengthen their own hands, but they were uncertain whether the Arab Executive would accept the proposal and insisted that there be no premature announcement: otherwise, their opponents could force the nominees to withdraw, as they had had to withdraw from the advisory council in 1923.

Chancellor intended to discuss the legislative council proposals in London in the summer of 1929, but the August disturbances wrecked these plans and reinforced Jewish opposition to any representative institutions. London denied Chancellor's appeal to resume constitutional discussions in October 1929,[34] although the colonial secretary did broach the issue with Jamal al-Husayni on November 19.[35]

The Passfield White Paper of 1930, however, mentioned that a legislative body should be established eventually in

---

32. Chancellor to CO, June 12, 1929, ibid.; see also J. S. Beckett, minute, July 15, 1929, ibid.

33. Chancellor to Shuckburgh, June 14, 1929, enclosing Luke's aide-memoire, ibid.; Porath, *Emergence,* pp. 256–257.

34. Chancellor, dispatch, Oct. 19, 1929, CO, reply, Oct. 21, Chancellor, reply, Oct. 23, ibid.

35. Jamal Effendi proposed an elected council based on proportional representation, with the high commissioner retaining a veto over certain matters. He was willing to consider the colonial secretary's insistence that officials must also be members of the council (minutes, Nov. 19, 1929, CO 733/178/67500).

order to correct the present situation whereby the Arabs lacked "any constitutional means for putting their views on social and economic matters before the Government"[36] and to improve Jewish-Arab relations through joint participation in a legislative body. Although the proposed legislature would be identical to the one suggested in 1922, the Arab Executive did not reject the proposal. Most of the Arabic newspapers in Palestine argued that participation would be a first step toward attaining their national aims and a means to demonstrate to "the civilized world" that the Arabs could adopt a constructive and positive approach.[37]

Radicalization

This cautious acceptance was shaken by the "black letter" of February 13, 1931, which, the Arab Executive asserted, violated the promises of the White Paper "before its ink was dried on the paper"[38] and confirmed their fears that Britain would capitulate to Zionist pressure.[39] Many Arab political activists argued that any further efforts to achieve a legislative council must be made not through persuasion and willingness to compromise, but through militancy and tough bargaining from a position of strength. This stance was uppermost at the Grand National Meeting in March 1933, which supported the principle of noncooperation and the use of "every legal means" to eliminate British rule.[40]

But efforts were still being made by the elders of the Arab Executive and the new high commissioner, Sir Arthur G.

36. Cmd. 3692, *Statement of Policy . . .* (Passfield) (London: HMSO, 1930).

37. Arabic press summary for week ending Oct. 31, 1930, CO 733/182/77050; Arab Executive memorandum on the White Paper, 71 pages, prepared by Awni Abd al-Hadi, Dec. 1929, enclosed in high commissioner, dispatch, Jan. 24, 1931, CO 733/197/87050/2.

38. Protest submitted by Arab Executive, Feb. 16, 1931, enclosed in Chancellor, dispatch, Feb. 17, 1931, CO 733/197/87050/4.

39. Arab Executive, manifesto to the Arab nation, Feb. 20, 1931, enclosed in Chancellor, dispatch, Feb. 21, 1931, ibid.

40. Resolutions enclosed in chief secretary, dispatch, April 1, 1933, CO 733/239/17356/4, pt. 1.

Wauchope, to formulate an agreement on a legislative council.[41] Wauchope based his talks on the Passfield White Paper, whose constitutional formulas had been ignored in the "black paper" and therefore, he assumed, remained applicable. Wauchope informed the Permanent Mandates Commission in November 1931 that he would formulate proposals for a legislative council as soon as the new local government ordinance came into operation.[42] By then, however, the Zionist leaders rejected the idea that the Arab community should have more representatives than they had and asserted that "parity" of representation was the only acceptable formula. Although the Jewish community within Palestine (the Yishuv) constituted only 20 percent of the population, they argued that the justice of parity would be recognized if Diaspora Jewry were counted and the Yishuv's important economic role considered.[43] The Zionist leaders were aware that the British would never permit a legislative council to veto immigration or other issues vital to the Jewish national home. Thus their insistence on parity and their opposition to the White Paper's terms really stemmed from their desire to delay discussion and the establishment of representative institutions until the Yishuv attained majority status. They were also concerned to prevent the Arabs from obtaining a legitimate forum in which they could air their grievances.[44]

By the middle of 1933, the British officials in Jerusalem and London had agreed informally on the structure of a legislature. The council would have an unofficial majority, based on the proportions of seven Muslims to one Christian and

41. Wauchope initiated private discussions with Arab and Jewish leaders in February 1932; see his dispatch, Feb. 13, 1932, CO 733/215/97050/9.

42. Minutes on Wauchope-CO discussion, London, Nov. 7, 1932; cabinet permission to make this statement to PMC granted, Nov. 9, CO 733/215/97054, pt. 1.

43. See, for example, resolution of the Jewish Elected Assembly in Palestine, enclosed in Wauchope, dispatch, April 9, 1932, and his telegram, April 8, criticizing parity, CO 733/219/97105/2.

44. See, for example, commentary in *Near East and India,* Dec. 15, 1932, attached to CO 733/223/97258, pt. 2.

three Jews.[45] They waited to discuss this proposal until municipal council elections were held in 1934. Wauchope was then pressed by Arab politicians to initiate such talks. The Arabs' sense of urgency mounted as Jewish immigration soared and the Zionists' insistence on parity hardened.[46]

Wauchope held informal discussions in July 1935 with Raghib al-Nashashibi, al-Hajj Amin al-Husayni, Jamal al-Husayni, Yaqub al-Farraj, and Francis Khayyat, a Catholic judge.[47] The British proposed a council with twenty-eight members, of whom only five would be officials. Half of the twenty-three nonofficials would be elected. There would be eleven Muslims (three nominated), three Christians (two nominated), eight Jews (five nominated), and one nominee to represent commercial interests. The high commissioner would retain the power to veto bills, promulgate legislation when the council was not in session, introduce financial bills, alter customs duties, and dissolve the council.[48]

The plan was modified during the discussions to reduce the number of Jews to seven and add a second commercial representative. Wauchope also agreed that the delegates could be allowed to criticize the mandate, although he emphasized that the high commissioner would veto any bills that ran counter to the mandate's terms. The Arab leaders disagreed among

45. The colonial secretary noted that, on a strictly proportional basis, there should be nine Muslims to one Christian and two Jews. He agreed with the assessment of Musa al-Alami (Wauchope's private secretary) that the Arabs would be less suspicious of a veto by the high commissioner than of a government-Jewish bloc that could overrule Arab motions (Wauchope, discussion with Colonial Secretary Sir Philip Cunliffe-Lister, Jerusalem, April 22, 1933, and the latter's discussion with Musa al-Alami, May 1, 1933, CO 733/235/17305).

46. See statements by Weizmann, Ben Gurion, and Moshe Shertok in Wauchope dispatches, May 7, June 6, 19, 21, 22, July 25, 1935, CO 733/275/75102. Raghib al-Nashashibi criticized Wauchope for yielding to Zionist opposition; see his letter to Wauchope, Jan. 28, 1935, reply, Feb. 11, enclosed in Wauchope, dispatch, March 4, 1935, CO 733/278/75156.

47. Wauchope, dispatches, July 25, Aug. 9, 1935, CO 733/275/75102.

48. Wauchope also agreed to the Arabs' suggestion that the high commissioner should not chair the council, but that the position should be held by a former official or a British citizen from outside Palestine.

themselves over such points as the number of members to be elected or nominated and the relative weight of the Christian community on the council.[49] The Husaynis also proposed that Arabs and Jews be added to the executive council, largely because they wanted the proposal to appear to be an improvement over the one offered in 1922.

Under Wauchope's prodding, the leaders of five political parties (all except Istiqlal) formed a common front in November 1935 to discuss the legislative council proposal on a formal basis. By then, however, the political mood was becoming explosive. Jewish immigration had peaked at sixty-two thousand; land purchases soared; and economic difficulties led Histadrut to enforce *avodah ivrit* with greater determination on Jewish farms and factories. Thus the demands presented by the five party leaders in late November were more far-reaching than merely for a legislative council. They called for a democratic government, the prohibition of land transfers, and an end to Jewish immigration. But they also grasped at the opportunity to defuse the crisis by means of a legislative council, and therefore they did not reject Britain's formal offer of a legislature, made in late December 1935.[50] By March 1936, the Christian Arab caucus pub-

49. Husaynis preferred all members to be elected, whereas Raghib Bey and Farraj wanted them nominated. Wauchope commented: "Knowing his weakness among the electorate Raghib proposed that all members should be nominated. Knowing his own strength the Mufti wishes the members to be all elected" (Wauchope, dispatch, July 25, 1935, ibid.). Farraj proposed, facetiously, that the Christians should claim "parity" if the Zionists insisted on it, thus resulting in equal representation for Muslims, Christians, and Jews (Wauchope, dispatch, Aug. 9, 1935, ibid.). Fakhri al-Nashashibi offered a wide-ranging proposal at this time: the formation of a cabinet with three Arab and two Jewish officers, each having a secretary of the opposite community. The president would be Arab, but the legislative council's president would be Jewish. Interdependence of the two communities would be fostered and independence would be gradually attained (his interview with Gail Hoffman, an American journalist, Aug. 8, 1935; her notes were taken by Leo Kohn of the Jewish Agency, who commented that he "induced her not to publish" them, CZA, S25/3051).

50. Great Britain, Colonial Office, Cmd. 5119, *Proposed New Constitution for Palestine* (London: HMSO, 1936).

licly accepted the offer,[51] and the political parties began to formulate qualified approvals.

Meanwhile, the Yishuv's unanimous opposition to the idea of a legislative council and the Zionists' vigorous lobbying against it caused the majority in the British Parliament to denounce the plan as "premature" for Palestine. The government was forced to shelve it, against the advice of the British officials in Palestine. The Arab political leaders belatedly regretted that they had not already spoken out in support of the plan. The National Defense party (Nashashibi) and National Bloc (Salah) quickly publicized their support,[52] and the Youth Congress (Ghusayn) indicated qualified approval. Jamal al-Husayni remained critical, but his party did not actually reject the plan.[53] Only Istiqlal held out against the council, arguing that it was a mere palliative that could not affect the fundamental situation in Palestine.[54]

Istiqlal leaders were also the first politicians to recognize the significance of the violence and strikes that broke out in mid-April. The other party leaders waited until the strike had been in process for a week before they abandoned their efforts to assemble a delegation to go to London to promote the legislative council plan. They were thereafter forced to turn their attention, once again, to the fundamental contradictions in the mandatory system.

A legislative council alone could have done little to further the aims of the national movement in Palestine. It was important only as a platform upon which the politicians could address and pressure the British government and as a first step in an evolutionary process. Arab politicians were con-

51. Letter, March 3, 1936, enclosed in Wauchope, dispatch, March 9, 1936; the dispatch also enclosed a report from the Northern District on the attitudes of a wide range of Arabs toward the legislative council, most of whom indicated qualified approval, CO 733/297/75156 pt. 1.

52. National Defense party, letter, April 1, 1936, National Bloc, letter, April 10, enclosed in Wauchope, dispatch, April 22, 1936, CO 733/293/75102 pt. 3.

53. Wauchope, telegram, Feb. 22, 1936, ibid., pt. 2.

54. Interview with Izzat Darwazah, Damascus, May 14, 1971; Porath, *Palestinian Movement*, p. 159.

tinually haunted by realization that its long-range impact would have been ambiguous. It could serve either as an initial step toward independence or as another step toward Zionist paramountcy in Palestine. As long as the council could not enact legislation to revise the mandate and to control immigration, the Arab politicians feared that the latter prospect was the more probable. Ultimately, the basic issue was not the legislature, but, rather, the political structure and the sovereignty on which its establishment was premised.

9 /
The Political Use
of Violence

When national movements failed in their diplomatic efforts, lacked any constitutional outlets, and felt themselves losing ground to a competing national movement, popular frustration was likely to erupt into mass violence.[1] A deep sense of injustice would lie at the root of such violence: the belief that the people's rights had been violated and that violence was the only way to redress these grievances.[2] If the feeling of injustice was not widespread or if only certain groups were affected, violence would remain scattered and sporadic. If, however, the general public was agitated or mobilized, even a trivial incident could serve as the "accelerator"[3] of a widespread rebellion. The results of such violence could be seriously counterproductive to the national movement. Mob violence might discredit politicians, even if they were not responsible for its excesses. The colonial power might crush the outbreak and ignore the underlying demands. Moreover, in a settler colony, the competitive movement would react vigorously against the violence, demanding arms to protect its own community or to attack the rebels and urging the ruling authorities to repress the rebellion.

1. Ted Robert Gurr, *Why Men Rebel* (Princeton: Princeton University Press, 1970), pp. 11, 92, 335.
2. Peter A. Lupsha, "Explanation of Political Violence: Some Psychological Theories versus Indignation," *Politics and Society,* 2 (Fall 1971), 89.
3. Chalmers Johnson, *Revolutionary Change* (Boston: Little, Brown, 1966), pp. 91, 99, 154.

Thus the settlers might strengthen their own position and prevent the colonial power from granting political concessions to the rebels' movement, in which case the violence would have exhausted them and brought them no gains.

In Palestine, sporadic rural violence under the Ottoman regime, resulting from conflicts over land sales and boundaries between villages and settlements, was followed by three serious outbreaks in 1920–1921 and major disturbances in 1929. Thereafter politicians began to consider the more deliberate use of violence. Clandestine groups were formed and illegal demonstrations were staged in 1933, resulting in clashes with the police. Prolonged periods of violence occurred during the six-month general strike in 1936 and the countrywide revolt of 1937–1939.

Each outbreak differed in cause, intensity, and duration. The constant factor remained the sense of political injustice and deprivation: the feeling that independence had been promised, only to be snatched away; the fear of submersion in a Zionist-dominated country; and the invidious comparison of Palestine's political stagnation with the acquisition of self-rule by neighboring Arab countries. These responses surfaced at moments when hopes were suddenly dashed or when fears of Zionist domination had escalated to the point where even a minor incident could have serious repercussions. One cannot make a clear correlation, however, between the occurrence of these outbreaks and either peaks in Jewish immigration or weaknesses in the British military forces, although in some instances they were coincident, and fear of Jewish immigration was certainly a continuously important factor.

Jewish opposition to the aspirations of the Palestine Arabs stiffened in direct proportion to this violence. Arab riots in the early 1920s caused the Yishuv to expand its self-defense forces (Haganah) in the towns and settlements and to try to hasten immigration. The 1929 violence, in particular, hardened the Zionist movement against any compromise with the Palestine Arabs. The 1936–1939 disturbances accelerated

Yishuv efforts to achieve economic autarky and build the Haganah into a military force capable not only of protecting the colonies and urban quarters but also of undertaking offensive moves against the Arabs. This buildup, when combined with the British military force's crushing of the Arab revolt, further eroded the Arabs' relative position. Even though the revolt won some political concessions from the British for the Arab community, this "victory" had little substance when compared to the disarray within Arab society and the militancy and consolidation of the Yishuv.

Attacks in Northern Galilee

The first major incidents after the British occupied Palestine occurred in the far north, in a region that fell under the formal jurisdiction of the French military forces and bordered on Faysal's Arab state in Syria.[4] Ever since Jewish companies began buying land there in 1892, there had been incidents involving the dispossessed Druze villagers. French military posts were established in late 1919 in the three Jewish colonies—Tel Hai, Kfar Giladi, and Metullah—against the wishes of the colonists, who feared Arab reprisals. These posts predictably aroused Arab villagers' fears of French-Zionist collusion.

On March 1, 1920, an Arab band came to Tel Hai looking for French soldiers, who by then had evacuated all the colonies. The colony's leader, Captain Joseph Trumpeldor, permitted the Arabs to search for the soldiers within the main buildings to demonstrate that none were there. He became apprehensive that the band would seize weapons from the storeroom and then launch an attack. He opened fire on those Arabs who remained in the courtyard; in the ensuing battle, Trumpeldor was mortally wounded. The enraged Arabs then summoned other villagers and attacked the two other colo-

---

4. A. Cohen, pp. 47–51, 56–58, 177–178; telegrams from general headquarters in Egypt and from the British consul in Beirut to London, 1920, in FO 371/5034, 5117, and 5118; Weizmann to Curzon, Feb. 2, 1929, FO 371/4187/2117.

nies as well. The settlers had to retreat south to the British military zone. They were unable to return to the settlements until late 1920, when the British arranged with the French that Britain should provide military protection over that area. Although this was an isolated occurrence of violence, it illustrated the rapid politicization of land disputes and the Arabs' ready association of the Zionists with the imperial powers.

The Jerusalem Riot of April 1920

The Arabs of Jerusalem, who lived close to the Jewish community, listened to the statements of the Zionist Commission and the behavior of the Jewish residents. Their fears were enhanced by articles in the Hebrew press that waxed enthusiastic about imminent massive Jewish immigration and about the Balfour Declaration, which was interpreted to mean immediate Zionist control over the entire country. The Arab politicians themselves discussed anxiously the meaning of these articles and assessed the prospects of Palestine's achieving political autonomy or unification with an independent Syria.

The leaders of the Jerusalem Muslim-Christian Society planned to hold a demonstration to protest Zionist claims on April 1, 1919. But the military authorities persuaded them to cancel the plans by threatening that they would be held responsible for any violence that resulted and by promising that the Paris peace conference would send a commission to ascertain the desires of the Syrian and Palestinian people.[5]

A year later, however, such arguments carried far less weight. The King-Crane Commission had assessed public opinion among the Arabs in Palestine, but its findings had not influenced the Paris conference, where the Zionist Organization had been allowed to post an influential lobby. And

5. The King-Crane Commission eventually came with only its American members. Clayton (CPO), telegram, March 26, 1919, telegrams from Muslim Christian Societies, March 28, 1919, FO 371/4153/275/49607, 48854, 50787; Clayton, April 5, 1919, transmitted chief administrator's report on his talk with Arab leaders on March 28, FO 371/4154/175/59775.

the chief administrator in Palestine was requested by the London government to make his first official reading of the Balfour Declaration to Arab notables, thereby validating the rumors that it would be enforced in Palestine. In response, al-Nadi al-Arabi and al-Muntada al-Adabi staged an orderly procession on February 27, 1920, of two thousand Arabs in Jerusalem.[6] The leaders of the Muslim-Christian Society also delivered a protest petition to the authorities. On March 8, Faysal's coronation and the proclamation of Syrian independence brought a more excited throng into the streets. Apprehensive that a third demonstration might become violent, the British military authorities prohibited any more outdoor rallies. They were particularly worried because three religious holidays—Passover, Easter, and Nabi Musa—coincided in early April.

The Muslim Nabi Musa celebrations were organized by the Husayni family, members of which at that time included the mufti and mayor of Jerusalem. Crowds entered Jerusalem on foot from the different towns, prayed at al-Aqsa mosque, and then walked to the traditional site of Moses' death near Jericho. On April 4, the first day of the celebration, the pilgrims walking from Hebron to Jerusalem were delayed on Jaffa Road near the entrance to the old walled city by speeches delivered from the headquarters of al-Nadi al-Arabi and the municipality balcony.[7] Instead of purely religious greetings, the politicians delivered political addresses, praising Faysal and denouncing the Zionists. The police, wishing to make up for the delay, diverted the pil-

6. Two thousand rallied in Jaffa and only two hundred fifty in Haifa (Porath, *Emergence,* p. 96).

7. Speeches were delivered by al-Hajj Amin al-Husayni and Arif al-Arif at al-Nadi al-Arabi and by Musa Kazim al-Husayni at the municipality. Musa Kazim Pasha lost his post as a result and the other two fled the country, being sentenced in absentia for responsibility for the outbreak (Palin Court of Inquiry, final report, July 1, 1920, transmitted from War Office to Foreign Office, Aug. 4, 1920, FO 371/5121; correspondence during and after the riots is in FO 371/5117 and 5118).

grims through Jaffa Gate into the Old City. This route to al-Haram al-Sharif would take them along the edge of the Jewish quarter, instead of the usual way through Damascus Gate and the Muslim quarter.

The politicians had wanted to use this legal public gathering to address an audience on political issues. They displayed pictures of Emir Faysal, pledged support for his regime, and encouraged shouts for Arab unity. But they had not anticipated that the route through the Old City would be altered to bring the pilgrims into contact with the Jewish residents. The politicians were still outside Jaffa Gate when there was a sudden volley of stones in the square inside. This outburst escalated into attacks on Jewish passersby and shop looting. Although the police hurried the Hebron pilgrims down to al-Haram al-Sharif and all the pilgrims left for the Nabi Musa site the next morning, Arabs living inside the Old City kept up the violence.

The older leaders, including Musa Kazim al-Husayni, immediately deplored the violence, fearing that it would damage the case they were making for self-rule.[8] In fact, the violence was seriously counterproductive. It hastened London's decision to replace the military administration with a civil administration guided by the Balfour Declaration because the British believed that uncertainty about the future regime was the root cause of the troubles.[9] The violence also accelerated the Yishuv's defense efforts. Rural self-defense groups had existed since the Ottoman period, but

8. Frances Newton, letter to chief administrator, April 25, 1920, ISA, Chief Secretary's Papers, POL/2195/I, 2/155; interview with Arif al-Arif, Ramallah, May 22, 1971; Zionist intelligence report, March 1920, stated that al-Muntada al-Adabi supported Arif al-Arif's demand that they "maintain order" during Nabi Musa and not attack Zionists, Z4/16078. See also Porath, *Emergence,* p. 98.

9. The Palin Court of Inquiry disagreed with this assessment and recommended the curtailment of the Zionist Commission's special privileges, in order to allay the Arabs' fears. Its report was not filed until the day civil administration was instituted. Samuel persuaded the FO not to publish the report (telegram, July 15, 1920, FO 371/5121).

203

the Haganah was not formed until the Arabs' demonstration in February. It trained openly in Jerusalem and thus increased Arab fears. Weizmann and other Zionist leaders denounced the April outbreak as a "pogrom," charged British officials with collusion, and proclaimed that vastly increased immigration was the only means to prevent its repetition. [10]

The Jaffa Riots of May 1921

The Jerusalem violence remained largely confined to the Old City, although villagers overran one nearby colony. An outbreak in Hebron was averted by quick military action and the squelching of rumors that Jews were attacking Arabs in Jerusalem. In contrast, violence in Jaffa on May 1, 1921, spread rapidly to outlying rural areas. These riots had clear political roots and lacked the religious overtones of the Nabi Musa outbreak.

Jaffa was the main port of Palestine and adjoined the rapidly growing Jewish suburbs of Tel Aviv and Petah Tiqvah. The Arab residents were acutely aware of Jewish immigration, much of which came through the port, and were antagonized by the announcement of the first official quota of Jewish labor immigrants that spring. They also observed political wrangles among Zionist groups in Tel Aviv, which included flareups between the main labor organization, Ahdut ha-Avodah, and a militant Marxist group. The Marxists distributed pamphlets in Arabic that fed Arabs' fears of "godless Bolshevik" influence.

Their anger and indignation at the political situation were deepened by Churchill's assertion in late March 1921 that Britain would rule Palestine for many generations. A British intelligence officer later reported: "Mr. Churchill's visit put the final touch to Arab hostility to Zionism. . . . In the state

10. C. Weizmann, pp. 255–257.

of extreme irritation of the whole Muslim and Christian population against the Zionists any kind of disturbance was sufficient to let loose the storm."[11]

The "storm" broke on May Day, at the close of labor demonstrations in Tel Aviv, during which the Marxist group clashed with Ahdut ha-Avodah. The police attempted to disperse the Marxists into an open area on the border between Tel Aviv and Jaffa. Arabs had gathered on the Jaffa side, growing increasingly concerned that the Jewish groups were about to march into Jaffa and attack them. When the police shot into the air, intending to disperse the Jewish demonstrators, the Arabs thought that the gunshots came from the Jews and were directed at themselves. Their anger peaked and a mob spread through northern Jaffa, smashing Jewish shops, attacking pedestrians, and breaking into the Immigration House that sheltered newly arrived Jews. The Arab policemen failed to stop the mob, and forty Jews were killed by the end of the second day.

The mayor of Jaffa and notables from the Muslim-Christian Society denounced the outbreak and toured the town to calm residents and dispel rumors. Despite these efforts, a large crowd gathered on May 2, responding to rumors that Jewish groups were planning reprisal attacks against Arabs. The crowd "forced the French, Italian and Spanish consuls to accompany them to the [district] governor and put forward as intermediaries their demand that British troops should be replaced by Indians and that the Arabs should be given arms to defend themselves against the armed Jews."[12] On May 4, a rumor that Muslim women and children were being killed by Jews caused crowds to assemble again, but this time the Arab

11. Captain C. D. Brunton, report to general headquarters of General Staff Intelligence, May 13, 1921, St. Antony's College, Private Paper Collection. Information on the riots is drawn from his report, correspondence in CO 733/3, and Great Britain, Parliamentary Papers, Cmd. 1540, *Palestine Disturbances of May, 1921: Reports of the Commissioners of Inquiry* . . . (London: HMSO, 1921).
12. Brunton, report, cited in n. 11.

notables and British district governor were able to calm and disperse them.

Similar rumors helped to spread the violence outside Jaffa to towns along the coast. Although the British were able to reassure a deputation of leading citizens in Gaza that their relatives in Jaffa were safe,[13] the Arab dignitaries and British officials were not always able to dispel such rumors in other towns. On May 4, over a thousand Arabs, armed with sticks and knives, overran two small colonies near Qalqilyah. The colonists retreated to Petah Tiqvah, which, in turn, was threatened the next day by bedouin of the Abu Kishk tribe. On May 6, Haderah colony was attacked unsuccessfully by villagers and residents of neighboring Tulkarm, who were reacting to rumors that Arab workers in the colony were being held hostage there.[14] Word of these attacks spread immediately to the area of Nablus and Jenin: "Anger and fear spread like fire. The fears which originated and stimulated these rumours were not simulated. Women, with their children, actually fled from villages supposed to be threatened [by Jewish attackers]."[15] The mayors and notables of Nablus and Jenin helped the British district governor to calm the townspeople.[16] But five hundred men set off from Nablus for Tulkarm in the evening of May 5 to aid its residents. The next day three thousand people, including bedouin from Ghawr Beisan and villagers from the surrounding hills, assembled in Nablus, prepared to move to the defence of Tulkarm. They dispersed only after several notables traveled to Tulkarm to verify that the town was not being attacked.

One important town near Jaffa remained quiet: in Ramlah

13. District Governor Lewis Nott to secretariat, Jerusalem, May 4, 1921, ISA, Chief Secretary's Papers, POL/2300, 2/144.

14. Separate reports on the Petah Tiqvah and Haderah raids were attached to Cmd. 1540. Porath, *Emergence*, pp. 129–130, questions whether the rumors were diffused deliberately or spontaneously.

15. Cmd. 1540.

16. Acting deputy district governor, B. Grew, to secretariat, Jerusalem, May 8, 1921, and Samaria district governor to secretariat, n.d., ISA, Chief Secretary's Papers, POL/2300, 2/144.

the influential Shaykh Sulayman al-Taji al-Faruqi appealed to the public to disbelieve the rumors and stay calm.[17] Similarly, Jerusalem remained quiet, with the help of the new mayor, Raghib al-Nashashibi, and al-Hajj Amin al-Husayni, the leading aspirant for the position of mufti. Al-Hajj Amin had already ensured tranquillity during the Nabi Musa celebration two weeks before.[18]

The 1920 violence had resulted in the imposition of a policy hostile to the Arab community, but this time the political repercussions favored the Arabs. The outbreak undercut Samuel's assumption that the Arab community would accept a fait accompli imposed by the British. He took immediate steps to restrict the activities of the Marxist labor group. More important, Samuel temporarily suspended the quota of Jewish labor immigration and articulated a somewhat limited conception of the Jewish national home, a conception that was formalized in the White Paper of 1922. Moreover, the British commission of inquiry concluded that the violence stemmed from the Arabs' basic political grievances.

Therefore the Arab delegation to London was treated as a serious complainant, if only because the Colonial Office feared that the delegates could stir up trouble if they went home dissatisfied. The likelihood of renewed violence was reduced, however, by the collective fines imposed on Arab villages that were implicated in the attack on Haderah and the imprisonment of the shaykh of the Abu Kishk tribe.[19] The impact of the fines—and of the political hopes raised by Samuel's actions and by the delegation to London—was evident in the rapid containment of an outbreak on November 2, 1921, the fourth anniversary of the Balfour Declaration. The outbreak was denounced by the Arab Executive, and its youthful organizers were promptly arrested and tried.[20]

17. Ibid.
18. Porath, "Al-Hajj Amin," p. 134.
19. Correspondence, Dec. 1921, between high commissioner and CO, CO 733/8.
20. Political report, Nov. 1921, chief secretary's report, Dec. 29, 1921, ibid.

The Wailing Wall Disturbances

The Arabs remained suspicious of the aims of the Zionist movement, despite the lack of violence in the mid-1920s. This distrust could be aroused to anger by an appropriate catalyst, such as the one that appeared on the Day of Atonement (September 24, 1938), when British police removed a screen from the pavement in front of the Wailing Wall in the midst of the Jewish service. The wall and pavement belonged to the Islamic *waqf,* but the Jewish community had traditionally used it for prayers. They did not, however, have permission to place a screen there, and the British authorities feared that permitting it to remain would establish a precedent and inflame the Muslim community.

The common reverence in which Muslims and Jews held the wall (al-Buraq to Muslims) made it a likely focus of antagonism. As early as 1918, Weizmann had proposed purchasing the area from the Muslim community.[21] Throughout the 1920s, there had been incidents in which Arabs threw rocks at Jewish worshipers and worshipers brought benches or screens onto the pavement. As the Jewish community expanded and become more self-confident, its claims at the wall grew. Thus the removal of the screen in 1928 prompted Jewish leaders in Palestine and abroad to demand not only benches and screens but also all the accoutrements necessary for a complete religious service.

Although the British authorities sought to maintain the status quo,[22] Jewish leaders continued to differ with Muslims as to what had been permitted in the past. The president of the Supreme Muslim Council, al-Hajj Amin al-Husayni, then formed the Committee for the Protection of al-Aqsa, which

21. Weizmann to Ormsby-Gore, May 1, 1918, enclosed in Storrs, memorandum tracing the controversy, which was enclosed in high commissioner, dispatch to CO, Oct. 31, 1925, CO 733/98; Clayton (CPO), telegrams to FO, June 16, Aug. 31, Oct. 1, Dec. 1, 1918, FO 371/3395/11053.

22. Cmd. 3229, *Statement of Policy* . . . (London: HMSO, November 1928).

issued strongly worded manifestos. He also took steps to assert Muslim proprietary rights at the wall, thereby irritating the Jewish community. A doorway was opened from al-Haram al-Sharif directly onto the pavement; sections of the wall were lowered so that the Jewish worshipers could be observed from above; and a small building nearby was converted into a *sufi* prayer room, complete with *muezzin* (crier) and clamorous gongs and cymbals. But al-Hajj Amin agreed to cease these provocations in the spring of 1929, when the high commissioner referred the issue of the status quo to the Law Officers in London.[23] Al-Hajj Amin did resume construction on one building in June, but only after the Law Officers had approved that construction. This renewed building activity drew strong protests from a Zionist official, Joseph Klausner, who was apparently unaware of London's approval. Klausner founded the Pro-Wailing Wall Committee in July and asserted that the Jewish community actually owned the wall area and that Muslims had no rights there.[24] By then the principal Zionist leaders had left for the biannual Zionist congress in Europe, and the high commissioner was in London on leave.

The conflict reached crisis proportions on August 15, the fast of Tisha Bav (the destruction of the Temple), and August 16, the beginning of Mawlad al-Nabi (the birth of the Prophet Muhammad). Youthful Jewish militants marched to the wall on August 15, ignoring the government's stipulation that they not unfurl the Zionist flag or sing "ha-Tiqvah," their national anthem. At noon the next day, two thousand Muslims moved from al-Haram al-Sharif to the wall, where

23. High commissioner, dispatches, April 20, May 10, 1929; chief secretary, dispatch, July 10, enclosing al-Hajj Amin's letter of July 7, 1929, CO 733/163/67013, pt. 1. Also see Cmd. 3530 on the period leading up to and including the outbreak.

24. Chief secretary, telegram, July 30, 1929, note on talk with Zionists about the building, Aug. 6; Weizmann had suggested purchasing the Wall area again, early that winter; see Shuckburgh, dispatch to high commissioner, Jan. 1, 1929, and the latter's reply, Jan. 12, CO 733/163/68013 pt. 1.

Shaykh Hasan Abu Suud, a rival of al-Hajj Amin, delivered an inflammatory speech.[25] The crowd remained within *waqf* property but destroyed Jewish prayer books and petitions placed in the crevices, spilled oil from the prayer lamps, and knocked over the beadles' table. Exaggerated reports of the damage inflamed the Jewish community.

Numerous small incidents occurred in the next days, until a Jewish funeral on August 21 developed into a vocal political demonstration against the government and the Arabs. Although al-Hajj Amin telephoned politicians in Jaffa and Gaza on August 16 to discourage Muslim counterdemonstrations, letters were circulated in villages near Jerusalem under his name (which he claimed was forged) that warned of trouble to occur in Jerusalem on Friday, August 23, and hinted that the villagers should come into town to protect their coreligionists. On August 22, the chief secretary met with three Jewish and three Arab leaders (including Jamal al-Husayni and Awni Abd al-Hadi) to negotiate an agreement on rights at the wall, but their plans to hold another meeting on August 26 were superseded by the ensuing violence.

On August 23, villagers came to the Friday services in Jerusalem carrying clubs, in response to the circulars warning of Jewish attacks on al-Aqsa. Al-Hajj Amin attempted to calm them by his address in al-Aqsa, but Shaykh Abu Suud denounced his stance and whipped up the congregants. The agitated crowd streamed out of the Old City into the orthodox Jewish quarter of Mea Shearim, where they clubbed residents at random.

Once again, exaggerated rumors spread rapidly throughout Palestine. Four colonies were destroyed, but the Haganah units in other colonies fended off assaults from villagers. On August 24, an Arab mob attacked the Jewish quarter in Hebron, killing sixty residents, many of whom were students at

25. The shaykhs of al-Aqsa had apparently initiated the procession while al-Hajj Amin was negotiating with the chief secretary (chief secretary, telegrams, Aug. 16, 17, 1929, ibid.; his dispatch, Aug. 22, 1929, CO 733/175/67411 pt. 1).

the Talmudic College.[26] Twenty Jewish residents of Safad, an isolated town in the far north, were killed on August 29 by Arab attackers. Both Hebron and Safad contained traditionalist Muslim communities,[27] previously remote from the center of political life in Palestine. The attacks were directed against longtime orthodox Jewish communities, whose residence long predated political Zionism and most of whom were critical of this secular movement. Neither town had many recent Jewish immigrants, but the attackers made no distinction between Zionist and non-Zionist Jews. Navy reinforcements arrived from Egypt on August 25 and maintained calm in the port towns, but the British troops were ill-equipped to counter violence throughout the interior.

The leaders of the Arab Executive hastily issued a manifesto on August 24 that called on the residents of Jerusalem to stop the bloodshed and concluded: "Be confident that we are making every possible effort to realise your demands and national aspirations by peaceful methods. Arm yourselves with mercy, wisdom and patience. For verily, God is with those who bear themselves in patience."[28] Al-Hajj Amin al-Husayni also signed the manifesto, although the Supreme Muslim Council had played a major role in exacerbating the conflict.

The outbreaks were a serious setback to the hope of political reform entertained by such leaders as Musa Kazim al-Husayni and Raghib al-Nashashibi. Not only did the Zionist leadership denounce the idea of cooperating in a legislative council with "pogrom-launching" Arabs, but the high commissioner's proclamation on September 1 implicated the entire Arab community in the attacks and declared that they

26. Press reports of grotesque crimes in Hebron proved to be unfounded, according to the official exhumation, which had been requested by Kisch (high commissioner, dispatch, Sept. 21, 1929, enclosing the doctors' report, CO 733/175/ 67411).

27. Porath, *Emergence*, p. 269.

28. Attached to Sir Harry Luke Papers, St. Antony's College, Private Paper Collection.

were unworthy of self-government. This antagonized both Christian Arabs, who had not participated in the attacks, and those politicians who had kept their towns quiet throughout the troubles. Acre's leaders, for example, protested to the government that they had managed to keep the town calm throughout the disturbances and yet they were being chastised along with the others.[29] The riots had the effect, however, of demonstrating not only the volatility of the Arab public but also their potential for mobilization. Arab politicians were later to view the 1929 violence as an important step in their struggle because of this renewed momentum.[30]

Militant Opposition

Political groups attempted to structure and channel this latent violence only after the disturbances of 1929. The forms ranged from guerrilla warfare in the countryside to clandestine cells and militant demonstrations in the towns.

In the winter of 1929–1930 a band called the Green Hand Gang, formed by men who had been implicated in the August 29 attack and had then become outlaws, assembled in the *wadis* (gorges) near Safad and fired sporadically on the Jewish quarter of Safad.[31] After police searches compelled them to move West into the Acre subdistrict, they operated in guerrilla fashion, ambushing police patrols and receiving provisions from the villagers. By spring, the band had been scattered by the combined action of the British troops, the Transjordanian Frontier Force, police patrols, and air reconnaissance. The group's exploits demonstrated the problems of fighting elusive and mobile bands, but they also demonstrated the limited military effectiveness of guerrilla forces.

Secret cells were formed in Haifa in the 1920s by Shaykh Izz

29. Ibid.

30. Porath, *Emergence*, pp. 270–271.

31. They were joined by some Syrian Druze who had participated in the 1925–1927 rebellion and were "well experienced in the harassing of Police and Military," as the British reported (high commissioner, dispatch, Feb. 22, 1930, CO 733/190/77171).

al-Din al-Qassam,[32] who was an influential leader of Haifa's Islamic school, mosque, *sharia* courts, and Muslim Society. He formed clandestine five-member cells that spied on the British to find out their military plans and police operations and studied the activities of Zionist groups. Shaykh al-Qassam denounced the violence of 1929 because it was anomic and unfocused. By building up militant cadres, he hoped to channel the Arabs' anger toward carefully selected targets and make precise plans before launching an attack.

The Ikhwan al-Qassam (Qassamite Brotherhood) divided over tactics. Abu Ibrahim al-Kabir (the code name for Khalil Muhammad Isa) argued after the 1929 outbreak that the group should lead a revolt immediately, before the Arab community could be further weakened by British force and the growth of the Jewish community. But Shaykh al-Qassam maintained that they had hardly begun preparations for a revolt and that the public must be educated and mobilized so that the people would rise up spontaneously when the Ikhwan gave the signal to revolt.

In defiance of the shaykh, Abu Ibrahim's cell attacked Nahalal colony in December 1932. Although Abu Ibrahim was later acquitted in court for lack of evidence, the case made the public aware of the existence of a revolutionary group in Haifa, which the court tried to link with the Muslim Society.[33] The Ikhwan al-Qassam only narrowly missed being exposed by this episode. It confirmed the shaykh's anxiety to remain secret until a more propitious moment.

By 1932 and 1933, a noncooperation movement was growing in Palestine in the wake of the prime minister's "black letter" of February 1931. Political activists pressured the Arab Executive into holding demonstrations in 1933 as well as boycotting government committees and Jewish produce. Because the British administration had banned public rallies after the

---

32. Yasin, *al-Thawrah*, pp. 30–42; see Chapter 5 for more details on Shaykh al-Qassam's background.
33. *Palestine Post*, summer 1933, passim.

1929 disturbances, even holding a demonstration would mean risking arrest. The young politicians derided the Arab Executive for always seeking government permission to hold demonstrations instead of asserting their right to protest.[34] By mid-1933 all the politicians had endorsed the policy of noncooperation, although many hesitated to act on it. Meanwhile, the surge in Jewish immigration in 1933, which included large numbers of illegal immigrants, spurred on the Istiqlal and Youth Congress activists and reawoke popular fears.

On October 8, the Arab Executive decided to hold a general strike and demonstration in Jerusalem on October 13, to be followed by successive demonstrations in Jaffa, Nablus, and other towns. This act of civil disobedience would emphasize their opposition to Jewish immigration,[35] indicate to the British the depth of public malaise, and "signal to the regime the threat of more disruptive violence if [their] claims were not met."[36]

Twenty-two members of the Executive—including the elderly Musa Kazim Pasha—participated in the Jerusalem demonstration on October 13. They attended noon prayers at al-Aqsa and then led nearly seven hundred people to Jaffa Gate. When they were blocked from proceeding out of the Old City to Government House, part of the crowd turned back toward New Gate and Damascus Gate. Twenty or thirty women were among the crowd. At both gates the police broke up the crowds with baton charges.

That evening the Executive decided to hold the next demonstration in Jaffa on October 27. Again people assembled in the principal mosque. The police then blocked the crowd from crossing the main square to the district commissioner's

34. The younger politicians persuaded the elders, at the close of the mid-August meeting of the Arab Executive, to deliver personally a petition protesting the government's development plan, walking between the Executive's office and Government House as a symbolic violation of the ban on demonstrations (high commissioner, telegram, Aug. 19, 1931, CO 733/209/87353).

35. Correspondence on the demonstrations, CO 733/239/17356/1; al-Kayyali, ed., *Wathaiq*, pp. 338–347.

36. Gurr, p. 356.

office, where Musa Kazim Pasha had planned to submit a petition. Blocked midway across the square, young people threw paving stones at the police and brandished sticks torn off shop awnings. After an initial baton charge, the police opened fire and killed fifteen demonstrators. That afternoon several members of the Executive were arrested in the Jaffa committee's office as they outlined plans for a third demonstration, scheduled for Nablus on November 10.

The word of bloodshed in Jaffa on October 27 spread rapidly, and crowds clashed with the police in Haifa, Nablus, and Jerusalem that day. Even though Musa Kazim Pasha sent telegrams to counter rumors that he had been killed in Jaffa, crowds gathered again on October 28 in Jerusalem and Haifa, and demonstrations were held in Beersheba, Lydda, and Gaza. British officials managed to prevent gatherings in Bethlehem, Hebron, and Ramallah, however, and town elders prevented the unrest from spreading to Ramlah and Acre.

The demonstrations represented a marked departure from the past. Hostility was directed at the British, who were the authority controlling immigration. No Jews were attacked. In contrast to 1920 and 1929, there was no religious dimension to this strife. Al-Hajj Amin was, in fact, abroad at the time. The demonstrations were purely urban in character and did not involve villagers. Most important, the rallies were organized in advance by the politicians and youth groups and were accompanied by the first week-long (rather than one day) general strike. Despite careful planning, they surged out of control once a direct confrontation took place with the police and exaggerated rumors spread through the country.

The results of the demonstrations were ambiguous for the Arab community. On the one hand, the government decided to allow them to hold demonstrations on December 9 and January 16, 1934, recognizing that the ban had denied them a needed outlet for their anger.[37] The government also acceler-

---

37. Parkinson (CO), minute criticizing the ban on demonstrations, Dec. 4, 1933, CO 733/239/17356/5; reports on the Jan. 1934 demonstrations, CO 733/248/17700.

ated its discussions of constitutional issues and reaffirmed its concern to prevent illegal Jewish immigration by increasing coastal patrols and tightening security. On the other hand, the Arab politicians did not take full advantage of the momentum provided by the demonstrations to press their case on the government. The politicians who were arrested that fall agreed to sign bonds promising not to undertake any illegal acts for three years. They were free to organize politically, but their credibility as self-sacrificing nationalist activists was damaged by their readiness to sign such bonds.[38]

More important, the death of Musa Kazim Pasha in March 1934, the distraction caused by the election campaign for the municipal councils, and the efforts to form new parties divided the politicians and postponed any concerted drive against the government. The initiative passed to youthful activist groups. Al-Hajj Amin al-Husayni exhorted the public to prevent land sales.[39] Scouts initiated nighttime patrols along the Mediterranean coast to block the landing of illegal immigrants.

In October 1935, believing that the time was ripe for a revolt, Shaykh al-Qassam sent an intermediary to ask al-Hajj Amin for his support. But, according to Subhi Yasin, al-Hajj Amin rejected the shaykh's plan, arguing that a revolt would alienate the British without achieving any political results.[40] Despite this apparent opposition from the leader of the Muslim community, the Ikhwan al-Qassam met in Haifa on November 12, 1935, and decided to launch a revolt immediately. Shaykh al-Qassam led fifteen men into the hills near Jenin. Although they planned to hide there for several days while they contacted villagers, they lost the essential element of secrecy when one member of their group shot a Jewish guard

38. See Chapter 5 for the names of those arrested. Only Shaykh al-Muzaffar refused to sign the bond and served six months in jail.
39. See his long speech quoted in *al-Jamiah al-Arabiyyah*, April 16, 1935, ISA, Chief Secretary's Papers, K/14/35, 295.
40. Yasin, *al-Thawrah*, p. 22; for a detailed analysis, see Porath, *Palestinian Movement*, pp. 138–139.

from the colony of Ein Harod, alerting the police to the presence of armed men in the hills. Several hundred policemen converged on the area, surrounding the village in which the shaykh and eleven followers were sleeping the night of November 18–19 and killing the shaykh and two others in a gun battle the next day. Another band, however, under the elderly Shaykh Farhan al-Saadi, was sleeping in a different village and managed to hide in the mountains all winter. Shaykh al-Qassam was eulogized as a national martyr. The emotional outpourings at his funeral and memorial service further excited and aroused the public.

The General Strike

The Ikhwan al-Qassam served as an important catalyst to the general strike of 1936. Shaykh al-Saadi's group stopped ten cars on the Tulkarm-Nablus road the night of April 15, robbed all the passengers, killed two Jewish travelers, and wounded a third.[41] This violence triggered a reprisal killing of two Arab workers in their hut near Petah Tiqvah the next night. A demonstration at the funeral service in Tel Aviv for one of the passengers swelled into an attempt to march on Jaffa and then random attacks on Arabs found in Tel Aviv. These acts, in turn, prompted Arabs from Jaffa to try to march on Tel Aviv after the district commissioner refused to grant them a permit to parade inside Jaffa. Fearing intercommunal violence, middle-class Arab professionals and merchants hastily formed local committees which they hoped could organize a nonviolent protest strike to channel the Arabs' explosive anger. The strike spread rapidly through the Palestinian towns and, a week later, the heads of the political parties gave it their support. They formed the Arab Higher Committee to serve as a coordinating body.

The strike escalated rapidly into violence. Three hundred

41. Information on the strike is drawn from correspondence files in CO 733/307/ 75348/1, CO 733/197/75156, CO 733/310/75528/6; *Palestine Post*, April–Oct. 1936, passim; Hurewitz, *Struggle*, pp. 68–71; Kalkas in Abu-Lughod, ed., *Transformation*, pp. 237–274.

Hawrani (Syrian) migrant laborers burned down the Yemenite Jewish quarter in Jaffa on April 20. Jewish residents of Jaffa sought refuge in all-Jewish Tel Aviv. On April 22, eight Arabs were killed and fifty-eight wounded when the police charged into a crowd in Jerusalem.

Support for the strike stiffened, especially after key Zionist leaders denounced the Arabs as barbaric, demanded separate facilities (such as opening a separate port at Tel Aviv), and urged the British to crush the strike as quickly and harshly as necessary. Certain British policies, in turn, propelled additional groups to support the strike. In mid-April, the British enacted regulations that authorized deportation, curfew, arrest and search without warrant, and collective punishment. They embittered the Arabs further by announcing a new labor immigration quota in mid-May and by demolishing a large section of Jaffa's Old City in mid-June to facilitate military operations there.[42]

The popular mood was vividly depicted in a private letter describing the villagers' reaction to the detention of a Tulkarm politician on May 23: the "news spread like wildfire into the surrounding villages." At least five hundred men and two hundred women streamed into town wielding sticks, iron rods, some "old Turkish sabres," and "knives fastened to the ends of sticks"; they had "grim faces, bent on taking revenge." The letter continued: "I believe that if any more of the popular men are arrested and deported the same will happen. In Nablus it will be worse, the fellahin round there are fiercer and better armed. Round Safad, conditions are still more favourable towards an armed revolt. In Jerusalem, Jaffa and Hebron, the pressure has been tested often enough."[43]

---

42. The Supreme Court in Palestine criticized this action (high commissioner, correspondence with CO about dismissing the chief justice, in CO 733/313/75528/24).

43. Letter about the arrest of Salim Abd al-Rahman al-Hajj Ibrahim, by Thabe Whalidi, Taiyibe (probably a teacher in the Kadoorie Agricultural School) to Sir Humphrey Bowman, former director of education, May 23, 1936, in Bowman Papers, St. Antony's College, Private Paper Collection.

In the towns, violence took the form of strewing nails on the streets to block cars and buses, stoning villagers who attempted to hawk their vegetables in the streets, and sniping at police patrols. Violence was more widespread in rural areas: crops in Jewish colonies were burned, trees planted by the Jewish National Fund were uprooted, some trains were derailed, and telephone lines were cut.

After the British announced a new Jewish immigration quota on May 18, guerrilla bands formed in the southern and central hills, particularly in the Nablus-Jenin-Tulkarm triangle. The first major engagement occurred on June 21, when sixty Arabs from the Nablus area ambushed a convoy of troops; a third of the Arabs died. Abd al-Qadir al-Husayni, the son of the late Musa Kazim Pasha, led a guerrilla band in the Bethlehem hills; he was captured on October 7, but jumped bail and escaped to Syria.[44] The local forces were supplemented by a band of about three hundred Syrians, Iraqis, and Palestinians led by the exiled Syrian guerrilla fighter Fawzi al-Qawuqji.[45] All the different guerrilla bands may have numbered a total of one or two thousand by September, equipped with rifles and hiding in the mountains. Against them, the British government fielded twenty thousand troops by the end of September and employed Royal Air Force spotter planes to locate the elusive bands in the hills.

By then strong pressures had mounted inside the Arab community to end the strike because the British were clearly unwilling to begin negotiations as long as the strike continued. Some Arabs hoped that the promised Royal Commission might support their cause now that they had emphasized its seriousness by a lengthy strike. Others were disturbed that

44. Abd al-Qadir had begun forming his clandestine band in 1931, according to Porath, *Palestinian Movement,* pp. 131–132, 179, 182.

45. His principal lieutenants were Fakhri Abd al-Hadi; Jasim Ali, an Iraqi; and Muhammad Saab, a Druze (Shimoni, p. 663). On the internal organization and tensions among the commanders, see Porath, *Palestinian Movement,* pp. 185–186, 188–192, and Tom Bowden, "The Politics of the Arab Rebellion in Palestine, 1936–39," *Middle Eastern Studies,* 11 (May 1975), 156–160.

the Jewish community had strengthened itself during the Arab strike by opening a port at Tel Aviv, enhancing its economic self-sufficiency and expanding its supply of legally held arms. Moreover, many Arabs were hurting economically from the strike. As the citrus season approached, landowners and merchants feared that they would lose their revenue from orange exports. The president of the Haifa strike committee, Khalil Taha, argued that orange merchants should stop striking and instead pay a tax to the Arab Higher Committee on each orange crate sold, thereby generating funds for the wider strike. But such arguments were silenced by the assassination of Taha on September 27.

The Arab Higher Committee was torn between those who opposed military action and those who felt that the political strike and guerrilla warfare were inseparable. Suddenly its members feared that the fighters' anger would turn against the committee if it tried to end the strike before any of the basic demands were met. Therefore the Arab Higher Committee turned to the Arab kings to lend their prestige to efforts to end the strike and attempt negotiations. They also sought, and obtained, the support of the local strike committees. After the strike ended in mid-October, the guerrilla bands dissolved into the countryside, but Qawuqji did not leave Palestine until late November, when the British permitted the non-Palestinian guerrillas to slip across the border into Syria.[46]

The six-month strike demonstrated the political will and desperation of the Palestine Arabs but failed to achieve their explicit goals. It neither halted Jewish immigration nor obtained guarantees that their demands would be met. The Arab community was weakened by the prolonged strike, and its economic life was slow to recuperate. On the positive side, the Arab rulers were introduced as interested parties, with the right to play an active diplomatic role. In addition,

46. Communiques by Qawuqji, Aug.–Nov. 1936, are found in al-Kayyali, ed., *Wathaiq*, pp. 433–461.

the Royal Commission recognized the depth of Arab nationalist feeling in Palestine and the impossibility of adhering to the terms of the mandate. But the commission's recommendation of a territorial partition of the country could not allay the Arabs' fears, much less satisfy their aspirations.

The Revolt

An undercurrent of disorder troubled Palestine through the winter and spring of 1937. Outbreaks were centered in Haifa, where bombs were thrown at the homes of several prominent residents who refused to contribute funds for underground cells.[47] Arab police inspectors and Arabs who traded with the Jewish community were harassed. Forty Haifa residents were arrested in February for complicity in this wave of intimidation. Those arrested included the successor to Shaykh al-Qassam as *imam* of Istiqlal mosque and as head of the local Muslim Society, as well as the secretary of the Haifa boy scouts and the Haifa correspondent for the Istiqlal party newspaper. In an additional attempt to control dissidence, several political activists in Tiberias, Safad, and Khan Yunis were exiled to other Palestinian towns under heavy bonds.

After the partition recommendation was announced in July, intimidation and violence resumed, reaching a climax with the assassination in Nazareth of the new district commissioner for Galilee on September 26. Since the partition plan called for Galilee to be transferred to the Jewish state and the Arab residents were threatened with mass eviction, this assassination had a strong symbolic significance. For the British, the act was also symbolic: the district commissioner was the highest British official to have been murdered in Palestine, and the act appeared to challenge Britain's basic authority. The government responded by rounding up political activists throughout the northern district and proscribing not

---

47. *Palestine Post*, Jan.–May 1937, passim. Three Arabs who had figured prominently on the government's side during the trial of Ikhwan al-Qassam for the 1932 attack on Nahalal were assassinated.

only the Arab Higher Committee but all the local committees in Palestine. This crackdown provided a stimulus for a full-scale revolt.

Two weeks later, al-Hajj Amin al-Husayni escaped from his sanctuary in Jerusalem to Lebanon, outside the reach of the British government. That very night, violence erupted throughout Palestine. The initial acts resembled those of 1936: wire-cutting, sniping at police and watchmen, and burning crops and forests. But guerrilla bands quickly formed in the hills, particularly in the north and in the southern mountains around Hebron. The first large-scale engagement did not occur until early March 1938, when a band of three or four hundred guerrillas suffered heavy casualties inflicted by two thousand British soldiers and police near Umm al-Fahum, a village west of Jenin.[48] The bands generally remained on the run, traveling long distances at night to avoid detection.[49] During the summer of 1938, however, the area under rebel control expanded swiftly. Guerrillas operated actively not only in the northern towns of Jenin and Nablus, but also in the central towns of Ramallah, Jerusalem, Jaffa, and Ramlah and to the south in Hebron, Beersheba, and Gaza. They raided post offices and banks for money, police stations for rifles and ammunition, and government offices for funds and typewriters.[50] The acting district commissioner of Jenin was assassinated at midday in his office on the second floor of the central police station. His assailants escaped undetected.

Most post offices and banks had to close by mid-September as a result of the thefts and lack of security. The British police

48. Ibid., March 4, 1938.
49. Yasin, *al-Thawrah,* p. 66; *Palestine Post,* April 13, 1938, describes an incident when a group entered a village near Nazareth, killed the headman, and took £P50 from the villagers, then crossed the Plain of Esdraelon, stopping to puncture the oil pipeline in several places, set fire to the leaking oil, and cut some telephone wires. The group finally disappeared into the hills east of Haifa.
50. In mid-August, the Barclays Bank in Nablus was robbed of £P5,020 at midday and another £P2000 was taken from an Arab postal employee there soon after. Thirty men raided the Nablus police station, taking four rifles as well as ammunition, cutting the phone line, and tying up the policemen.

evacuated Beersheba after rebels burned the radio station, the quarantine station, and the post office; after the British departed, the town's government offices and police barracks were destroyed. The general officer commanding the British troops reported that by September "the situation was such that civil administration and control of the country was, to all practical purposes, non-existent."[51]

Not until late October, when the Munich agreement enabled the British government to release troops from the European front for action in Palestine, were the British forces actively able to confront the rebels. The Old City of Jerusalem was reoccupied by British troops after a five-day cordon and search, as were Jaffa and Acre soon after, and Beersheba on November 21. The Jerusalem-Lydda railway line was reopened in late December, and troops slowly fanned out from the towns and communications routes into the villages to reassert control. As the British pressed villagers to cooperate and the situation became increasingly difficult for the guerrilla bands, support for them diminished in the countryside. They had to demand food from villagers and extort money from merchants. Rivalries among guerrilla leaders were exacerbated,[52] and some villages formed "peace" bands that clashed with the guerrillas and with rival villages.[53]

The titular commander in chief of the guerrillas was Abd al-Rahim al-Hajj Muhammad. His own band did not exceed fifty permanent members, out of some two thousand full-time guerrillas in Palestine. Al-Hajj Muhammad divided his efforts between purchasing arms in Damascus and carrying out military operations in the Nablus-Jenin area. He at-

---

51. General Robert Haining, report, Aug. 30, 1938, St. Antony's College, Private Paper Collection.
52. Ibid. Fakhri Abd al-Hadi, Qawuqji's former aide, was one who turned against the rebellion, forming a "pro-Government" group in the Jenin area. See also Porath, *Palestinian Movement*, pp. 249–256.
53. Miss H. Wilson, teacher at Bir Zayt private school, diary, p. 71, St. Antony's College, Private Paper Collection.

tempted to exert his authority over the other commanders by coordinating arms distribution and by presiding over the rebel military courts that handled both treason cases and local village disputes.[54] He opposed political assassination and issued special notices that announced debt moratoriums for the peasants, warned creditors not to visit villages, alerted Arabs not to help the British build police posts, and called on Arab policemen and watchmen to resign.[55] He also ordered townspeople to adopt the *kaffiyah* and *agal* headgear, both as the nationalist headdress (instead of the Ottoman fez) and to enable the *kaffiyah*-wearing guerrillas to blend with the civilians in the towns.

Abd al-Qadir al-Husayni returned to Palestine in the spring of 1938. He assumed command over the Hebron sector in May and added Jerusalem to his operations in August, after the previous commanders had died.[56] No other regional commanders consolidated their authority to the same extent as Abd al-Qadir, although Arif Abd al-Raziq, the commander of the Tulkarm-Ramallah sector, vied for leadership with the nominal commander in chief al-Hajj Muhammad and forced aside the commander of the Lydda-Ramlah-Jaffa area, Shaykh Hasan Salamah. As an example of the factional nature of many of these bands, two local families in northern Palestine—Abu Dura and Zuubi—formed rival forces that attacked each others' villages as well as harassing British patrols and Jewish colonies.[57] Moreover, assassinations against opponents of al-Hajj Amin al-Husayni occurred in November and December 1938, largely carried out by Abd al-

54. High commissioner, dispatch, Dec. 29, 1938, CO 733/398/75156, pt. 1; Haining, report, Nov. 30, 1938, and Wilson diary, St. Antony's College, Private Paper Collection; correspondence on a conflict in Ramah village, ISA, Chief Secretary's Papers, O/73/40, 336.

55. Communiques in al-Kayyali, ed., *Wathaiq,* pp. 613–616, and attached to high commissioner, dispatch, Sept. 20, 1938, CO 733/372/75156/93.

56. The previous commander in Hebron was Isa al-Hajj Sulayman al-Battat; in Jerusalem, Muhammad Taha Zubani, alias Abu Mansur.

57. Shimoni, pp. 402–403.

Raziq's men.[58] Many prominent opponents of the Husaynis found it prudent to go abroad for several months.

Many of the British measures that were designed to curb the revolt actually accelerated it by antagonizing villagers and townspeople. Under the martial law introduced in November 1937, military courts imposed the death penalty on men found with a rifle or bomb, houses were demolished if shots were fired from them or any warmaking material found in them, people were detained without trial (over five thousand were under detention by 1939), and collective fines were imposed on villages and quarters of towns. Midnight searches of villages, during which all the men were rounded up for a lineup, proved particularly galling. On one occasion, the military gathered all fifteen hundred men in the Ramlah market for an identity check and interrogation.[59] Over a hundred men were hanged during the course of the revolt, the first being the Qassamite leader Shaykh al-Saadi. But one district commissioner argued that these hangings were "ineffective as a means of checking the revolt. The more martyrs who were killed, the more Arabs there were ready to take their places."[60] The practice of using detainees as human minesweepers angered both the public and the Colonial Office in London.[61] The British use of Jewish soldiers, not only to defend settlements but to fight the Arab guerrillas,[62] further raised interracial passions.

58. Abd al-Raziq's band murdered Hasan Sidqi al-Dajani, a prominent Jerusalemite and supporter of the Nashashibis, in November 1938, which triggered Fakhri al-Nashashibi's repudiation of the revolt and his effort to build himself up as an alternative (pro-British) leader to al-Hajj Amin.

59. I. Lloyd-Phillips to general officer commanding, Oct. 8, 1938; Wilson, diary, pp. 34–35, St. Antony's College, Private Paper Collection. For criticism of the policy see Donald McGillivray to high commissioner, Sept. 14, 1938, ibid.

60. Alec S. Kirkbride, *A Crackle of Thorns* (London: John Murray, 1956), p. 106.

61. High commissioner, dispatch, Nov. 4, 1938, enclosing a protest from Acre religious leaders, Sept. 22, and CO minutes; acting high commissioner, dispatch, Jan. 23, 1939, and CO minutes, CO 733/368/75156/23 pt. 2; interview with Walid Khalidi, Beirut, May 13, 1971.

62. Such as Major Orde Wingate's Special Night Squads. See Lloyd-Phillips to general officer commanding, Oct. 8, 1938; General Haining, reports, Aug. 24, Nov. 30, 1938, St. Antony's College, Private Paper Collection.

Relatively effective measures to contain the rebellion included the construction, in the late spring of 1938, of a seventy-kilometer barbed wire fence along the north-northeast border, which reduced infiltration from Syria. In November 1938, a rigorous traffic control system was instituted to hamper the movement of men and ammunition from one district to another within Palestine. And permanent military occupation of villages was facilitated by massive troop reinforcements in late 1938 and 1939, which brought the troop level back up to twenty thousand.[63]

By the beginning of 1939, the southern and central parts of Palestine were under British control again, and Abd al-Qadir al-Husayni had retreated to Damascus. The other commanders also left for Damascus in January to discuss the strategy that the Arab negotiators should adopt at the upcoming London conference. By March the revolt had degenerated into sporadic incidents of sniping and the settling of scores between families.[64] Although the situation was relatively secure, a final spate of assassination attempts occurred in June 1939 after most of the Nashashibi supporters had returned from their self-imposed exile abroad.[65]

British forces outnumbered the rebels by ten to one and had far superior military and logistical equipment, thus dooming the revolt militarily. Its motivating force, however, had always been political: to compel the British to accommodate Arab grievances. These political ends were reflected in the White Paper of May 1939, which came nearer to meeting Arab demands than any previous policy statement. A second motivating factor was social unrest within Palestinian Arab society. Indebted and dispossessed peasants asserted themselves against

63. Kirkbride, pp. 104, 106; Haining, reports, Aug. 24, Nov. 30, 1938, St. Antony's College, Private Paper Collection.

64. Al-Hajj Muhammad and Abd al-Raziq returned to Palestine in early March, but the former was killed trying to escape a village cordon on March 27 and the latter surrendered to a French military post in Syria in mid-April, with only sixteen men left in his band.

65. Attempts were made against members of the Bitar family of Jaffa, and a son of Shaykh Asad al-Shuqayri of Acre was murdered (*Palestine Post,* June 1939, passim).

the conservative landowning elite. The guerrilla forces controlled the countryside, but they still needed the elite to articulate the political demands and negotiate with the British. No alternative political structure emerged in the countryside, and the social revolt petered out amid intervillage feuds.

The political victory in 1939 had to be measured against the serious economic and social disintegration suffered by the Arab community and the marked political and military consolidation of the Yishuv.[66] Jewish militants had turned to violence for the first time: the Irgun placed bombs in Arab markets in Haifa, Jerusalem, and Jaffa in 1938 and, after the publication of the White Paper, sabotaged government buildings and raided Arab villages at night.[67] The established politicians of the Yishuv were so alienated by the White Paper that many advocated civil disobedience against the British authorities. They accelerated efforts to bring in illegal immigrants and refused to assist the British authorities in locating Jews responsible for the bombings and raids.

The violence in Palestine dramatized the Arabs' grievances and contributed to British reassessment of policies. The brief riots of the early 1920s might have induced a serious policy reevaluation if Britain had not been committed to ruling Palestine and allowing the Zionist movement to become established there. This British policy, however, meant that the underlying grievances of the Arabs could never be effectively redressed. Thus the possibility—and inevitability—of violence persisted. Such violence, however, was self-defeating if it did not bring independence nearer and especially if it did not weaken the Yishuv. In fact, the Yishuv became stronger and more determined in its aims with each violent outbreak. Violence proved to be a double-edged weapon: although useful to pressure the colonial power, it accelerated the mobilization of the rival national movement and thus further undermined the position of the indigenous group.

66. Hurewitz, *Struggle*, pp. 84–85.
67. Ibid., pp. 92, 107–109.

10 / Concluding Reflections

The Palestine Arab national movement reached the height of its vigor and accomplishments in the 1930s. The general strike and rebellion compelled the British government to re-interpret its policy to the extent of issuing a White Paper in 1939 that held out the possibility of independence for the mandated territory and restricted Jewish immigration and land purchases. This White Paper appeared unsatisfactory to most of the Palestinian leaders because they wanted Britain to agree to rule by the Arab majority and to abrogate the Balfour Declaration. But the Arab community would have co-operated with the policy enunciated in the White Paper if circumstances had permitted its implementation.

The onset of World War II, however, radically altered the context in which Britain operated, restructuring the international milieu, undercutting the bases of the British Empire, and enhancing the moral case of the Zionist movement. At the close of the war, the American and Soviet superpowers were in the ascendant. Britain was dismantling its Indian empire, had lost the will and capacity to rule Palestine, and was increasingly inclined to wash its hands of the task of reconciling Arab and Jewish claims. The deep sympathy for the plight of the Jewish people after the holocaust brought the Zionist movement international support for the establishment of a Jewish state and the ingathering of the remnants of European Jewry. The Zionist movement displayed great resiliency and flexibility in its tactics, keeping the

Yishuv in a high state of mobilization and accommodating itself to the international demand for partition at the critical period in 1946–1947.

The Palestine Arab political movement had been fractured since 1939.[1] The Palestine Arabs had become fatally dependent on the neighboring Arab states, who took the lead diplomatically and militarily on their behalf. Moreover, al-Hajj Amin al-Husayni's defection to Nazi Germany damaged the moral case of the Palestinians in the eyes of the victorious Allied powers.

During the war, the Arab community could not organize politically because the British government banned all such activities and kept the leaders of the Arab Higher Committee in exile or detention. The Husayni supporters fell into disarray after al-Hajj Amin fled to Germany and Jamal al-Husayni was detained by the British in Southern Rhodesia. The Nashashibis initially wanted to cooperate with the British war effort, but they fell silent after Raghib Bey's outspoken cousin Fakhri was assassinated in late 1941. Only the leaders of the Istiqlal party attempted to organize inside Palestine. Because political parties were outlawed, the Istiqlal party tried to use such channels as the Arab National Bank, left-wing labor societies, and chambers of commerce, but these groups had limited impact and minimal coordination.

The Arab states had to intervene three times to impose a semblance of unity on the Palestinian movement. In 1944, the Syrian leader, Jamil Mardam, induced the Istiqlal and Husayni activists to accept the appointment of Musa al-Alami as the Palestinian delegate to the Alexandria conference, which drew up plans for the League of Arab States. Alami then took charge of Arab League efforts to establish information offices abroad and promote land buying in Palestine. He earned the

---

1. The following section is adapted from Ann Mosely Lesch, "The Palestine Arab Nationalist Movement under the Mandate," in William B. Quandt, Fuad Jabber, and Ann Mosely Lesch, *The Politics of Palestinian Nationalism* (Berkeley: University of California Press, 1973), pp. 40–42, and largely based on Hurewitz, *Struggle*, chaps. 8–23.

enmity of both the Husaynis and Istiqlalists when he refused to allow them to control his activities.

In the fall of 1945, Mardam imposed a twelve-member Arab Higher Committee on the Palestinian politicians, but Jamal al-Husayni reorganized this committee as soon as he was allowed to return to Palestine in the spring of 1946. He expanded the committee to twenty-eight members, one-third from the Husayni camp, one-third from other parties, and one-third representing various economic groups. The Istiqlal refused to participate and formed a rival committee in June. The situation was further complicated by al-Hajj Amin's sudden arrival in Cairo at the end of May, having escaped from detention in France. The Arab League seized this opportunity to revise the membership of the Higher Committee again, this time placing it firmly under the control of al-Hajj Amin and Jamal Effendi. The Arab League funded its activities and placed Musa al-Alami's projects under its direct supervision. The British government officially recognized this body as the spokesman of the Arab community in Palestine, but refused to allow al-Hajj Amin to return.

The Arab Higher Committee never succeeded in organizing effectively within Palestine. It could not command the support of the Istiqlalists, Nashashibis, and left-wing organizations, such as the League of National Liberation. Most important, it never developed a strategy for presenting its case to the international community or for counteracting the Jewish rebellion that was gathering force inside Palestine. The Palestine Arabs failed to present their case before—or effectively to oppose afterward—the Anglo-American Committee of Inquiry in May 1946, which called for a period of trusteeship to be followed by independence under a unitary state, with no restriction on land buying by Jews and the immediate admission of one hundred thousand Jewish refugees from Europe. The Palestinian leaders supported the concept of a unitary state, but opposed the immigration and land-buying provisions. They also failed to make their case before the United Nations Special Committee on Palestine, which recommended partition in September 1947. Only the Communist-affiliated League of National Liberation accepted the principle of partition, a viewpoint that appeared treasonous to most of the Arab public.

The local-level nationalist committees that had formed the backbone of the 1936 strike were not revived until December 1947, weeks after the UN General Assembly upheld partition. And not until April 1948 did the Arab Higher Committee propose that Arab civil servants assume control of the departments in which they served after Britain evacuated in May. Efforts to renew guerrilla warfare were nearly as ineffective as the political actions.[2] Abd al-Qadir al-Husayni, a guerrilla leader in the late 1930s, organized village bands in central Palestine. And Fawzi al-Qawuqji, the Syrian fighter in 1936, headed the Arab League–sponsored Arab Liberation Army, which operated in the Nablus–Jenin hill region. Qawuqji received little support from the Arab states and never managed any successful operations against the Jewish settlements. Abd al-Qadir was held in high esteem by the Palestinians, but he was killed in the April offensive of the Haganah. This offensive broke the Arabs' hold over communication routes and overran such major Arab centers as Acre, Haifa, Tiberias, Safad, and Jaffa, all before the British withdrew on May 14 and the state of Israel was proclaimed.

Although the Palestine Arab community was disorganized and its military efforts confined to village-level combat, al-Hajj Amin was loath to approve military intervention by the Arab states. He feared that they would use the fighting for their own political ends and as an arena for their dynastic rivalries, turning the Palestinians into their pawns. As the situation deteriorated inside Palestine, however, he had no

2. For firsthand accounts of the fighting in 1948, see Nafez Nazzal, "The Zionist Occupation of Western Galilee, 1948," *Journal of Palestine Studies*, 11 (Spring 1974), 58–76; Fauzi el-Qawuqji, "Memoirs, 1948," *Journal of Palestine Studies*, 4 and 5 (Summer and Autumn 1972), 27–58 and 3–33; and Elias Shoufani, "The Fall of a Village," *Journal of Palestine Studies*, 4 (Summer 1972), 108–121.

choice but to accept Arab League intervention. Emir Abdullah of Transjordan joined the fighting to gain control over the hill districts and Jerusalem. His de facto acceptance of partition was understood by the Israeli leadership and supported by his British mentors. The Egyptian regime was embroiled in its conflict with Britain over the stationing of British troops at the Suez Canal and was therefore hesitant to undertake a military adventure in Palestine. But, at the last minute, Egyptian troops were sent to Gaza and the Hebron hills, largely to check Abdullah's ambitions.

In the ensuing fighting, only the seacoast around Gaza and the central hill region were retained by the Arabs, in the hands of the Egyptian and Jordanian armies, respectively. The Arab Higher Committee formed a short-lived "government of all Palestine" in Gaza in September 1948, with al-Hajj Amin as president of the assembly. But Abdullah countered by annexing the hill districts and cemented his alliance with Raghib al-Nashashibi by appointing him military governor of this area, thereafter known as the West Bank. As a result of *an-nakba* (the disaster), Palestine Arab society was fractured and became dependent on the Arab regimes and on the international dole.

In Chapter 1, I proposed that the tactics adopted and the manner in which policy dilemmas were faced established the patterns of interaction between the nationalist movement and the European authorities and settlers, but that, in the final analysis, these actions alone could not determine the outcome of the nationalist struggle. Rather, the balance of force and influence between the indigenous movement and the settlers, the strategic requirements of the ruling power, and the international attitude toward colonialism were the overriding determinants. An examination of the interwar years reveals that these three factors coalesced to the detriment of the Arab community in Palestine.

First, the dominant international environment in the interwar years supported the system of imperial rule by European states over non-European peoples. Although the unself-conscious assumptions of superiority that underlay the British mastery of India and Africa were tempered after World War I, and lip service was given to the need for a gradual move toward self-rule, the paternalistic ethos was not seriously challenged. The view that European settlers would contribute to the betterment of the indigenous population was largely unquestioned. Thus there was no moral pressure on Britain to relinquish control over Palestine. In fact, the European powers' interest lay in maintaining the balance in the imperial system and limiting the demands being made by such expanding powers as Germany.

Second, the British government viewed Palestine as an essential part of its strategic holdings linking Europe with Asia and Africa. It hesitated to relinquish its substantial interests in Palestine, such as the Haifa port and Lydda air base. Particularly after Egypt and Iraq gained a measure of independence, Britain wanted to ensure control of at least one military entrepôt. One rationale that British officials used to retain Palestine was their fear that hostile European states would step into the vacuum created after their departure. In the 1920s, France was the competitor; in the 1930s, German and Italian designs were feared. As Arab-Jewish tensions escalated inside Palestine, the real danger emerged that no stable regime could be established if the British withdrew and that outside powers would be drawn into the conflict. Thus Britain's own policies in Palestine and the resulting dilemmas made it increasingly difficult for Britain to extricate itself from the territory.

Third, the Zionist movement's claim that the Jewish people had the right to settle in Palestine and establish autonomous communal institutions won official recognition in London and at the League of Nations. Extensive immigration, the creation of a largely autarkic society, and the formation of a quasi-government and semiclandestine military force all served to consolidate the Yishuv. The Zionist movement viewed as illegitimate the indigenous Arab community's aspiration to political independence. The mainstream Zionist leadership was willing to concede civil and religious rights to the Arabs, but not national rights. Even those who supported binationalism refused to compromise the Jewish community's right to immigrate and buy land and were therefore viewed by Arab leaders as little different from the majoritarian Zionists. Moreover, when partition was first suggested in 1937, the Zionist leadership insisted that the Arab residents be evicted from the zone intended for the Jewish state, even though that would cause large-scale dislocation. This insistence indicated that they disregarded not only the nationalist aspirations of the Arabs, but also the peasantry's bonds to their ancestral lands. They had little comprehension that the Arabs' ties to Palestine were as profound as their own and would be guarded as zealously.

The importance of the psychological gap between the Jews and Arabs in Palestine should not be underestimated. Not only was there a marked disparity in living standards, social mores, and political structure, but there was also a completely different *Weltanschauung*. The Yishuv's belief in its innate right to regain Palestine, when coupled with the colonialist attitude toward the "natives," resulted in disregard for the status and needs of that indigenous people. The Arabs were made to feel inferior to the Jewish community, which only made more acute their resentment against the Jewish immigrants and the Zionist movement.

Fear of Zionism accelerated the growth of a national movement among the Palestine Arabs. In the last decades of the Ottoman Empire, the conventional modes of protest—petitions by notables and sporadic rural outbreaks—were supplemented by protests that utilized newly emerging institutions and modes of action, namely, the press, political societies, and the parliament in Istanbul. These forms of protest became more fully developed in the 1920s, but were less effective vis-à-vis the British than they had been under the Ottoman regime. Articles in the Arabic press, the convening of national congresses, and the submission of petitions to the British authorities served more to structure the Arab political community and develop its national awareness than to influence British policy. Delegations were sent to London so infrequently that their impact could only be ephemeral. Even riots in the towns, general strikes, and the rural rebellion could be contained, although at a rising cost.

The Palestine Arab community became highly politicized, active in arguing its case, and well aware of the dangers facing it. Why then did its national movement fail? The answers may lie, in part, in the nature of Arab society at that historical period. The society was highly stratified vertically and localized horizontally. Primary allegiances were to the family, clan, village, and religious sect. The population was largely illiterate, with limited horizons. Peasants defended their own land, but could not coordinate their efforts throughout the country, much less respond to a threat in another district. Antagonisms among villages and clans and rivalries among elite families attenuated the effectiveness of political institutions and limited the possibility of unified action. The landed elite could mobilize villagers through its patron-client ties, which had the benefit of ensuring rapid mobilization, but had the weakness of perpetuating social cleavages. Although the community shared the same ultimate political aspirations and fears, they were unable to structure a movement to work consistently and effectively toward those goals. Thus the mass rebellion degenerated into feuding among villages and families. And the political elite adhered to maximalist goals even though it lacked the power to realize them. This inflexibility—and the disjunction between means and ends—are often viewed as the major weaknesses of the Palestinian national movement, but they are hardly a sufficient explanation for its failure. The neighboring Arab countries were at approximately the same level of social development and suffered comparable internal cleavages. They also went through long struggles and internal convulsions in the process of obtaining independence. And yet, by the 1930s, they had all obtained a degree of internal autonomy, and their politicians were in the position to exert increasing leverage against the European rulers.

The fact that the neighboring Arab countries obtained such institutions, through which their politicians could gain experience and exert power, points to another area in which the Palestinians were disadvantaged. Observers have argued that the Arab politicians should have accepted British offers to participate in a legislative council and thereby gain some influence over British policy. In this way the Arabs would have acquired some real leverage vis-à-vis the British and the Yishuv. Failure to grasp such opportunities has been seen as a sign of the immaturity of the Arab political movement and the inflexibility of its leadership. While the lack of such institutions did greatly hamper the development and consolidation of the Arab political structure, the charge must be placed in context. In 1922–1923, when the Arab Executive rejected the legislative council, the mandate had not yet come into force and the Arabs still had grounds for hoping that its terms could be altered. Acceptance of a council, at that critical juncture, would have undermined their entire case and made them look like political opportunists who merely sought the perquisites of office. When, starting in 1926, the Arab leaders began to propose formulas for a legislative council, the British and subsequently the Zionists opposed establishing such a forum. The British government preferred to remain as the arbitrator between the Jews and Arabs and realized that it could not give the Arabs any control over Jewish immigration or land purchases. In other words, anything related to implementing the policy of the Jewish national home would have to remain outside the purview of the council, and thus its role would be meaningless. If a legislative council had been established, the Arabs would have made a major compromise on principle while gaining no real power in return. But the resulting institutional vacuum further weakened the Arab efforts to maintain an effective political movement.

As late as 1939, Britain called for the establishment of a state which neither Arab nor Jew would dominate. But Britain never devised a strategy to realize that objective. British officials realized that the human dislocations that would result from partition made that option excessively costly. But how could they persuade the Arabs and Jews to share Palestine?

The aspirations of the two communities were fundamentally irreconcilable, and the overall constellation of forces was weighed against the Arab community. Although in the late 1930s—and even in the 1940s—the Arabs were still the majority in Palestine, they were fighting a defensive battle, trying to maintain their demographic edge and their economic base. The Arabs had no means to prevent the Yishuv from taking root in the 1920s and 1930s, given Britain's military and diplomatic support. When the British hold weakened in the 1940s and British policy began to shift, the Yishuv was capable of standing on its own and of undermining any major concession that Britain might make to the Arabs.

Two nations claiming the same territory must either compromise their goals or clash head-on. Neither the Arabs nor the Zionists were willing to accept less than majority status, thereby ruling out a binational solution. The Zionist leaders, but not those of the Arabs, were willing to consider partition, which would give the Jewish community a secure geographical base but take from the Arabs substantial lands and displace many people. The irreconcilability of aspirations made confrontation unavoidable. Though it was feared that the confrontation might cause dislocation within the Arab society, such a wholesale uprooting was incomprehensible beforehand. The Arabs had reacted in disbelief and outrage to the partition plans of 1937 and 1947: the war in 1948, which fragmented and dispersed the entire society, magnified their grievances immeasurably. Another fifteen years would pass

237

before the Palestinians could begin to restore their political movement and rebuild their fractured community. By then, the localized conflict between the Arab and Jewish communities had been transformed into a major confrontation with world wide ramifications.

Bibliography

Primary Sources

Archives

American University of Beirut
  Library, special file on Palestine
Central Zionist Archives, Jerusalem
  File of Political Department of the Jewish Agency (S25)
  File of the Central Office of the Zionist Organization, London (Z4)
Israel State Archives, Jerusalem
  Chief Secretary's Office Papers, Palestine Government Arab Documents
Middle East Centre, St. Antony's College, Oxford
  Private Paper Collection: George Antonius; Arif al-Arif, Gaza Diary 1939–1940 (in Arabic); Humphrey Bowman: Captain William Brunton; Sir Wyndham Deedes; General Robert Haining; David G. Hogarth; I. Lloyd-Phillips; Sir Harry Luke; Sir Harold MacMichael; Donald McGillivray; Reginald Monckton; Sir Herbert Samuel; Sir Mark Sykes; Miss H. Wilson diary, Bir Zayt, 1938–1939; William Yale
Oberlin College, Oberlin, Ohio
  Henry Churchill King Papers
Public Record Office, London
  Correspondence files of the War Office (1917–1921), Foreign Office (1917–1921, 1939), and Colonial Office (1921–1940) relating to Palestine

British Government Publications

Great Britain. Colonial Office. *Report by His Majesty's Government in the United Kingdom of Great Britain and Northern Ireland to the Council of the League of Nations on the Administration of Palestine and Transjordan, 1922–1938.* Colonial Numbers 5, 9, 12, 20, 26, 31, 40, 47, 59, 75, 82, 94, 104, 112, 129, 146, 166. London: HMSO, 1923–1939.
——. Parliamentary Papers. Cmd. 1499: *An Interim Report on the Civil Administration of Palestine during the Period 1st July, 1920–30th June, 1921.* London: HMSO, 1921.

——. Cmd. 1500: *Mandates, Final Drafts.* London: HMSO, 1921.

——.Cmd. 1540: *Palestine Disturbances of May, 1921: Reports of the Commissioners of Inquiry* . . . (Haycraft) London: HMSO, 1921.

——.Cmd. 1700: *Correspondence with the Palestine Arab Delegation and the Zionist Organization.* (Churchill) London: HMSO, 1922.

——.Cmd. 1785: *Mandate for Palestine (and Note on Application to Transjordan).* London: HMSO, July 1922.

——. Cmd. 1889: *Papers Relating to the Elections for the Palestine Legislative Council.* London: HMSO, 1923.

——. Cmd. 1989: *Proposed Formation of an Arab Agency. Correspondence with High Commissioner for Palestine.* London: HMSO, November 1923.

——. Cmd. 3229: *Statement of Policy* . . . (Wailing Wall) London: HMSO, November 1928.

——. Cmd. 3530: *Report of the Commission* (Palestine Disturbances of August 1929; Shaw). London: HMSO, 1930.

——. Cmd. 3582: *Palestine, Statement with Regard to British Policy.* London: HMSO, May 1930.

——. Cmd. 3683–3687: *Report on Immigration, Land Settlement and Development by Sir John Hope Simpson* . . . London: HMSO, 1930.

——. Cmd. 3692: *Statement of Policy by His Majesty's Government in the United Kingdom Presented by the Secretary of State for the Colonies to Parliament by Command of His Majesty.* (Passfield) London: HMSO, 1930.

——. Cmd. 5119: *Proposed New Constitution for Palestine.* London: HMSO, March 1936.

——. Cmd. 5479: *Report of the Palestine Royal Commission* . . . (Peel) London: HMSO, 1937.

——. Cmd. 5513: *Statement of Policy* . . . *Presented by the Secretary of State for the Colonies* . . . London: HMSO, 1937.

——. Cmd. 5854: *Report of the Palestine Partition Commission.* (Woodhead) London: HMSO, 1938.

——. Cmd. 5893: *Statement of Policy* . . . *Presented by the Secretary of State for the Colonies* . . . London: HMSO, 1938.

——. Cmd. 5957: *Correspondence between Sir Henry McMahon and the Sharif of Mecca, July, 1915–March, 1916.* London: HMSO, 1939.

——. Cmd. 5974: *Report of a Committee Set up to Consider Certain Correspondences between Sir Henry McMahon and the Sharif of Mecca in 1915 and 1916.* London: HMSO, 1939.

——. Cmd. 6019: *Statement of Policy Presented by the Secretary of State for the Colonies* . . . (MacDonald) London: HMSO, 1939.

——. *Report of the High Commissioner on the Administration of Palestine, 1920–1925.* Colonial Number 15. London: HMSO, 1925.

Palestine Government. *A Survey of Palestine for the Information of the Anglo-*

American Committee of Inquiry. 2 vols. Jerusalem: Government Printer, 1946.
Woodward, E. L., and Rohan Butler, eds. *Documents on British Foreign Policy, 1919–1939.* 1st ser., IV. London: HMSO, 1952.

League of Nations Publications

Permanent Mandates Commission. Fourteenth session; *Minutes,* 1928. Geneva, 1928.
——. Seventeenth (Extraordinary) session; *Minutes,* 1930. Geneva, 1930.
——. Twenty-ninth session; *Minutes,* 1936. Geneva, 1936.
——. Thirty-second (Extraordinary) session; *Minutes,* 1937. Geneva, 1937.
——. Thirty-sixth session; *Minutes,* 1939. Geneva, 1939.

Newspapers

British Museum, London, Newspaper Collection
  News Bulletin of the Palestine Daily Mail, April–May 1921
  Palestine Bulletin, Jerusalem, 1926–1928, 1932
  Palestine Post, Jerusalem, 1932–1939
Royal Institute of International Affairs, London, Newspaper Collection
  Manchester Guardian, 1923–1930
  Morning Post, 1923–1930
  Times, 1923–1930

Interviews

al-Arif, Arif. Ramallah, May 22, 1971.
Darwazah, Muhammad Izzat. Damascus, May 14, 1971.
Darwish, Ishaq. Jerusalem, June 5, 1971.
Dudiin, Akram Aysa. Hebron, June 5, 1971.
Duwayk, Arafat. Hebron, June 5, 1971.
Faris, Abd al-Rauf. Nablus, June 3, 1971.
al-Husayni, Jamal. Beirut, May 8, 1971.
al-Jaabari, Shaykh Muhammad. Hebron, May 29, 1971.
Khalidi, Walid. Beirut, May 13, 1971.
al-Masri, Hikmat. Nablus, June 3, 1971.
Qamhawi, Dr. Walid. Nablus, June 3, 1971.
Shihadeh, Aziz. Ramallah, May 22, 1971.
Sultan, Hamdi. Hebron, May 29, 1971.
al-Taji al-Faruqi, Dr. Hamdi. Ramallah, May 22, 1971.

Secondary Literature

Abbas, Abdul Majid. "Palestine (1933–39)." In *Challenge and Response in Internal Conflict,* ed. D. M. Condit and Bert H. Cooper, Jr. Washington, D.C.: American University Center for Research in Social Systems, 1967.

Abboushi, Wasef F. "The Road to Rebellion: Arab Palestine in the 1930's." *Journal of Palestine Studies,* 23 (Spring 1977), 23–46.

Abcarius, Michael F. *Palestine through the Fog of Propaganda.* London: Hutchison, 1946.

Abu Ghazaleh, Adnan Mohammad. "Arab Cultural Nationalism in Palestine, 1919–1948." Ph.D. dissertation, New York University, 1967.

———. "Arab Cultural Nationalism in Palestine during the British Mandate." *Journal of Palestine Studies,* 3 (Spring 1972), 37–63.

Abu-Lughod, Ibrahim, ed. *The Transformation of Palestine.* Evanston, Ill.: Northwestern University Press, 1971.

al-Alami, Musa. *Ibrat Filastin.* Beirut, 1949.

———. *al-Mashru al-Inshai al-Arabi.* Baghdad, 1946.

Allubah, Muhammad Ali. *Filastin wal-Dhamir al-Insani.* Cairo: n.d. (late 1940s).

AlRoy, Gil Carl. *The Involvement of Peasants in Internal Wars.* Princeton: Center of International Studies, Research Monograph No. 24, 1966.

Alush, Naji. *Al-Muqawwamah al-Arabiyyah fi Filastin, 1914–1948.* Beirut: Palestine Research Center, 1967.

Andrews, Fannie Fern. *The Holy Land under Mandate.* 2 vols. Boston: Houghton, Mifflin, 1931.

The Annals of the American Academy of Political and Social Science, "Palestine: A Decade of Development," ed. Harry Viteles and Khalil Totah. Philadelphia: Vol. 164, November 1932.

Antonius, George. *The Arab Awakening.* New York: Capricorn, 1965. (First published 1938.)

Arab Students League. English Supplement to *al Ghad* (Bethlehem), no. 1 (February 1940).

Arab Women's Society of Jerusalem. *The Holy Land.* Jerusalem, February 5, 1938.

Asfour, Edmund, et al. *Backdrop to Tragedy: The Struggle for Palestine.* Boston: Beacon Hill Press, 1957.

Aurel, Alexander, and Peretz Cornfield, eds. *The Near East and Middle East Who's Who.* Vol. 1: *Palestine Trans-Jordan 1945–1946.* Jerusalem: Near and Middle East Who's Who Publishing Co., 1945.

Barbour, Nevill. *Nisi Dominus: A Survey of the Palestine Controversy.* London: George Harrap, 1946.

———. "Some Less Familiar Aspects of the Palestine Problem." *Journal of the Royal Central Asian Society,* 25 (October 1938), 554–570.

Ben Gurion, David. *My Talks with Arab Leaders.* New York: Third Press, 1973.

Bentwich, Norman. "The Bi-National Solution." *New Outlook,* 13 (March–April 1970), 44–48.

——. *England in Palestine.* London: Kegan Paul, Trench, Trubner, 1932.

Bertram, Sir Anton, and Harry Charles Luke. *Report of the Commission Appointed by the Government of Palestine to Inquire into the Affairs of the Orthodox Patriarchate of Jerusalem.* London: Oxford University Press, 1921.

Boustany, Wedi F. *The Palestine Mandate: Invalid and Impracticable.* Beirut: American Press, 1936.

Bovis, H. Eugene. *The Jerusalem Question, 1917–1968.* Stanford, Calif: Hoover Institution Press, 1971.

Bowden, Tom. "The Politics of the Arab Rebellion in Palestine 1936–39." *Middle Eastern Studies,* 11 (1975), 147–174.

Bowle, John. *Viscount Samuel.* London: Victor Gollancz, 1957.

Bowman, Humphrey. *Middle East Window.* New York: Longmans, Green, 1942.

Canaan, Muhammad Tawfiq. *The Palestine Arab Cause.* Jerusalem: Modern Press, 1936.

Cattan, Henry. *Palestine, the Arabs and Israel, the Search for Justice.* London: Longmans, 1969.

Cohen, Aharon. *Israel and the Arab World.* New York: Funk and Wagnalls, 1970.

Cohen, Israel. *The Zionist Movement.* New York: Zionist Organization of America, 1946.

Cohen, Michael J. "British Strategy and the Palestine Question: 1936–1939." *Journal of Contemporary History,* 7 (July–October 1972), 157–184.

——. "Secret Diplomacy and Rebellion in Palestine, 1936–1939." *International Journal of Middle East Studies,* 8 (July 1977), 379–404.

Cottam, Richard W. *Nationalism in Iran.* Pittsburgh: University of Pittsburgh Press, 1964.

Crozier, Brian. *The Rebels: A Study of Post-War Insurrections.* London: Chatto and Windus, 1960.

Cust, Archer. "Cantonization: A Plan for Palestine." *Journal of the Royal Central Asian Society,* 23 (April 1936), 194–220.

Darwazah, Muhammad Izzat. *al-Qadiyyah al-Filastiniyyah fi Mukhtalif Marahiliha.* 2 vols. Sidon, 1951.

Dawn, C. Ernest. *From Ottomanism to Arabism.* Urbana: University of Illinois Press, 1973.

——. "The Rise of Arabism in Syria." *Middle East Journal,* 16 (1962), 145–168.

Dawson, William Harbutt. *The Future of Empire and the World Price of Peace.* London: Williams and Norgate, 1930.

Dayri, A. "The Fall of Nazareth and Galilee: The Role of the Hittin and Ajnadin Brigades." *Shuun Filastiniyya,* 21 (May 1973), 82–91.

Deutsch, Karl W. *Nationalism and Social Communication.* Cambridge, Mass.: M.I.T. Press, 1966.

Emerson, Rupert. *From Empire to Nation: The Rise to Self-Assertion of Asian and African Peoples.* Boston: Beacon Press, 1966.

ESCO Foundation for Palestine. *Palestine: A Study of Jewish, Arab and British Policies.* 2 vols. New Haven: Yale University Press, 1947.

Evans, E. W. *The British Yoke: Reflections on the Colonial Empire.* London: William Hodge, 1949.

Feiwel, T. R. *No Ease in Zion.* London: Secher and Warburg, 1938.

Finn, James. *Stirring Times, or Records from Jerusalem Consular Chronicles of 1853 to 1856.* 2 vols. London: Kegan Paul, 1878.

Furlonge, Geoffrey. *Palestine Is My Country: The Story of Musa Alami.* London: John Murray, 1969.

Gann, L. H., and Peter Duignan. *Burden of Empire: An Appraisal of Western Colonialism in Africa South of the Sahara.* Stanford, Calif.: Hoover Institution Press, 1971.

al-Ghuri, Emile. *Filastin.* Baghdad, 1962.

——. *Jihad al-Filastiniyyin didd al-Istimar wal-Harakah al-Yahudiyyah min 1918 ila 1948.* Arab Higher Committee, n.d.

Gibb, H. A. R. "The Islamic Congress at Jerusalem in December 1931." In *Survey of International Affairs 1934,* pp. 99–105. London: Oxford University Press, 1935.

Goodrich, Leland M. *The United Nations.* New York: Crowell, 1959.

Granovsky (Granott), Abraham. *The Land System in Palestine.* Rev. ed. London: Eyre and Spottiswoode, 1952.

Graves, Philip. *Palestine: The Land of the Three Faiths.* London: Jonathan Cape, 1923.

Gurr, Ted Robert. *Why Men Rebel.* Princeton: Princeton University Press, 1970.

Hadawi, Sami. *Bitter Harvest: Palestine between 1914–1967.* New York: New World Press, 1967.

Haddad, Elias N. "Political Parties in Syria and Palestine (Qaisi and Yemeni)." *Journal of the Palestine Oriental Society,* 1 (1921).

Hanna, Paul L. *British Policy in Palestine.* Washington: American Council on Public Affairs, 1942.

Hattis, Susan Lee. *The Bi-National Idea in Palestine during Mandatory Times.* Haifa: Shikmona, 1970.

Haykal, Yusif. *al-Qadiyyah al-Filastiniyyah Takhlil wa Naqd.* Jaffa: n.d. [1937].

Hertzberg, Arthur, ed. *The Zionist Idea.* New York: Atheneum, 1969.

Herzl, Theodor. *Diaries.* Trans. Marvin Lowenthal. New York: Dial Press, 1956.

Himadeh, Said, ed. *Economic Organization of Palestine.* Beirut: American Press, 1938.

Holt, P. M. *Egypt and the Fertile Crescent 1516–1922: A Political History.* Ithaca, N.Y.: Cornell University Press, 1966.

Horowitz, David, and Rita Hinden. *Economic Survey of Palestine, with Special Reference to 1936 and 1937.* Tel Aviv: Jewish Agency, 1938.

Howard, Harry N. *The King-Crane Commission.* Beirut: Khayats, 1963.

Hurewitz, J. C. *Diplomacy in the Near and Middle East.* 2 vols. New York: Van Nostrand, 1956.

——. *The Struggle for Palestine.* New York: Norton, 1950.

al-Husayni, Muhammad Amin. *Haqaiq an Qadiyyah Filastin.* Cairo: Library of the Arab Higher Committee, 1957.

Hyamson, Albert Montefiore. *Palestine under the Mandate, 1920–1948.* London: Methuen, 1950.

Jabbour, George. *Settler Colonialism in Southern Africa and the Middle East.* Beirut: Palestine Research Center, 1970.

Jeffries, Joseph M. N. *Palestine: The Reality.* London: Longmans, Green, 1939.

Jennings, William Ivor. *The Approach to Self-Government.* Cambridge: Cambridge University Press, 1956.

John, Robert, and Sami Hadawi. *The Palestine Diary.* 2 vols. Beirut: Palestine Research Center, 1970.

Johnson, Chalmers. *Revolutionary Change.* Boston: Little, Brown, 1966.

Joseph, Bernard (Dov). *British Rule in Palestine.* Washington, D.C.: Public Affairs Press, 1948.

al-Joundi, Sami. *Le Drame palestinien: Pour sortir de l'impasse.* Paris: Artheme Fayard, 1969.

Judd, Denis O'N. *Balfour and the British Empire: A Study in Imperial Evolution, 1874–1932.* New York: St. Martin's Press, 1968.

Kanafani, Ghassan. *The 1936–39 Revolt in Palestine.* Committee for Democratic Palestine, n.d.

Karpat, Kemal H. "The Transformation of the Ottoman State, 1789–1908." *International Journal of Middle East Studies,* 3 (July 1972), 243–281.

al-Kayyali, Abd al-Wahhab, ed. *Wathaiq al-Muqawwamah al-Filastiniyyah didd al-Ihtilal al-Britani wal-Sahyuniyyah, 1918–1939.* Beirut: Institute for Palestine Studies, 1968.

——. *Tarikh Filastin al-Hadith.* Beirut: al-Muassah al-Arabiyyah li-Dirasah wal-Nushr, 1970.

Kedourie, Elie. *Nationalism.* New York: Praeger, 1960.

——. "Religion and Politics: The Diaries of Khalil Sakakini." In *Middle Eastern Affairs,* 1, *St. Antony's Papers,* 4 (1958).

———. "Sir Herbert Samuel and the Government of Palestine." *Middle Eastern Studies,* 5 (January 1969), 44–68.

Kendall, Henry, and K. H. Baruth. *Village Development in Palestine during the British Mandate.* London: Crown Agents for the Colonies, 1949.

Khadduri, Majid. *Arab Contemporaries: The Role of Personalities in Politics.* Baltimore: Johns Hopkins Press, 1973.

Khalidi, Walid, ed. *From Haven to Conquest: Readings in Zionism and the Palestine Problem until 1948.* Beirut: Institute for Palestine Studies, 1971.

———. "Plan Dalet." *Arab World,* 15 (October–November 1969), 15–20.

Khammar, Qustantin. *al-Mujaz fi Tarikh al-Qadiyyah al-Filastiniyyah.* Beirut: al-Maktab al-Tajari, 1964.

Khouri, Fred. *The Arab-Israeli Dilemma.* Syracuse, N.Y.: Syracuse University Press, 1968.

Kirkbride, Alec S. *A Crackle of Thorns.* London: John Murray, 1956.

Kisch, Frederick H. *Palestine Diary.* London: Victor Gollancz, 1938.

Klieman, Aaron. *Foundations of British Policy in the Arab World: The Cairo Conference of 1921.* Baltimore: Johns Hopkins Press, 1971.

Kohn, Hans. *History of Nationalism in the East.* London: George Routledge, 1929.

Lee, John M. *Colonial Development and Good Government.* Oxford: Clarendon Press, 1967.

Lesch, Ann Mosely. "The Origins of Palestine Arab Nationalism." In *Nationalism in a Non-National State: The Dissolution of the Ottoman Empire,* ed. William W. Haddad and William L. Ochsenwald. Columbus: Ohio State University Press, 1977.

———. "The Palestine Arab Nationalist Movement under the Mandate." In William B. Quandt, Fuad Jabber, and Ann Mosely Lesch, *The Politics of Palestinian Nationalism.* Berkeley: University of California Press, 1973.

Lupsha, Peter A. "Explanation of Political Violence: Some Psychological Theories versus Indignation." *Politics and Society,* 2 (Fall 1971), 89–104.

Mandel, Neville J. *The Arabs and Zionism before World War I.* Berkeley: University of California Press, 1976.

———. "Attempts at an Arab-Zionist Entente, 1913–1914." *Middle Eastern Studies,* 1 (April 1965), 238–267.

———. "Turks, Arabs and Jewish Immigration into Palestine, 1882–1914." *Middle Eastern Affairs,* 4 (1968), and *St. Antony's Papers,* 17 (1965), 77–108.

Mansur, George. *The Arab Worker under the Palestine Mandate.* Jerusalem: Commercial Press, 1937.

Ma'oz, Moshe. *Ottoman Reform in Syria and Palestine, 1840–1861: The Impact of the Tanzimat on Politics and Society.* Oxford: Oxford University Press, 1968.

——, ed. *Studies on Palestine during the Ottoman Period,* Jerusalem: Magnes Press, 1975.

Marlowe, John. *The Seat of Pilate: An Account of the Palestine Mandate.* London: Cresset Press, 1959.

McTague, John J., Jr. "The British Military Administration in Palestine, 1917–1920." *Journal of Palestine Studies,* 27 (Spring 1978), 55–76.

Meinertzhagen, Richard. *Middle East Diary, 1917–1956.* London: Cresset Press, 1959.

Mogannam, Matiel. *The Arab Woman and the Palestine Problem.* London: Herbert Joseph, 1937.

*Monroe, Elizabeth. *Britain's Moment in the Middle East.* Baltimore: Johns Hopkins Press, 1963.

Nashif, Taysir. "The Bases of Arab and Jewish Leadership during the Mandate Period." *Journal of Palestine Studies,* 24 (Summer 1977), 113–121.

Nasser, Gamal Abdul. "Memoirs of the First Palestine War." *Journal of Palestine Studies,* 6 (Winter 1973), 3–32.

Nation Associates. *The Arab Higher Committee, Its Origins, Personnel and Purposes.* New York, 1947.

Nazzal, Nafez. "The Zionist Occupation of Western Galilee, 1948." *Journal of Palestine Studies,* 11 (Spring 1974), 58–76.

Newton, Frances E. *Fifty Years in Palestine.* London: Coldharbor Press, 1948.

Novomeysky, Moise Abramovich. *Given to Salt: The Struggle for the Dead Sea Concession.* London: Max Parrish, 1958.

Nuh, Ibrahim. Untitled collection of poems in Arabic. Preface by Fawzi al-Qawuqji. Damascus: n.d. [1938–1939].

Ochsenwald, William L. "Arab Muslims and the Palestine Problem." *Muslim World,* 66 (1976), 287–296.

——. "Opposition to Political Centralization in South Jordan and the Hijaz, 1900–1914." Paper delivered at the Middle East Studies Association convention, November 1971.

Ofer, Pinhas. "The Role of the High Commissioner in British Policy in Palestine: Sir John Chancellor, 1928–1931." Ph.D. dissertation, University of London, 1971.

Oliphant, Laurence. *Haifa or Life in Modern Palestine.* New York: Harper, 1887.

Palestine Arab Party. *Appeal to Members of the British Parliament.* Jerusalem: Arab Federation Printing Press, April 1935.

Parkes, James. *The Emergence of the Jewish Problem, 1878–1939.* London: Oxford University Press, 1946.

Parkinson, Cosmo. *The Colonial Office from Within: 1909–1945.* London: Faber and Faber, 1947.

Patai, Raphael. *On Culture Contact and Its Working in Modern Palestine.* American Anthropological Association, No. 67, 1947.

Pennock, J. Roland, ed. *Self-Government in Modernizing Nations.* Englewood Cliffs, N.J.: Prentice-Hall, 1964.

Perham, Margery. *Colonial Sequence, 1930 to 1949.* London: Methuen, 1967.

Porath, Yehoshua. *The Emergence of the Palestinian-Arab National Movement, 1918–1929.* London: Frank Cass, 1974.

———. "Al-Hajj Amin al-Husayni, Mufti of Jerusalem—His Rise to Power and the Consolidation of His Position." *Asian and African Studies,* 7 (1971), 121–156.

———. *The Palestinian Arab National Movement, 1929–1939.* London: Frank Cass, 1977.

———. "The Palestinians and the Negotiations for the British-Hijazi Treaty, 1920–1925." *Asian and African Studies,* 8 (1972), 20–48.

———. "The Political Organization of the Palestinian Arabs under the British Mandate." In *Palestinian Arab Politics,* ed. Moshe Ma'oz. Jerusalem: Jerusalem Academic Press, 1975.

Pye, Lucian W. *Politics, Personality and Nation-Building: Burma's Search for Identity.* New Haven: Yale University Press, 1962.

Qasimiya, K. "History of the Palestinian Struggle Movement during the Mandate Period." *Shuun Filastiniyya,* 41–42 (January–February 1975), 468–483.

el-Qawuqji, Fauzi. "Memoirs, 1948: Part I." *Journal of Palestine Studies,* 4 (Summer 1972), 27–58.

———. "Memoirs, 1948: Part II." *Journal of Palestine Studies,* 5 (Autumn 1972), 3–33.

Quandt, William B. *Revolution and Political Leadership: Algeria, 1954–1968.* Cambridge, Mass.: M.I.T. Press, 1969.

Razzouk, Ass'ad. "Zionism and Arab Human Rights." In *Zionism and Arab Resistance.* Beirut: Palestine Research Center, Monograph No. 54, 1969.

Rihani, Ameen. *The Fate of Palestine.* Beirut: Rihani, 1967.

Robinson, Kenneth, and Frederick Madden, eds. *Essays in Imperial Government.* Oxford: Basil Blackwell, 1963.

Ro'i, Yaacov. "The Zionist Attitude to the Arabs, 1908–1914." *Middle Eastern Studies,* 4 (April 1968), 198–242.

Rosberg, Carl G., Jr., and John Nottingham. *The Myth of Mau Mau: Nationalism in Kenya.* New York: Praeger, 1966.

Rose, Norman Anthony, "The Arab Rulers and Palestine, 1936: The British Reaction." *Journal of Modern History,* 44 (June 1972), 312–331.

———. *The Gentile Zionists: A Study in Anglo-Zionist Diplomacy, 1929–1939.* London: Frank Cass, 1973.

Sachar, Howard Morley. *The Emergence of the Middle East, 1914–1924.* New York: Knopf, 1969.

Sadaqah, Najib. *Qadiyyah Filastin.* Beirut: Dar al-Kitab, 1946.

Samuel, Edwin. *A Lifetime in Jerusalem.* London: Vallentine, Mitchell, 1970.

Samuel, Herbert, *Memoirs.* London: Cresset Press, 1945.

Samuel, Horace. *Unholy Memories of the Holy Land.* London: Hogarth Press, 1930.

Schmidt, H. D. "The Nazi Party in Palestine and the Levant, 1932–9." *International Affairs,* 28 (October 1952), 460–469.

Sheffer, Gabriel. "The Involvement of Arab States in the Palestine Conflict and British-Arab Relationship before World War II." *Asian and African Studies,* 10 (1974–1975), 59–78.

Shimoni, Jacob. *The Arabs in Israel.* New Haven: Human Relations Area Files, 1956.

Shoufani, Elias. "The Fall of a Village." *Journal of Palestine Studies,* 4 (Summer 1972), 108–121.

Sidebotham, Herbert. *Great Britain and Palestine.* London: MacMillan, 1937.

al-Sifri, Isa. *Filastin al-Arabiyyah bayn al-Intidab wa al-Sahyuniyyah.* Jaffa, 1929.

——. *Risalati.* Jaffa, 1937.

Simson, H. J. *British Rule, and Rebellion.* London: William Blackwood, 1938.

Stein, Leonard. *The Balfour Declaration.* New York: Simon and Schuster, 1961.

——. *Memorandum on "Report of Commission on Palestine Disturbances of August 1929."* London: Jewish Agency, 1930.

Stevens, Richard P., ed. *Zionism and Palestine before the Mandate: A Phase of Western Imperialism.* Beirut: Institute for Palestine Studies, 1972.

Storrs, Ronald. *Memoirs: Orientations.* London: Nicholson and Watson, 1937.

Supreme Muslim Council, *Report of Arab Doctors on Exhumation of the Bodies of the Jewish Corpses Exhumed at Hebron, on September 11, 1929, and Report of Committee on Reference Nominated by the Government of Palestine.* Jerusalem: Bayt al-Makdes Press, 1929.

Sykes, Christopher. *Crossroads to Israel: Palestine from Balfour to Bevin.* London: Collins, 1965.

Taylor, Alan R. *Prelude to Israel: An Analysis of Zionist Diplomacy, 1897–1947.* Beirut: Institute for Palestine Studies, 1970.

Thomas, Hugh. *The Spanish Civil War.* New York: Harper and Row, 1961.

Tibawi, Abdul Latif. *Arab Education in Mandatory Palestine: A Study of Three Decades of British Administration.* London: Luzac, 1956.

Tolkowsky, Samuel. *The Gateway to Palestine: A History of Jaffa.* London: George Routledge, 1924.

Tuqan, Subhi Said. *Al-Musuah al-Filastiniyyah.* Cairo, 1969.

Vester, Bertha Spafford. *Our Jerusalem: An American Family in the Holy City, 1881–1949.* Beirut: Middle East Export Press, 1950.

Watt, D. C. *Personalities and Policies: Studies of the Formulation of British Foreign Policy in the Twentieth Century.* London: Longmans, 1965.

Wavell, Archibald P. *The Palestine Campaigns.* Rev. ed. London: Constable, 1941.

Weiner, Myron. *Party Building in a New Nation: The Indian National Congress.* Chicago: University of Chicago Press, 1967.

Weinstock, Nathan. "The Impact of Zionist Colonization on Palestinian Arab Society before 1948." *Journal of Palestine Studies,* 6 (Winter 1973), 49–63.

Weisgal, Meyer W., and Joel Carmichael, eds. *Chaim Weizmann: A Biography by Several Hands.* New York: Atheneum, 1963.

Weizmann, Chaim. *Trial and Error.* New York: Harper, 1949.

Weizmann, Vera. *The Impossible Takes Longer.* London: Hamish Hamilton, 1967.

Worsfold, William Basil. *Palestine of the Mandate.* London: T. Fisher Unwin, 1925.

Wright, Quincy. *Mandates under the League of Nations.* Chicago: University of Chicago Press, 1930.

Yasin, Subhi. *Harb al-Isabat fi Filastin.* Cairo: Dar al-Katib al-Arabi, 1967.

———. *al-Thawrah al-Arabiyyah al-Kubra fi Filastin, 1936–1939.* Rev. ed. Cairo: Dar al-Katib, 1967.

Zeine, Zeine N. *The Emergence of Arab Nationalism.* Beirut: Khayats, 1966.

Index

251

This book is Number 11 in *The Modern Middle East Series*, sponsored by the Middle East Institute, Columbia University, New York. The other books that have appeared in this series are:

Nationalities of the Soviet East, by Edward Allworth. Columbia University Press, 1971.

Poverty and Plenty on the Turkish Farm: A Study of Income Distribution in Turkish Agriculture, by Eva Hirsch. Middle East Institute of Columbia University, 1970.

The Commander of the Faithful: The Moroccan Political Elite—A Study in Segmented Politics, by John Waterbury. Columbia University Press, 1970.

Iran Faces the Seventies, edited by Ehsan Yar-Shater. Praeger, 1971.

Recession As a Policy Instrument: Israel, 1965–1969, by Carol Schwartz Greenwald. C. Hurst and Company, 1973

The Soviet Union and the Arab East under Khrushchev, by Oles M. Smolansky. Bucknell University Press, 1974.

A Tacit Alliance: France and Israel from Suez to the Six Day War, by Sylvia Kowitt Crosbie. Princeton University Press, 1974.

Bedouin Village: A Study of a Saudi Arabian People in Transition, by Motoko Katakura. University of Tokyo Press, 1977.

Tradition and Politics: The Religious Parties of Israel, by Gary S. Schiff. Wayne State University Press, 1977.

The Modern Middle East: A Guide to Research Tools in the Social Sciences, by Reeva S. Simon. Westview Press, 1978.

Arab Politics in Palestine, 1917–1939

Designed by Richard E. Rosenbaum.
Composed by Huron Valley Graphics
in 11 point VIP Bembo, 2 points leaded,
with display lines in Bembo.
Printed offset by Thomson/Shore, Inc.
on Warren's Number 66 Antique Offset, 50 pound basis.
Bound by John H. Dekker & Sons, Inc.
in Joanna book cloth
and stamped in All Purpose foil.